LIFE AND CAREER SKILLS
SERIES

Volume 4

Social Skills

LIFE AND CAREER SKILLS
SERIES

Volume 4
Social Skills

Miranda Herbert Ferrara and Michele P. LaMeau,
Project Editors

GALE
CENGAGE Learning®

Farmington Hills, Mich • San Francisco • New York • Waterville, Maine
Meriden, Conn • Mason, Ohio • Chicago

**Life and Career Skills Series,
Volume 4: Social Skills**

Project Editors: Miranda Herbert
   Ferrara and Michele P. LaMeau

Editorial Service : Thomas Riggs &
   Company

Indexing Service: Laura Dorricott

Production Technology Support:
   Mike Weaver

Rights Acquisition and Management:
   Moriam M. Aigoro, Ashley
   M. Maynard

Imaging: John Watkins

Product Design: Kristine Julien

Manufacturing: Wendy Blurton

Vice President and Publisher,
   New Products and GVRL:
   Patricia Coryell

For product information and technology assistance, contact us at
Gale Customer Support, 1-800-877-4253.
For permission to use material from this text or product,
submit all requests online at **www.cengage.com/permissions.**
Further permissions questions can be emailed to
permissionrequest@cengage.com

Cover images: ©PureSolution/Shutterstock.com (icon) and ©Dean Drobot/
Shutterstock.com (business team).

While every effort has been made to ensure the reliability of the information
presented in this publication, Gale, a part of Cengage Learning, does not
guarantee the accuracy of the data contained herein. Gale accepts no payment
for listing; and inclusion in the publication of any organization, agency,
institution, publication, service, or individual does not imply endorsement of the
editors or publisher. Errors brought to the attention of the publisher and verified
to the satisfaction of the publisher will be corrected in future editions.

EDITORIAL DATA PRIVACY POLICY: Does this product contain information
about you as an individual? If so, for more information about our editorial data
privacy policies, please see our Privacy Statement at http://solutions.cengage
.com/Gale/Data-Privacy-Policy/.

LIBRARY OF CONGRESS CATALOGING-IN-PUBLICATION DATA

Social skills / Miranda Herbert Ferrara and Michele P. LaMeau,
project editors. — 001
      pages cm. — (Life and career skills series ; volume 4)
   Includes bibliographical references and index.
   ISBN 978-1-4103-1764-3 — ISBN 1-4103-1764-1
   1. Social skills. 2. Interpersonal relations. I. Ferrara, Miranda Herbert, 1950- II.
LaMeau, Michele P.

HM691.S64 2016
302—dc23

                                                            2015001661

Gale
27500 Drake Rd.
Farmington Hills, MI, 48331-3535

ISBN-13: 978-1-4103-1764-3
ISBN-10: 1-4103-1764-1

This title is also available as an e-book.
ISBN-13: 978-1-4103-1773-5   ISBN-10: 1-4103-1773-0
Contact your Gale sales representative for ordering information.

Printed in China
1 2 3 4 5 6 7 19 18 17 16 15

Contents

WRITTEN AND GRAPHIC COMMUNICATION

ORGANIZATIONAL, PROBLEM-SOLVING AND DECISION-MAKING, AND CONFLICT RESOLUTION SKILLS

GETTING ORGANIZED AND PROJECT MANAGEMENT SKILLS

PROBLEM SOLVING AND DECISION MAKING

CONFLICT RESOLUTION SKILLS

ENTERING THE WORKPLACE: PROFESSIONAL ETHICS, ETIQUETTE, AND CONDUCT

PROFESSIONAL ETHICS

WORKPLACE ETIQUETTE AND CONDUCT

TEAMWORK, COLLABORATION, AND LEADERSHIP SKILLS

TEAMWORK SKILLS AND DEVELOPING HEALTHY TEAM DYNAMICS

Preface

The *Life and Career Skills Series (LCSS)* is designed to supply foundational information in an accessible format to provide direction for personal life decisions. This collection of thematically focused volumes centers on the life and career issues people face on a day-to-day basis, as well as key organizations and suggested resources for further reading. Written in an engaging, approachable, and informative question-and-answer style, the series provides users with the tactical information needed to accomplish their life goals—whether in the context of transitioning from school and/or college into the workplace or transitioning into the next stage of life.

Topic Selection

The first four volumes of the series contain topics that consist of the most relevant, current, and useful subjects surveyed in the market. Entry topics have been selected for the *Life and Career Skills Series* through a variety of methods to assure that the most timely and useful information would be provided. When needed or warranted, the list of topics was reviewed by subject matter experts to ensure that the materials being covered were presented accurately and appropriately.

LCSS Entry Features

Each volume of *LCSS* includes entries on topics appropriate to that volume's particular theme. Entries have been divided into four major sections, then the individual essays grouped under thematic subsections so that like topics fall together. Each of the major sections begins with a **table of contents** outlining the essay coverage immediately followed by an **overview essay** that sets out the themes for the section. The overview entry is followed by two or three **composite entries** bringing together information on that particular theme. Each composite entry is followed by a list of books, periodicals, and websites where the reader can find more information.

Each composite entry in an *LCSS* volume begins with an **In This Section listing** that clearly outlines the topics and key concepts covered.

Throughout the text of the entry the reader will find **icons** used as visual cues to indicate paragraphs or sections of text where key terms or particularly important or helpful information can be found. The icons are more fully explained in the User's Guide following this preface.

LCSS entries feature **in-text key terms** that the authors and editors feel will aid overall reader comprehension of the topic.

Many *LCSS* entries also contain **sidebars**. Sidebars highlight information such as historical data about the entry topic, biographical information about people involved with the topic, case studies, statistics, hints, and "fun facts."

The entries are **heavily illustrated** with color photos, charts, tables, and other graphics, allowing users to further contextualize the information they are being provided.

Authoritative Sources

Entries have been compiled by combining authoritative data from government sources, professional associations, original research, and publicly accessible sources both in print and on the Internet. These sources include periodicals, white papers, and books, as well as websites and blogs.

The *Life and Career Skills Series* overview and composite entries contain a selection of relevant print and electronic sources where the reader can find further information on the topic. In addition, there is a list of **Resources for More Information** at the end of each volume listing books, periodicals, and websites that can be used for further research.

Organizations

A **List of Key Organizations** follows the Resources for More Information. Although not an exhaustive list, these organizations are important in the field and provide another source of information for interested readers. The list gives the address and home page url of each organization and has a short description of the organization when available.

Fully Indexed

Each *LCSS* volume has a comprehensive index of concepts, names, and terms enabling readers to locate topics throughout the volume. Because many subjects are not treated in separate entries but are discussed within the context of larger composite entries, the index guides readers to discussions of these subjects quickly.

About *Life and Career Skills Series, Volume 4: Social Skills*

Life and Career Skills Series, Volume 4: Social Skills helps readers understand and hone the social skills necessary for success. Although the essays offer advice applicable to many aspects of life, the focus is primarily on the workplace. The essays guide readers in effective communication and conduct, emphasizing the characteristics of verbal, nonverbal, and written communication; stress the importance of ethics and etiquette; and provide tips for conflict resolution and teamwork. They offer information that can help readers identify and develop important leadership, organizational, and problem-solving skills.

Questions addressed in this volume include "What Is Team Culture?," "What Does It Mean to Have Good Verbal Communication Skills?," "What Are Some Different Types of Body Language?," and "What Are Examples of Meeting Behaviors That Should Be Avoided?" The essays draw on both foundational and contemporary scholarship about communication. They consider the impact of modern technology such as e-mail and video conferencing on communication and workplace etiquette.

Suggestions Welcome

Comments on this *LCSS* volume and suggestions on topics for future volumes are cordially invited. Please write:

The Editors
Life and Career Skills Series
Gale, Cengage Learning
27500 Drake Rd.
Farmington Hills, Michigan 48331-3535

Gale, Cengage Learning, does not endorse any of the organizations, products, or methods mentioned in this title.

The websites appearing in the *Life and Career Skills* Series have been reviewed by Gale, Cengage Learning, to provide additional information. Gale is not responsible for the content or operations policies of these websites. Further, Gale is not responsible for the conduct of website providers who offer electronic texts that may infringe on the legal right of copyright holders.

User's Guide

Throughout the text of each entry in the *Life and Career Skills Series*, there are three icons used as visual cues to indicate paragraphs or sections of text where key terms or particularly important or helpful information can be found.

Icons

Know This — Indicates a paragraph where a key concept or larger theme that must be known to understand the main idea of the entry is located.

Helpful Hint — Indicates a paragraph where a helpful tip or idea, a suggestion for consideration, or a best practice is located. These suggestions may be helpful when putting concepts presented in the entry into practice.

Key Term — Indicates the paragraph and provides the definition of an essential term in an entry necessary to understand the overall topic and core concepts presented.

Interpersonal Communication Skills

Overview: Interpersonal Communication Skills

What Does It Mean to Have Good Verbal Communication Skills?

Many jobs require that applicants have "good communication skills," but they are not always clear about what this means. Although the ability to communicate comes naturally to human beings, there are a number of skills that you can learn and practice in order to become a more effective communicator. Before you list "excellent communication skills" on a résumé or job application, you should understand what specific skills are involved so that you can demonstrate to your employer that you recognize the essentials of successful communication. Understanding and improving communication skills can also have a positive impact on your personal relationships with friends and family.

The most important elements of communication are knowing what you want to say and expressing it as clearly as possible. This involves putting thought and consideration into your words, and it often means slowing down your reactions so that you can be sure that you are saying what you mean as directly and calmly as you can. In some cases, good communication may involve doing research to improve your knowledge of the subject you will be discussing. You should also make sure that you know the correct vocabulary, such as technical or industry terms.

A major part of developing communication skills is understanding the difference between intentional and unintentional communication. Unintentional communication may occur when you speak or write without thinking. It may also be transmitted through such automatic and unconscious means as body language, tone of voice, or facial expression. Even punctuation and capitalization in an e-mail may convey an unintentional message about your mood or attitude. In order to become a good communicator, you should become aware of all the ways you

© HONZA HRUBY/
SHUTTERSTOCK.COM.

transmit information to your listeners or readers in order to ensure that your communication is as intentional as possible.

Another vital element of good communication is the art of listening. Good listening skills include being attentive to the words of others, clarifying their meaning through respectful questions, and responding to others in ways that demonstrate that you understand what they have said. You should be careful not to fall into the habit of planning what you are going to say next while someone else is talking. This is discourteous, and it places you at a disadvantage, since you are not paying careful attention to the flow of discussion. Like good communication, good listening involves an understanding of body language. If you maintain an open posture and facial expression, this can help speakers know that you are paying attention, and studying their body language as they talk can give you a deeper understanding of their emotional state and attitude. You can apply the principles of good listening to written communication as well, by paying careful attention when you read e-mails, letters, or other documents. Good listening skills can help you show respect and improve your contribution to the conversation.

How Has Communication Changed in the Modern World?

Speech and writing have been important forms of human communication for thousands of years. Technological changes during the nineteenth, twentieth, and early twenty-first centuries have greatly expanded the accessibility, immediacy, and reach of communication. The invention of the telephone and telegraph during the late 1800s first made communication over long distances broadly available, and advances in cellular and computer technology during the late 1900s and early 2000s have made almost instant worldwide communication possible among large numbers of people.

Before the computer age, people generally communicated by speaking in person, writing letters, or conversing over the telephone. The introduction of the Internet during the last decade of the twentieth century led to the popularization of e-mail as an efficient way to communicate with individuals or groups within the same office or across the world. Much faster than postal mail, e-mail quickly became the preferred method of communication for both business and personal purposes. E-mailers have created their own linguistic shortcuts and rules of etiquette that have helped to develop computer communication as a medium different from traditional letters.

During the first decades of the twenty-first century, the increasing popularity of cellular phones made widespread communication even more readily available to private individuals. Texting and instant messaging has allowed users to communicate quickly, to keep in close touch, and make and change plans with ease. By the beginning of 2014, the Pew Research Center's Internet Project estimated that 90 percent of American adults owned cell phones and that almost a third of those could not imagine life without their mobile phone.

Continued technological development has seen the introduction of smartphones that have a wide range of computer capabilities, as well as dozens of social media websites that provide platforms for sharing information among friends, family, and strangers with similar interests. Software applications such as Skype and FaceTime allow users to have real-time, face-to-face conversations over great distances through the cameras and microphones on their computerized devices. Scientific advancements have increased the speed and scope of modern communication. However, technology is not a substitute for the human elements of empathy and consideration, and basic communication skills remain necessary in ensuring clarity and respect in interpersonal interactions.

What Are Obstacles to Good Communication?

A number of things may interfere with your ability to communicate easily, but most of these can be overcome with attention, education, and effort. Shyness or a lack of confidence in your verbal or written communication skills may be a barrier to your ability to express yourself. A lack of interest in or hostility toward a particular subject may make communication difficult. Many people find it hard to talk about controversial subjects, such as religion, politics, or sexuality, and communicating about these topics may require special sensitivity. When people have very different opinions on a subject, it may be challenging for them to discuss it, but concentrating on listening skills and maintaining a respectful tone help.

Cultural and language differences can also impede communication. If you and your listeners or readers do not share a language, you may need to find ways to accommodate that difference in order to ensure that both sides are understood. Some differences may require interpreters or translators to bridge the gap, but in many cases attention to speaking or writing simply and clearly may be enough. People from different cultures may also have varying ideas of acceptable communication practices. For example, in some Asian, African, and Latin American cultures, direct eye contact may be viewed as challenging or insulting, while in the United States, looking someone in the eye is a sign of honesty and openness. In order to communicate respectfully with those of different cultures or language groups, you may need to research cultural communication differences.

Even when all parties are proficient in English, language can still present an obstacle to effective communication. The use of slang, jargon, or technical terms can make your communication unclear to someone who does not belong to your generation or field of work. Some people develop the habit of using a lot of long words in order to seem more educated or intelligent. In reality, however, this type of writing or speaking may have the undesired effect of making you appear pretentious and could irritate your audience. Unless you are communicating with academics or experts in your field, you should avoid technical jargon and obscure words.

What Are Some Types of Communication?

Numerous forms of communication are part of your daily life, and developing skills of attentiveness and clarity can help improve them all. In your personal life, you might communicate with family and friends through conversation, handwritten notes, e-mail, phone calls, voice messages, or texts. You may write letters to those who live far away, or you might keep in touch through a variety of social media, such as Facebook, Twitter, or Pinterest.

At work, you are likely to use one-to-one conversation as well as phone calls to communicate with coworkers and clients. You may also have to communicate in groups in work meetings and conferences. Some jobs require that you deliver presentations before an audience or even speak on the radio or television. Most positions involve some writing, and many require frequent written communications. In addition to texts, memos, and e-mails, on-the-job writing could include creating reports and proposals that may be read by coworkers, your supervisor, the board of your company, or other industry leaders.

What Are the Differences between Verbal and Written Communication?

One of the major differences between verbal and written communication is the element of time. Except for voice mails, which may be heard much later than they are delivered, most verbal communication takes place in real time. That is, you speak to a person or group of people and they respond right away. Because it is immediate, verbal communication requires practice in thinking clearly, being aware of nonverbal messages such as body language, and slowing your response in order to consider your words and meaning before you speak.

Written communication, on the other hand, often takes place over a longer period of time. Even when using the fairly rapid media of e-mail or texting, you generally have more time to collect your thoughts and plan your response. However, written communication does not allow you to see your audience's response immediately the way you can during a verbal conversation, and you must use both reasoning and imagination to attempt to predict how your words will be received.

When you communicate verbally, you can use a number of tools that are not available to the writer. Body language, changes in the tone and pitch of your voice, and facial expression are all important parts of delivering a spoken message. A smile and a warm, lively tone can engage your audience immediately, even in a radio interview when you cannot be seen. A writer must draw readers in using only words and phrasing, although written work may include graphic images, such as pictures, graphs, and charts, to illustrate the words and help clarify their meaning.

Spoken communication is also more forgiving in terms of form and structure. Though you should follow general rules of grammar and use vocabulary correctly, verbal presentations and conversations are generally more relaxed than written communication. In speech you may break some of the more formal rules of grammar by using incomplete sentences. In all but the most casual letters, e-mails, and texts, written communication must follow formal rules of grammar and structure. However, a disadvantage of spoken communication is that you must gain your audience's attention and communicate clearly in the moment; in written communication, your work can be read later, or repeatedly, at the reader's convenience.

What Skills Do I Need for Group Communication?

Even if you are not a public personality or even a very social person, much of your communication will take place in groups. Your interactions with family and coworkers will frequently require group communication skills in order to create harmony, maintain group identity, and build teamwork. Understanding some of the fundamental principles of group communication may make your participation in business, civic, social, or church events more rewarding and successful.

Communicating in groups presents special challenges, because you must learn to be attentive to a number of different communication styles. Listening becomes even more important in a group discussion, as does careful consideration of what you say and the attitude you project. A good rule in any group discussion is to listen more than you talk.

It may be useful to agree upon some sort of group communication process to ensure that everyone is heard and that no one dominates the conversation. This may be as simple as going around the room and offering everyone the chance to speak. A good way to begin a group discussion is for all participants to introduce themselves and explain why they came and what they would like to accomplish during the meeting. As the discussion progresses, it is a good idea to check in with members of the group to ensure that everyone feels included and heard. You may wish to choose a facilitator or moderator to focus the discussion and call on speakers in order. If a group meets regularly, rotating the responsibility of facilitation can give everyone the opportunity to learn group management skills.

Some work groups require a more formal process. Very structured meetings can be conducted in accordance with Robert's Rules of Order, which are based on the procedures of the British Parliament. The Robert's Rules of Order website (http://www.robertsrules.org/) provides an overview of the rules and guidelines for using them. Other groups may prefer to use less formal structures for discussion and decision making. One of these is consensus decision making, in which group members work through discussion and compromise to reach a decision that is acceptable to all.

Where Can I Learn Communication Skills?

There are a number of resources available to help you improve your ability to communicate. Most local colleges and universities offer communication programs and may have classes available to the public. A benefit of in-person classes is that they offer you the opportunity to practice your new skills in a group. However, if you are very self-motivated or simply do not have the time to attend a scheduled class, there are numerous online resources for learning communication skills. The Education Portal website (http://education-portal.com/articles/List_of_Free_Online_Communications_Courses_and_Classes.html) provides a list of free communication classes available online.

If you would like to improve your communication on the job, the website of the American Management Association (http://www.amanet.org/training/seminars/communication-skills-training.aspx) offers free online training seminars in communication skills for business. You may want to suggest to your employer that business efficiency and success could be increased by involving the whole workforce in improving interpersonal communications. Organizations such as Skillpath (https://www.skillpath.com/) and Business Training Works (http://www.business trainingworks.com/onsite-training-courses-directories/communication-skills-training-courses-directory) offer on-site training programs that can teach communication skills in your workplace.

Improving your communication skills is a lifelong process, and you should not be discouraged if you are not immediately successful. Your everyday life will offer endless opportunities for practicing and refining your skills of reading and using body language, expressing yourself clearly and thoughtfully, and listening respectfully. If you learn the principles of effective communication and apply them as consistently as you can in your interactions with your partner, children, friends, coworkers, and new acquaintances, you will see gradual but significant improvement in your personal and work relationships and in your own sense of personal effectiveness.

For More Information

BOOKS

Lerner, Marcia. *Writing Smart: Your Guide to Great Writing*. 2nd ed. New York: Princeton Review, 2001.

McKay, Matthew, Martha Davis, and Patrick Fanning. *Messages: The Communication Skills Book*. 3rd ed. Oakland, CA: New Harbinger Publications, 2009.

Nazario, Luis, Deborah Borchers, and William Lewis. *Bridges to Better Writing*. 2nd ed. Boston: Wadsworth, 2013.

O'Hair, Dan, and Mary Wiemann. *Real Communication: An Introduction*. 2nd ed.Boston: Bedford/St. Martin's, 2012.

PERIODICALS

Burg, Natalie. "How Technology Has Changed Workplace Communication." *Forbes*. December 10, 2013. This article can also be found online at http://www.forbes.com/sites/unify/2013/12/10/how-technology-has-changed-workplace-communication/.

Moulesong, Bob. "Listening Skills Are an Important Part of Effective Communication." *Times of Northwest Indiana*. December 19, 2010. This article can also be found online at http://www.nwitimes.com/business/jobs-and-employment/listening-skills-are-an-important-part-of-effective-communication/article_b4d0940a-f919-5d1a-be45-05da2c6752c2.html.

Stewart, Jill. "The Most Enjoyable Way to Improve Your Writing Skills." *Ragan's PR Daily*. December 30, 2013. This article can also be found online at http://www.prdaily.com/Main/Articles/The_most_enjoyable_way_to_improve_your_writing_ski_14300.aspx.

Suttle, Rick. "Importance of Writing Skills in Business." *Houston Chronicle.* This article can also be found online at http://smallbusiness.chron.com/importance-writing-skills-business-845.html.

WEBSITES

"List of Free Online Communications Courses and Classes." *Education Portal.* http://education-portal.com/articles/List_of_Free_Online_Communications_Courses_and_Classes.html (accessed December 16, 2014).

Rivers, Dennis. "The Seven Challenges Workbook: Communication Skills for Success at Home and Work." *The New Conversations Initiative.* 2012. http://www.newconversations.net/ (accessed December 16, 2014).

Robinson, Lawrence, Jeanne Segal, and Robert Segal. "Effective Communication: Improving Communication Skills in Business and Relationships." December 2014. *Helpguide.org: Your Guide to Better Mental and Emotional Health.* http://www.helpguide.org/articles/relationships/effective-communication.htm (accessed December 16, 2014).

"The Seven Cs of Communication: A Checklist for Clear Communication." *Mind Tools: Essential Skills for an Excellent Career.* http://www.mindtools.com/pages/article/newCS_85.htm (accessed December 16, 2014).

Wetanson, Burt. "Why Communication Skills Should Matter to You." *Working World.* http://www.workingworld.com/articles/why-communication-skills-should-matter-to-you (accessed December 16, 2014).

Verbal or Spoken

How Is Language Defined?

Language is the basic system of human communication. It is the way we put words, symbols, and gestures together to convey thoughts and ideas to each other. Though we generally think of language as being spoken or written, there are other types of language as well. Body language, in which ideas and attitudes are communicated by body position and gestures, and American Sign Language, a standardized system of hand gestures used by many people who are hearing impaired, are examples of non spoken languages. Some experts believe that human beings are defined by our need to communicate with each other and by the sophisticated systems of language we have created in order to do it.

Over the course of history, thousands of different language systems have evolved around the world. Some of these have similarities to each other, such as French, Spanish, and Italian, which are all based on the Latin language, while others, such as African and Asian languages, come from quite different roots. All languages have rules to ensure some sort of uniformity, but all also grow and change over time. For example, with

Knowing what you want to say, the words you use, and your body language lead to successful communication, one-on-one or in front of a group like this one. © PAVEL L PHOTO AND VIDEO/ SHUTTERSTOCK.COM.

the development of new technologies, new words entered languages. *Photoshopping*, which means editing a photograph with a computer program, and *spam*, which refers to unsolicited advertisements received through e-mail, are examples of words that have been added to the English language in the twentieth century.

In What Ways Does Language Affect My Verbal Communication Skills?

Because language is the most basic ingredient of communication, considering your use of language is the place to start when developing communication skills. The fundamental elements of communication are knowing what you want to say and expressing it as clearly as possible. Language is your most important tool for accomplishing this. When people communicate well, they are said to "speak the same language." Quite literally, you will want to make sure that those to whom you speak will understand your words. If you are a non-native speaker of English, this may mean working to improve your pronunciation and to minimize your accent. For both native and non-native English speakers, it may mean slowing down your speech and pronouncing your words more distinctly. If you do not share a language with your audience, you may want to engage an interpreter to ensure that you are understood.

Using Colloquial Language

Colloquial language is informal language that is generally used in casual, everyday speech. Although it is not considered as informal as slang, colloquial language should be avoided in most formal situations, including most business settings. In such situations such as meetings and presentations, using colloquial language could inadvertently convey to your audience that you are unprofessional, disinterested, or uneducated about your topic.

There are some occasions, however, in which colloquial language is acceptable and, in fact, in which it might be preferable to more formal language. For example, if you are conversing with someone who employs colloquialisms frequently in his or her own speech, you may find that conversation flows more naturally if you are less formal in choosing your own words. Tread carefully, however. People can easily pick up when your use of colloquialisms feels rehearsed, forced, or insincere. In these cases, your use of colloquial language may insult or offend your audience.

The words you use are an important factor in successful communication. Unless you are speaking to colleagues in your field, you should avoid technical terms or uncommon words that your listeners may not understand. Your choice of words may vary depending on the situation. For example, if you are talking to a friend or group of friends, you may use colloquial speech and language shortcuts you know they will understand. However, when speaking at a business meeting, you should use more formal language. The larger the group, the more care you should take to make sure that your language is clear and simple and that you keep your speech as brief as possible. You may also wish to check in with your listeners occasionally to ensure that they understand you.

Body language is also a significant part of communication. Your body may send a wide variety of unintended messages through your stance, facial expression, and the position of your arms and hands. For example, arms crossed over your chest because you are cold may make you appear unreceptive to an idea. As you speak, either in a small group or before a crowd, be aware of your body, take steps to stand or sit in a relaxed manner, and avoid nervous habits, such as finger tapping or nail biting, that can arouse nervousness in your audience or make you appear insecure.

What Does Tone Mean?

Tone is the term used to express *how* something is said. Also called intonation or tone of voice, tone generally describes the emotion or attitude conveyed in the words you use, the volume and sound of your voice, and your facial expression. Your tone of voice can express excitement, anger, humor, and boredom, even when your words may be saying something quite different. While your words may express what you are thinking, your tone expresses what you are feeling and may reveal a lot about your personality.

Tone may also express qualities in your voice that are unconscious, like those that are part of a regional accent. These qualities may have an impact on your ability to communicate effectively. For example, a nasal tone may be perceived as irritating, while a musical voice might attract positive notice. In some cases it is possible to improve the quality of your voice with attention, practice, or speech therapy.

How Does Tone Affect Communication?

Because tone is an expression of emotion, your tone of voice has the power to stir emotions in your listeners as well. Excitement in your voice can increase enthusiasm for your ideas, while a bored or angry tone can inspire hostility in your audience. This is true no matter who you are talking to. Your conversations with friends and family can quickly become unpleasant confrontations if they perceive your tone as harsh, exasperated, or hostile. Tone becomes even more important in business situations, when you cannot expect your associates to make allowances for a sharp or impatient comment. In addressing larger groups, a positive, animated tone can make your audience much more receptive to what you are saying.

 In order to make effective use of tone in your interactions, you must first become aware of your tone of voice and what it communicates to others. Practice being mindful of how your voice sounds when you speak, and work to keep it level, calm, and pleasant. Taking a breath or two before responding may help you to adjust your tone and your attitude. Keep in mind that attitude is also expressed in body language. Widening or rolling your eyes, shaking your head, or gesturing with your hands all convey a negative tone, while nodding slightly, smiling, and relaxing your face and body will help you communicate a more positive and open tone.

What Does Pitch Mean?

Pitch, or inflection, describes whether your voice sounds high or low to a listener. Your voice is created by the vibration of air on folds of membrane (called vocal cords) in your throat. A fast vibration produces a high pitch, and a slow vibration produces a low pitch. Though you can alter the pitch of your voice intentionally, as is done in singing, the pitch of your natural speaking voice is largely determined by the size of your vocal cords. In general, men have deeper voices than women do because hormonal changes in male bodies cause their vocal cords to become longer as they reach puberty.

As you speak, your pitch may rise and fall for various reasons. Typically, in English, your voice rises at the end of question or when you express surprise or disbelief. In some languages, such as many of those spoken in China, the pitch of a word can determine its meaning. Pitch may also be affected by your emotional state or by your stress level. Fear, tension, and anger can all cause a rise in pitch.

How Does Pitch Affect Communication?

The pitch of your voice may affect how others view you. Perhaps because of cultural prejudices, a lower pitch is often associated with authority and success. This view has tended to place women at a disadvantage in the business world, which has been traditionally dominated by men. However, women and men who do not have naturally low-pitched voices may moderate their pitch by calming themselves before speaking, breathing deeply, and projecting their voices with confidence.

In your personal conversations, a heavily inflected speech pattern in which the voice rises and falls repeatedly may be lively and engaging. However, for effective business communication, you may want to work toward a more evenly pitched delivery that projects stability and composure. This is especially important in group situations, such as meetings, where a rising pitch may escalate tension. If you speak before a large group, you may find that using slightly more inflection than you would in conversation adds interest to your delivery. In all but the most informal situations, you should avoid the habit of speech called "uptalk," the practice of ending all your sentences with a high inflection, so that statements sound like questions. Although it is common among young people in various locations, uptalk projects uncertainty and insecurity and is widely considered an annoying speech pattern.

What Does Audience Mean?

Your audience is the individual or group with whom you wish to communicate effectively. Audiences may be formal, such as an auditorium full of people, or informal, such as a group sitting around your kitchen table. Your audience may be members of your family with whom you want to build satisfying relationships, a friend with whom you need to have a difficult conversation, or a group of friends at a party where you would like to reduce your shyness and make yourself heard.

Human resources:
The department in a company that is responsible for hiring and managing employees.

In business, your audience may be a ***human resources*** director who interviews you for a job or a boss who receives your regular reports. If you attend meetings, you are usually required to speak before an audience, even if it consists of only two or three other people. You may also be called upon to address larger audiences at conferences or professional gatherings.

How Might My Audience Affect the Way I Communicate?

As an effective communicator, your primary job is to engage your audience. There are two major elements to accomplishing this goal. One is to develop a conscious understanding of your audience, and the other is to have a confident grasp of what it is you want to communicate.

One of the first rules of teachers of communication is "know your audience." In informal situations with family and friends, this knowledge may be quite personal. You may know that your children stop listening when you use a lecturing tone or that your partner becomes defensive when you begin a conversation with "I wish you wouldn't…" Similarly, you may quickly learn that, with a certain group of talkative friends, you must speak up forcefully or you will not be heard.

In work situations, you may not have an intimate understanding of your audience's communication needs, but you should spend some time thinking about who is listening to you and what you want to communicate to them. What is their level of expertise? If you are speaking to a client group with limited understanding of their field, you will want to speak simply and explain any technical terms you use. If you are speaking to colleagues, you may annoy your audience if you spend too much time explaining things they already know.

In any case, it is important to remember that you are speaking to people much like yourself who are taking the time to listen to you.

In order to hold their interest, you must be both respectful and entertaining. In order to do this, you must know what you want to say. This may involve writing your speech out and practicing it a number of times until you can deliver it using your notes as little as possible. Knowing your subject shows respect for your audience. Even the most fascinating material will quickly lose the audience's attention if it is read in a monotone by a speaker who rarely looks up from his or her notes.

Audiences tend to reflect the interest and emotion that a speaker projects. In addition to maintaining a respectful and attentive tone, you may wish to use humor to engage and relax your audience. However, be cautious, since not everyone finds the same things funny. The most effective use of humor may be a brief story from your own experience that your audience may relate to. Do not tell long, irrelevant stories, and never tell a joke that ridicules any group or individual or could be considered offensive or indecent.

Face-to-Face Conversations

What Is a Face-to-Face Conversation?

A conversation is a talk or discussion between two or more people. A conversation is typically small and informal, whereas a meeting or conference tends to be larger, more formal, and more structured. Sometimes the word *conversation* is used in a broader sense to describe a free and open exchange of ideas. For example a large public event may be described as "a community conversation about safety" to encourage attendance and public input. A business meeting may be characterized as a conversation in order to impart a more relaxed and open tone.

 In a face-to-face conversation, all of the people involved are present in person and taking part in the dialogue. You probably have face-to-face conversations regularly with your friends and family. Unless you work from home, most of your interactions with coworkers and customers is likely to be in the form of face-to-face conversation. The introduction of such computer programs and smartphone apps as Skype and FaceTime has made face-to-face interaction possible even over long distances. Because of this, improving your face-to-face conversational skills can help you communicate clearly and make a lasting impression both in your personal life and the business world.

What Are the Benefits of Face-to-Face Communication?

Face-to-face communication is generally more intimate and personal than an exchange carried out over the telephone or through e-mail and may offer a greater opportunity for understanding. If you can see the person to whom you are speaking, you can judge your listener's level of interest by paying attention to body language, also called nonverbal cues, which may include leaning toward or away from the speaker, yawning, or looking at one's watch. Facial expression can also be revealing, as a smile may demonstrate agreement, and a wrinkled brow may show

Bill Clinton converses one-on-one with Reverend Otis Moss at the Olivet Baptist Church in Cleveland, Ohio, during the Clinton/Gore 1992 Buscapade Great Lakes campaign tour.
© AMERICAN SPIRIT/
SHUTTERSTOCK.COM.

confusion even if someone does not speak. Being able to see and respond to nonverbal cues can help clarify intended meaning and pinpoint conversational problems.

In your personal relationships, face-to-face conversations can build closeness and help you avoid misunderstandings that can arise during text and e-mail communications. For example when discussing a difficult issue, e-mail may allow you to express anger and hostility more freely. In contrast, being face-to-face with your listeners may encourage you to adopt a more restrained and cooperative tone.

At work, face-to-face conversations tend to increase efficiency and productivity. Face-to-face interactions promote attentiveness, as participants are generally not able to check e-mail, play computer games, or perform other activities in addition to listening. A group of people in a face-to-face meeting may be able to share ideas and arrive at solutions more efficiently than they could by exchanging numerous e-mails. Personal interaction also helps build durable business relationships, as friendly conversations before and after a business meeting allow you to learn more about your coworkers' or clients' lives.

Are There Disadvantages to Face-to-Face Communication?

Although the immediacy of response in face-to-face conversation may increase efficiency, it can become a disadvantage in some situations.

Smartphones and Face-to-Face Conversations

Smartphones have made it easy to connect with friends, family, colleagues, and acquaintances via telephone, text message, e-mail, and social media. However, many people have noted that, as smartphones have become more popular, they have affected the quality of face-to-face conversations.

Face-to-face conversations require active listening, receptive body language, and immediate responses. When a participant in a face-to-face conversation is focusing on his or her smartphone instead of the person to whom they are speaking, the outcome of the conversation is often lackluster or negative. For example, two old friends, Jenna and Lee, met for coffee to catch up. While they stood in line waiting to order coffee, Jenna noticed that Lee often checked her phone, swiping its screen every time it beeped. As Lee's attention wavered from their conversation, Jenna felt dejected. "Am I not interesting enough for Lee?" Jenna asked herself as Lee typed away on her phone. Throughout their coffee date, Lee continued to check her phone, responding to text messages immediately and absentmindedly scrolling through her Twitter and Facebook feeds. Jenna left the coffee date feeling frustrated. She found it hard to connect emotionally with Lee because her attention was clearly elsewhere.

If you have a difficult time ignoring your smartphone during face-to-face conversations, it may be useful to silence your phone or turn it off altogether. Zipping the phone away in a pocket or purse may also be helpful. Although such preventive measures may initially be challenging, they will most likely improve face-to-face conversations and, consequently, your relationships with other people.

If you do not think carefully before speaking and do not work to control your emotions, you may make a hasty comment in a face-to-face interaction. You might regret this action almost immediately, but the damage can be hard to undo. In addition, face-to-face communication requires you to think clearly and quickly when you are asked to respond to comments or questions that you do not expect.

In a business context, one drawback of face-to-face discussion is that there is usually no written record of what was said. This may open the door to misunderstanding if the participants have different recollections of the conversation. Another disadvantage to talking face-to-face is that it generally requires more logistical planning than telephone or e-mail communication. Participants must agree on an acceptable location that provides a quiet and comfortable place to talk, and they must set aside enough time to meet there. Privacy may also be an issue in face-to-face conversations because they might be overheard by those nearby.

Face-to-face conversation is often an impractical communication method for large groups or businesses. Large corporations are frequently too spread out to allow easy face-to-face connections, and large events, even those billed as "conversations," are simply too unwieldy for real face-to-face exchange. Such events usually become question-and-answer sessions directed toward a speaker or panel of speakers rather than a true conversation. Some large event planners attempt to avoid this dynamic by having the audience break down into more manageable conversational groups for a discussion period.

What Are Some Situations That Call for Face-to-Face Conversation?

Although electronic communication such as texting or e-mailing has become more and more popular and is considered acceptable in an increasing number of situations, there are many situations that require face-to-face contact. Any topic that is sensitive or that lends itself to misunderstanding should be discussed in a face-to-face conversation where you can express yourself most clearly and directly and recognize immediately whether your listener understands you or not.

In business, a face-to-face discussion may increase your chances of making a favorable and memorable impression. If you are seeking a job, a promotion, or a raise in pay, you should make every effort to make your case in person. This will give you the opportunity to maximize your persuasive skills and ensure that your supervisor recognizes and listens to you. Likewise, if you are a supervisor, you should conduct all employee evaluations face-to-face in order to make sure that your meaning is understood. Other important meetings, such as general planning sessions, should also be conducted face-to-face to ensure clarity and engage participation. Workers are more likely to feel ownership of a policy or plan if they have participated in a face-to-face conversation about it.

Relations with customers or clients can also benefit from face-to-face communication. A skillful face-to-face interaction can help you make a sale or increase a client's confidence in your company. The personal touch can be especially important in solving customer service problems. Once you become aware of body language and other verbal and nonverbal cues, you can be more sensitive to your customers' frustrations and more convincing about your willingness to resolve problems.

What Are Important Skills for Face-to-Face Communication?

A number of communication skills come into play when you have a conversation. One of the most significant skills particular to face-to-face interactions is attention to body language. Our bodies give subtle clues to our emotions and attitudes, and learning to interpret body language can be an important factor in understanding why a conversation develops the way it does. If you approach a conversation with crossed arms or clenched fists, you will appear closed or angry, even though you may only be exhibiting nervous habits. It is possible to introduce a more relaxed note into a conversation by using your body language to indicate openness with a relaxed stance and a friendly facial expression.

 Perhaps the most important skill in face-to-face conversation is the art of listening. Make direct eye contact and nod to indicate that you are listening to the person with whom you are speaking. You may also show interest and increase comprehension by asking questions or making comments that demonstrate you understand what is being said. This technique is called active listening and is an important part of international diplomacy, mediation, and other advanced communication practices.

Courtesy is also important for successful face-to-face communication. The word *courtesy* is generally defined as showing consideration and respect for others. Not interrupting other speakers and controlling the tone and volume of your voice are important gestures of politeness that can make face-to-face conversations more pleasant and effective. The use of politeness and consideration can frequently calm a tense situation and affect the mood of those with whom you engage in conversation.

What Can I Do to Improve My Face-to-Face Conversational Skills?

Whether consciously or unconsciously, you are probably already using a number of conversational skills in your face-to-face interactions. Pay attention to the skills you use in normal conversation, and work to improve them. A conversation is a cooperative effort, and skills you develop can produce a more positive experience for everyone involved.

 One of the first steps to improving your communication skills is to pay more attention both to your own behavior and to the responses you receive. A number of self-help books and websites, such as Mindtools (http://www.mindtools.com/pages/article/Body_Language.htm), can give you suggestions about how to become more sensitive to body language cues. Practice reading the body language of those around you so that noting the subtle clues to emotions and attitude becomes second nature.

Work to practice active listening in your conversations. It is important to try to understand what your conversational partner is saying before demanding that he or she understand what you are saying. Applying this technique in your daily interactions can help you develop listening skills that can transform arguments into constructive discussions that build acceptance and connection.

Another important part of face-to-face interaction is paying attention. When you converse in person rather than through written or telephone conversations, the person you are talking with can see if you are distracted, and this will affect the quality of your conversation. Before starting a face-to-face conversation, put away all electronic devices, and ask other participants to do the same. Approach the conversation with an open body posture, and look directly at those to whom you are listening or speaking. Resist the impulse to gaze out the window or doodle in your notebook. Even in informal chats with friends, practice the discipline of not interrupting other speakers in order to show respect and demonstrate your willingness to listen. Develop the habit of regulating your voice so that you do not project anger or impatience or make yourself the center of attention. Conversational skills you develop with your friends and family can not only result in more satisfying personal relationships but can make you a more effective worker and community member.

Telephone or Remote Web Conference

How Is Talking on the Telephone Different from Other Forms of Communication?

The telephone has been a major communication medium in the United States since the early 1900s. Unlike written correspondence, such as letters and e-mail, speaking on the telephone allows you to hear the voice of the person with whom you are communicating. Unlike face-to-face interactions, telephone communication does not generally allow you to see the person you are talking with.

These facts give telephone communication some advantages and some disadvantages when compared to other forms of communication. Speaking by phone is usually considered more warm and personal than written communication. A variety of nonverbal information, such as emotion and attitude, can be transmitted through the tone and volume of your voice. However, when talking on the telephone, you do not receive important *body language* cues, which can allow misunderstandings to arise more easily. These body-language cues help people understand each other when they talk face to face.

Body language: *The gestures, movements, and mannerisms by which a person communicates with others including facial expressions, tone of voice, and posture.*

Telephone communication has changed dramatically since the invention of the telephone in the 1870s. Early telephones were all landlines; that is, they were connected to a network of wires across the country, and speakers' voices were transmitted through electric pulses over the wires. Though landlines have remained an important part of telephone technology, the popularity of wireless phones, or cell phones, at the end of the twentieth century revolutionized telephone communication. By the beginning of the twenty-first century, many people carried cell phones with them at all times. To many citizens of the modern world, a form of communication once reserved for emergencies and special occasions has become a daily lifeline that serves a number of personal and business purposes.

What Are Some Situations That Call for Communication by Telephone?

In your personal relationships, there is a wide variety of occasions when telephone communication is either necessary or used socially. You may use a telephone to make plans to get together with a friend or to find each other in a crowded area when you arrive for a date. Longer telephone conversations can take the place of friendly face-to-face chats so that you can maintain closeness when distance or busy schedules prevent you from visiting friends in person. Frequent telephone calls can help maintain closeness with your family, as well as providing a convenient means of solving logistical problems, such as arranging rides or asking someone to run an errand. When discussing a difficult issue, using the telephone may also provide a compromise between face-to-face interaction and written communication.

Video conferencing allows people from different locations to collaborate on a project as if they were in the same room. © BLEND IMAGES/ SHUTTERSTOCK.COM.

Telephone communication has long been used in the business world to provide immediate and efficient connections between colleagues and clients. Because the voice-to-voice connection is more personal than e-mail and other forms of written communication, the telephone is often the preferred means of contacting customers to make sales or resolve problems. Although you may communicate with your coworkers primarily by e-mail, you may find that telephone communication allows you to clarify issues more easily and resolve them more quickly than waiting for an e-mail response. Using the telephone may impart a "human touch" to your communications. If you are unable to speak in person, discussing a personal or delicate matter by telephone may seem kinder and more sympathetic than using e-mail.

Though telephones are used primarily for conversations between two people, the technology does allow conference calling, in which several people may take part in the same phone call. Conference calls can usually be arranged through your telephone service provider. In your personal life, conference calls may be used to facilitate a group arrangement, such as planning a family trip or chatting informally with distant friends. Businesses frequently use conference calling as an

Interviewing for a Job via the Web

The wide availability of web conferencing software has revolutionized the job interview process. Many companies have turned to these programs to conduct initial job interviews, particularly for positions that draw applicants from across the country or even around the globe. Remote web conferencing allows employers and applicants to avoid the travel expenses associated with in-person job interviews while still allowing "face-to-face" contact. The screen-sharing tools that are built into most web conferencing software allow applicants to give formal presentations if required. Applicants who impress in their online interviews may be invited to interview in person. Some employers make hiring decisions from web interviews alone.

If you are asked to interview online, there are several important things that you should keep in mind. If you will be interviewing through software such as Skype that you also use for personal communications, make sure that any images associated with your account are professional and appropriate for a corporate audience. You also will want to use an account name, or "handle," that is professional. If possible, use your full name in your online I.D. If you are unfamiliar with the technology or uncomfortable with video conferencing, you may want to make a test call with a friend before your interview. You can practice using the software, and your friend can let you know how you look and sound.

For the online interview, dress as though you are meeting in person, and make sure that the parts of your home that will be visible during the call are neat and free from clutter. In addition, try to look at your camera rather than your screen. This is the online equivalent of making direct eye contact with your interviewers.

economical and efficient way to hold a meeting or make announcements to employees or customers.

What Is Texting?

Texting, also called text messaging or short message service (SMS), means sending and receiving written messages using your telephone. Texting is mainly carried out using cell phones. You cannot send or receive a text on most landlines without subscribing to a special service. Many cell phones provide keyboards to make texting easier, but texting can also be accomplished on standard phone keypads on which each number also represents three or four letters. The number key must be struck several times to indicate which letter is desired. Predictive or autocomplete text programs, included on your cell phone, make texting more efficient by suggesting common words before they are completely spelled out.

Telephone Tips for Successful Calls

No munching on gum, candy, or lunch.

Take a deep breath. You don't want to sound breathless or rushed.

Identify yourself by name and company so the person knows who you are or that s/he has reached the right person.

Put a smile in your voice and be sincere. Your listener can hear grumpiness or insincerity in the way you sound.

Listen to the other person and address any concerns. If you need to, take notes to remember what the person at the other end of the line said.

Summarize what happened during the call and thank the person for taking the time to speak with you.

SOURCE: Compiled by the staff of *Life and Career Skills Series*.

ILLUSTRATION BY LUMINA DATAMATICS LTD. © 2015 CENGAGE LEARNING.

Texting has become increasingly popular, especially among young people, who may text far more often than they talk by telephone. Many use a special texting jargon in which certain abbreviations for words and phrases are widely understood, such as RNN, for "reply not necessary," or RUS, meaning "are you serious?" A number of websites, such as NetLingo (http://www.netlingo.com/acronyms.php) provide glossaries of common abbreviations to help you understand texting shorthand.

In What Situations Is Texting Appropriate?

Even if you generally use the telephone for spoken conversations, you may find texting an efficient way to send brief messages when you do not have the time or are not at an appropriate location for a voice call. Texting is especially useful for sending addresses and telephone numbers as it avoids such errors as misspellings and transposing numbers that may occur when information is given orally. In addition, the information is stored in the phone for easy retrieval. If you have children or other young people in your life, you may need to learn to text in order to facilitate communication. Texting can also be useful for communicating with hearing-impaired people who may be unable to speak on the telephone.

Texting can have important business uses as well. Especially if you work with or do business with people under the age of 30, you may find that texts form an increasing percentage of your office communication. Texting can be an efficient way to confirm the delivery of a shipment, set up a meeting, or announce a new product or service.

However, when texting in both business and personal situations, be aware of your environment. Not only is constant attention to sending and receiving texts often perceived as rude, but it can present a safety hazard if you are distracted from your surroundings. Texting and driving, for example, is extremely dangerous.

What Skills Are Necessary for Effective Telephone Communication?

Telephone communication requires many of the same skills of courtesy and consideration that are necessary for face-to-face interactions. Speaking on the telephone demands special attention to the tone and volume of your voice. In both your personal and business use of the phone, it is important to have a pleasant and distinctive speaking voice. If you are naturally soft spoken, make an effort to speak loudly enough to be easily heard. If you have a naturally loud voice, tone it down or move the mouthpiece of the phone away from your mouth so that you do not jar your listener. Be aware that your voice conveys emotion and attitude, and learn to become conscious of how you sound. A rising volume may indicate excitement, but it may also be perceived as angry. In the absence of visual cues, you must be aware of what your voice may reveal about you.

When using the telephone on the job, understand the frustrations that may erupt when you speak with a client or coworker on the phone. Be as polite and informative as you can, introduce yourself by name and position, and use courteous language, such as "please" and "thank you". Do not be overly familiar or introduce unnecessary personal topics into the conversation. Speak slowly and clearly, using simple, direct language, and allow the caller to talk without interruption. You may wish to take notes to help you recall what was said.

Telephone etiquette suggests that you ask the caller's permission before placing him or her on hold or transferring a call to another line and that you supply the caller with the appropriate direct number in case you are cut off. If you have received a call, it is a good idea to ask for a number where you may call the person back if the call is interrupted. Before ending a call, make sure that you have said everything you wanted to say and that the next step is clear to both of you. Say good-bye politely and suggest that the caller telephone you again if there are further problems or questions.

What Is Remote Web Conferencing and How Is It Used?

Web conferencing is a form of interactive computer communication through which people in remote locations may be connected over the Internet. Web conferencing generally includes audio and video connection as well as the ability to transmit documents and pictures. Participants all view the same information on their computer screens, and each can take a turn at presenting information to the others. Web conferences are generally organized through web conferencing services and require all participants to have high-speed Internet connections. Businesses that employ web conferencing on a regular basis may establish an ongoing contract with a conferencing hosting service.

Web conferencing is frequently used to arrange meetings among people in different locations. It may also be used to organize interactive computer gatherings, called webinars, or web-based seminars. Webinars allow people in distant locations to meet in real time for training and workshops. Web conferencing allows participants to ask questions and participate in discussion through multiple audio and video connections.

What Skills Are Necessary for Effective Web Conferencing?

Participating in a web conference requires a slightly different focus from either telephone or in-person communications. If the conference includes a video component, you must keep in mind the basic rules of face-to-face interactions, which include appropriate dress and respectful and open body language. Before a conference begins, assess your workspace to ensure that it will be quiet during the event. Close doors and windows to shut out external noise, turn off your cell phone, and make sure that no inappropriate posters or personal items are visible. Take steps to prevent interruption, such as notifying coworkers that you will be unavailable for the duration of the conference. When the conference begins, pay attention and do not try to do other tasks, such as checking e-mail, while it is going on.

In your audio communications, practice monitoring the tone and volume of your voice to reflect confidence, composure, and consideration. Do not interrupt or talk over other speakers. Make notes as you listen to organize your thoughts and remember any questions that arise.

If you are a presenter at a web conference, keep in mind that you are attempting to make a connection with a number of widely scattered people. Carefully organize your presentation in advance so that any visual aids you use will appear when and how you want them to as you talk. Anticipate areas where your listeners may have questions. Keep your presentation short and instructive, and maintain a conversational and interesting tone. Frequently ask for specific feedback to ensure that you are being understood.

Verbal Communication via Other Media

Why Are Media Communication Skills Useful?

Broadcast radio and television are two of the most important media for communication and entertainment. Though most people use a radio or TV to receive information, you might one day find yourself on the other end of the microphone. You may witness a news event and be asked to describe your experience on the air. If you are a musician or another type of performer, you might at some point perform on a radio or television program. If you win an award or achieve some other distinction, you may be invited to give an interview.

You may also have the opportunity to speak on the radio or on television as part of your job. Your company may ask you to serve as spokesperson for a new product or development, or you may go on a broadcast program to publicize an event, such as a sale or a charity auction. If your business is in the public eye, you may be called upon to speak to the media to offer an opinion or to provide background information about your company or profession.

What Skills Do I Need for Speaking on the Radio?

If you are planning ahead for a radio interview, you should do your best to be prepared. Even if you are asked to speak on a fairly informal program, you should spend time thinking about what you want to say and make notes to keep your thoughts in order. If you are giving a prepared talk, you should practice it repeatedly so that you are familiar and comfortable with its content. It is a good idea to keep notes close at hand in case you forget a detail while you are on the air. If you will have a short time to speak, you should be sure to make your point quickly and resist the impulse to fit more ideas into a short time by talking faster. Hurrying can

Unlike speaking on television, when you are speaking on the radio, you will have to use your voice effectively as your audience cannot see your facial expressions.
© DMITRIMARUTA/
SHUTTERSTOCK.COM

cause you to trip over your words, and it can also increase your nervousness and prevent your audience from understanding you. You should try to take regular, quiet breaths and speak slowly, using short sentences and simple vocabulary.

When you are speaking on the radio, keep in mind that your audience is unable to see you. Because you cannot use visual cues to communicate, you will have to use your voice effectively. Changes in the volume and tone of your voice can make it more expressive. Some experts recommend smiling broadly as you speak in order to give your voice warmth and liveliness. Others suggest that you give each answer to a question as if you are telling a story in order to make your delivery more interesting. If there are other speakers present, such as in an interview or an on-air panel discussion, you should be careful not to interrupt them. It is best to use the time when you are not speaking to gather your thoughts, but you should also listen closely so that you are able to respond to what is being said. If you are on a program with others who have opposing viewpoints, you should resist getting drawn into an angry exchange and do your best to state your opinions clearly and calmly.

Before going on the air, it is a good idea to make sure that you understand the technology you will be using. If you are in a studio, you should ask for instructions about how to speak into the microphone and remember to follow them closely throughout the interview. Turning your face away or moving too far from the microphone may make it difficult for the audience to hear you. If you will be speaking over the telephone from a remote location, you should try to make sure that you will be heard clearly. Be sure to turn your radio off at home, as there is a time lag between what you say into the phone and what you hear on the air that can confuse and distract you. You should also make sure that you will be speaking from a quiet location with no disruptions.

What Skills Do I Need for Speaking on Television?

Speaking on television requires many of the same preparations that you would make to speak on the radio. Careful planning ahead of time can help you to be less nervous and improve the effectiveness of your delivery. Many of the same rules, including slowing your speech, saying each word clearly, and animating your voice, also apply to television. However, when you are on television, your audience can see you, which means that you may not be able to use notes. You should practice what you want to say beforehand so that you will be able to remember it. You may also wish to *brainstorm* possible questions that you may be asked and prepare answers in advance.

When appearing on television, you should pay attention to what are doing with your body, head, and hands. Nervous habits, such as pulling at your clothes, touching your hair, or biting your nails, will become more noticeable on a television screen. Taking slow breaths may help you remain composed. You should pay attention to body language and avoid defensive positions, such as sitting with your arms crossed in front of your chest. It is best to sit in a relaxed position with your hands loosely folded and your feet crossed at the ankles under your chair. You should not wear clothing with bold patterns, since they can be visually distracting. Simple clothing in rich colors or a dark suit and a white or light-colored shirt are better choices for appearing in front of a camera. If there is a makeup professional connected with the program you will be appearing on, you may wish to ask him or her for advice about appropriate makeup. Without makeup, your complexion may appear washed out or discolored under television lights.

It may be helpful for you to watch other television speakers, such as those on news programs, to learn good techniques of speech and presentation. You should definitely watch the program that you will appear on, so that you will know what to expect and what type of audience the show attracts, as well as the name of the host and producer. When you arrive at the studio, you should ask for advice on how to use the technology, where to look when you are talking, and how microphones will be used. A good general rule is to look at the interviewer or the person you are addressing rather than looking into the camera.

What Is a Podcast?

Podcasts are audio or video broadcasts that are distributed online, either as regular programming or in individual transmissions that can be streamed or downloaded. The word *podcast* was created by combining the words *broadcast* and *iPod*. Created by technology company Apple

Brainstorming:
A session where employees either individually or in a group contribute their ideas for solving a problem or meeting a company objective without fear of retribution or ridicule.

in 2001, the iPod was one of the first portable devices for playing digital media, and the earliest podcasts were created specifically for transmission through it. However, in years since, the term *podcast* has come into general use to describe any broadcast intended for digital devices. Podcasts may be produced in a variety of formats, but the most common format for audio podcasts is MP3, while MP4 is used for video podcasts. These designations refer to the technology used to compress the broadcast content into a file that is small enough to be easily transmitted and stored.

Podcasts can be heard or viewed on a wide variety of devices, from a desktop computer to a mobile phone or pocket media player. Some podcasts are ongoing programs that are available by subscription, while others are one-time events that are made available to a broad audience. Some are distributed by respected establishment media sources such as the *New York Times* and National Public Radio, while others are independently made by alternative media. Most podcast subscriptions are free, although some podcast creators charge a fee for their programs. Many commercial websites, such as Podcast Pickle (http://podcastpickle .com/), Podcast Alley (http://www.podcastalley.com/), and the video-sharing website YouTube (www.youtube.com), offer extensive listings of free podcasts. A number of commercial sites, including Apple, Google, and the iTunes store, also provide a variety of podcasts at no charge.

How Are Podcasts Used?

Podcasts provide a wider audience for traditional radio and television shows by allowing listeners or viewers to tune in at their own convenience rather than at a scheduled time. Podcasts may also allow regular broadcast programs to release expanded editions or extra episodes. Some institutions, such as universities, use podcasting to provide audio and video tours of their facilities. Podcasts may also be used by businesses to provide tutorials for new equipment or processes.

The wide availability of affordable digital audio and video recording technology has made it possible for nearly anyone to produce a podcast. With the greatly reduced financial limitations and the almost unlimited accessibility provided by the Internet, podcasts have contributed greatly to broadcast diversity. Anyone with the appropriate recording equipment can produce a radio or television program on any subject.

How Can I Make a Podcast?

In order to create a podcast, you need little more than a recording device and a website for storage and distribution. There are a number of online resources available that offer instruction in producing podcasts, such as Joe Donovan's 2014 article "How to Make a Successful Podcast" on the Digital Trends website (http://www.digitaltrends.com/how-to/how-to-make-a-podcast/).

The skills needed for hosting a podcast are similar to the voice and body management skills used in radio and television appearances. Podcasting may even help you hone your presentation skills and overcome timidity and nervousness. If you have a hobby or interest, such as music, art, or politics, creating a podcast can give you the opportunity to launch your own television or radio show on that subject, featuring commentary on issues of importance to you. Once you learn to create an effective podcast, you may even be able to find a way to use podcasting at your job as a tool for training, advertising, or communication.

Presentations

What Is a Presentation?

A presentation is a type of verbal communication used for transmitting information to a group of people. A presentation usually involves a person or group of people (presenters) who are reporting to or instructing a group of people (the audience) who are present chiefly to receive information on some subject in an organized manner. Presentations may be formal or informal, and audiences may be large or small. Presenters may use a variety of audiovisual aids, or they may simply convey their information verbally.

Presentations are used for a wide range of personal, civic, and business needs. Effective presentations can be entertaining, informative, and persuasive. However, presentations require a number of communication skills in order to be effective, and a poorly planned, boring, or unfocused presentation can lose your audience's attention and reduce their openness to your subject. A well-executed presentation shows respect for your audience and is likely to earn their interest and receptiveness to your ideas.

In What Kinds of Situations Might I Be Expected to Give a Presentation?

Though you may not think of yourself as a public speaker, chances are that you will be called upon to present information to others at some point in your life. This may be as simple and informal as presenting a slideshow of your vacation photos. If you are involved in community work, you may be asked to present an issue before the school board, parent-teacher association, or city council. If you are active in your church, occasions may arise when you are required to make a report to the congregation or to church leaders. Presentation skills may serve you well if you decide to challenge a traffic citation or parking ticket and must make your case in court before a judge.

You should tailor your presentation to the type of the presentation (formal or informal) and the type and size of your audience (colleagues or strangers, a few people or many). © AFRICA STUDIO/ SHUTTERSTOCK.COM.

Presentations arise in the business world even more frequently than in your personal life. Project results are frequently announced in the form of presentations to committees or boards. New polices may gain quicker acceptance if they are formally presented to the workforce. Although most presentations are given before groups, sometimes you may perform a presentation before an audience of one. For example, if you make a suggestion about something at work, you may be asked to create a presentation to demonstrate the value of your idea to your supervisor.

What Planning Skills Are Involved in Giving a Presentation?

The most important factor in a successful presentation is planning. Because the purpose of most presentations is the transmission of information, it is important to study and research your topic thoroughly in order to ensure that your information is correct and up to date. Once you obtain the information you need, you must organize it so that it can be easily understood.

Keep in mind your goals for the presentation. What is it that you want your audience to learn from your presentation? What results do you hope to achieve? Plan your presentation so that it has an introduction that will engage your listeners' interest and a conclusion that ties

Becoming a More Confident Public Speaker

Be Prepared
- Write out your presentation either in outline form or in full.
- Practice your presentation—the more comfortable you are with your presentation, the less room for stage fright.
  - Rehearse your presentation out loud several times. This gives you a chance to find out how the presentation flows, if you need to rewrite or reorder your topics, what words work best, and how long it takes to deliver.
  - Record yourself giving your presentation. How do you sound? How do you look?
  - Ask a friend to critique a trial run of your presentation and use the feedback to polish it.

Take a Course
- Many community colleges and universities offer courses in public speaking or acting.
- Your local school system may offer adult education courses for presenters.
- Use the Internet to find private public speaking coaches and classes.

Join a Group
- Toastmasters International is the best-known group focused on developing communication skills.
- Local community theater groups often offer classes in acting and other stagecraft that can boost confidence for performing in public.

SOURCE: Compiled by the staff of *Life and Career Skills Series*.

ILLUSTRATION BY LUMINA DATAMATICS LTD. © 2015 CENGAGE LEARNING.

together the information you have presented. Throughout this process, it is important to take into account your audience's needs and abilities. Place yourself in your listeners' position. How much information can you realistically expect them to absorb in one sitting? Take care to gear your language to your audience's level of understanding. Unless you are speaking to professionals in a field, explain all technical terms and acronyms or abbreviations you use in your presentation.

Once you have organized your information and written out what you want to say, practice it repeatedly. Although you may use notes to keep you on track and remind you of important points, reading from a prepared script tends to make your presentation less engaging. As you put your ideas together, try to imagine what questions your listeners may raise, and prepare answers to these questions.

Another part of giving an effective presentation is to be familiar with the place where you will perform it. Visit the venue in advance and plan where you will stand and what arrangements you need to make for audiovisual aids and any other equipment you may need. If you will be using a microphone, try to practice with it in advance so that you will be comfortable using it correctly during your presentation. Ask a technician the proper way to speak through the microphone you will be using.

Using PowerPoint Effectively

Microsoft PowerPoint is often used as a visual aid during a presentation. However, many people undermine their presentation by relying too heavily on the program. Here are some helpful tips to use PowerPoint so it enhances your speech.

- Use PowerPoint slides sparingly. You don't need slides for your entire speech, so use them only to highlight important information such as quotations, photos, graphs, maps, and charts. PowerPoint should supplement, not replace, your speech.

- Aim for no more than four lines of text per slide. The text could be a quotation, a key point, or a short bulleted list.

- Avoid sliding transitions, bouncing text, and other kinds of graphic animation. These visual tricks appear unprofessional and are distracting.

- Ensure words and images are clear and readable. For example, don't put dark-blue text on a black background. Only include high-resolution images so they do not appear fuzzy on the screen.

- Rehearse, rehearse, rehearse. It takes practice to coordinate your speech with the slides, and your presentation will be more effective if all goes smoothly.

- Maintain the audience's focus. Position yourself in front of your listeners so they have to look primarily at you. Instead of using a laser pointer to refer to the screen, walk over and point to it with your hand.

- Remember that technology can fail. Make sure you can do your presentation without PowerPoint in case your computer or the software stops working.

Although you may be reluctant to use a microphone, be aware that it will be annoying to your listeners if they cannot hear you clearly.

What Communication Skills Are Involved in Giving a Presentation?

Presenting information to an audience requires the use of a broad range of communication skills. Although some people are naturally more comfortable speaking in public than others, verbal communication skills can be learned with attention and practice. Acquiring basic skills can help you build confidence and make speaking before a group of people far less challenging.

One of the first things your listeners will note about you, consciously or unconsciously, is how you present yourself. Personal presentation is used to describe the way you appear to your audience and includes dressing properly for the occasion. This does not necessarily mean "dressing up." Dressing in a suit and tie to show your vacation photos to a small group of friends is just as inappropriate as dressing in a t-shirt and blue jeans for a formal work presentation. Both will cause the same feelings of discomfort in your audience. Gear your clothes to your audience, but always make sure that you are well groomed and tidy.

Your speaking voice is probably the most important factor in giving a successful presentation. Practice speaking slowly and pronouncing your words carefully. Use tone and volume consciously to add interest to your delivery. Lowering the pitch of your voice may draw listener interest, while a slight rise in volume may reinforce an important point. Keep in mind that your presentation is competing for your listeners' attention with a number of outside distractions. If your voice is monotone, you risk losing your audience. Speak as naturally as you can, as if you were telling a story. Practice projecting your voice so that you can be heard without shouting. Check with your audience initially to make sure everyone can hear you well. If you are soft-spoken and cannot easily project, arrange beforehand to have a microphone available.

Body language: *The gestures, movements, and mannerisms by which a person communicates with others, including facial expressions, tone of voice, and posture.*

Just as you may use your voice to add interest to your presentation, you should also be aware of your *body language* and facial expressions. A warm, smiling face and lively gestures can animate even a routine work presentation. Avoid closed body positions, such as standing with your arms crossed, which may convey anger or tension. Do not pace excessively or flail your arms about, but gesture naturally and move around the stage when appropriate. Do not look down at your notes for long periods or too frequently. Looking directly at your listeners can make your delivery more personal. If you are shy or uncomfortable speaking in front of others, practicing in front of a mirror or with your family can help you develop relaxed, open body language.

What Do I Need to Know When Working with Other People on a Presentation?

In addition to honing your personal communication and planning skills, working with others on a presentation requires interpersonal skills. Although more complicated than planning a presentation on your own, working with others can reduce your workload, decrease the weight of responsibility, and build teamwork skills.

It is important to engage all members of the team in the planning stages of a presentation. You may wish to agree on the overall goals of the presentation and plan the general format, then divide the information to be presented into sections, giving each team member one section to work on. Each person can then present his or her own section, while sharing responsibility for the introduction, conclusion, and question-and-answer session. Take care to ensure that all tasks and credit are shared equally among the team members.

Communication is vital to any shared project. Your team may wish to discuss the strengths and weaknesses of your individual presentation styles in order to anticipate and troubleshoot possible problems. For example, if one member is very verbal and comfortable speaking in public and another is shy and reluctant to speak up, the more verbal worker may naturally take over the speaking tasks and let the shy worker to do most of the planning. However, a more constructive approach may be for the more verbal person to work on curbing his or her tendency to dominate the stage and encourage the timid teammate to practice speaking.

What Kinds of Aids Can I Use for a Presentation?

There are many audiovisual aids you can use to enliven your talk and reinforce the information you are presenting. Audiovisual aids can be important, because it is often difficult for listeners to process and retain the large quantities of information they receive in a short time. In addition, some kinds of information are difficult to explain orally, so an illustration, a graph, or a photo may make a concept quickly accessible. Even when visual aids only illustrate the information that is being delivered orally, they can help the audience understand and remember the information by engaging a different part of the brain. One example of an aid you might use for a personal presentation, such as a slideshow of photographs, is a music soundtrack. An appropriate choice of music can add emotion, energy, and interest to a series of photos. Presentation programs, such as Microsoft PowerPoint, enable you to create a series of slides with text, graphics, photos, animation, and other features. The slideshow can accompany a spoken presentation or take the place of one, enabling the presentation to be sent via e-mail to a wide audience that people can view it at their leisure.

You may also use an overhead projector, in which you place slides or papers that are then projected in large size on a wall screen. The overhead projector allows you to create slides as you speak, so that your listeners can see your writing or drawing on the paper being projected, which may add interest to your presentation. Interactive whiteboards, or smartboards, work in a similar way. You may also use videos to add a visual element to your presentation. If you choose to use video in your talk, practice beforehand to ensure that you know exactly how to use the equipment and that you can easily find the section of the video you want to show. Audiences will have little patience if you keep them waiting while you search for your visual aids.

You may also use non technological visual aids such as whiteboards and blackboards to illustrate points as you speak, or you can write down information on them beforehand. Flip charts, or large pads of paper set on a stand, may be used in the same way and often provide a satisfying sense of progression because you can turn the pages over once you are done with them to reveal a new blank space. Writing boards and flip charts have the advantage of being simple to use and inexpensive to obtain, but you must have legible handwriting and be comfortable writing or drawing while standing up.

Perhaps the most useful visual aid is the handout. Handouts are papers printed in advance that contain information that you give to each member of the audience. Handouts may elaborate on your presentation, provide resources for finding further information, or simply reproduce what you have said so that your listeners can refer to it later. In addition to being inexpensive and simple to produce, handouts have the advantage of being something your listeners can take with them to help them remember the content of your presentation.

For More Information

BOOKS

Davis, Jeannie. *Beyond "Hello": A Practical Guide for Excellent Telephone Communication and Quality Customer Service*. Aurora, CO: Now Hear This, 2000.

Duarte, Nancy. *HBR Guide to Persuasive Presentations*. Boston: Harvard Business School Publishing, 2012.

Ellis, Donald G. *From Language to Communication*. New York: Routledge, 2012.

Keller, Ed, and Brad Fay. *The Face-to-Face Book: Why Real Relationships Rule in a Digital Marketplace*. New York: Free Press, 2012.

RoAne, Susan. *Face to Face: How to Reclaim the Personal Touch in a Digital World*. New York: Fireside, 2008.

Stephenson, Alan R., David E. Reese, and Mary E. Beadle. *Broadcast Announcing Worktext: Performing for Radio, Television, and Cable.* Burlington, MA: Focal Press, 2004.

PERIODICALS

Johnson, Chandra. "Face Time vs. Screen Time: The Technological Impact on Communication." *Deseret News*, August 29, 2014. This article can also be found online at http://national.deseretnews.com/article/2235/Face-time-vs-screen-time-The-technological-impact-on-communication.html#Vz4TEhyEQ3UO6TGX.99.

Jowitt, Angela L. "Creating Communities with Podcasting." *Computers in Libraries* 28, no. 4 (2008): 14+.

"Pulse Financial: Importance of Telephone Skills in Practice." *Pulse*, May 4, 2006: 28.

Russell, Joyce E. A. "Career Coach: The Wrong Tone Can Spoil the Message." *Washington Post*, February 7, 2011. This article can also be found online at http://www.washingtonpost.com/wp-dyn/content/article/2011/02/04/AR2011020406095.html.

WEBSITES

Chapman, Gary. "Thoughts on Using PowerPoint Effectively." *University of Texas at Austin.* http://www.utexas.edu/lbj/21cp/syllabus/powerpoint_tips2.htm (accessed November 11, 2014).

Donovan, Joe. "How to Make a Successful Podcast." *Digital Trends.* July 17, 2014. http://www.digitaltrends.com/how-to/how-to-make-a-podcast/ (accessed November 10, 2014).

"Five Tips for a Better Web Conference." *Microsoft Business.* http://www.microsoft.com/business/en-us/resources/technology/communications/5-tips-for-a-better-Web-conference.aspx?fbid=iUa8eFHaH6X (accessed November 6, 2014).

"How to Engage Your Audience and Keep Them with You." *Hamilton College.* http://www.hamilton.edu/oralcommunication/how-to-engage-your-audience-and-keep-them-with-you (accessed November 3, 2014).

"How to Improve Listening and Conversation Skills." *Erupting Mind: Intelligent Advice for Intelligent People.* http://www.eruptingmind.com/how-to-improve-listening-skills-in-conversations/ (accessed November 4, 2014).

"Presentation Skills." *University of Surrey.* http://libweb.surrey.ac.uk/library/skills/Presentation%20Skills%20Leicester/index.php (accessed November 11, 2014).

Rosenthal, Bill. "Making an Effective Presentation." *Forbes.* February 24, 2010. http://www.forbes.com/2010/02/24/effective-presentation-skills-leadership-careers-rosenthal.html (accessed November 11, 2014).

Nonverbal

What Is Nonverbal Communication?

While nearly everyone uses language, words are not the only way people communicate. We all send nonverbal cues that may provide as much information as speech. This nonverbal communication, sometimes called body language, includes facial expressions, posture, eye contact, gestures, and touch. It can also incorporate mannerisms such as how fast you talk or how close you stand to others. These signals give the listener hints about who you are as well as what you are saying.

While estimates vary as to how much of our communication is nonverbal, most experts place the overall amount at more than half. Nonverbal communication is usually subconscious, and most scientists agree that basic facial expressions are inherited behaviors. People in all cultures use the same expressions for emotions such as anger, happiness, sadness, fear, surprise, and disgust. Other kinds of nonverbal communication vary from culture to culture. People in Latin America typically stand closer to each other when talking than people do in Europe and the United States, for example. Eye contact is thought to be disrespectful

Probably the most effective nonverbal communicators are mimes like this one. © KORIONOV/ SHUTTERSTOCK.COM.

or rude in some Asian and Middle Eastern countries, as well as for some Native Americans.

What Can I Learn about Others from Their Nonverbal Communication?

Even before a person speaks, you receive clues from his or her body language that add to the meaning of spoken words. Standing tall with feet apart signals power and confidence, especially when combined with hands on hips. A hunched, head-down posture can communicate weakness, submissiveness, or sadness. In most conversations, leaning in toward the listener can show that the speaker is interested and engaged, while leaning out or looking away may show the opposite. When the speaker is angry or confrontational, leaning in can signal aggression.

You can also learn about a person by noticing how far away he or she stands from you during a conversation. The amount of space between you and another person is called personal space, and it can indicate how that person feels about you. In U.S. culture, most personal conversations occur at a distance that is generally between 18 inches and four feet. More intimate exchanges can take place at less than 18 inches apart, and people who don't know each other well, such as guests at a social gathering, are likely to stand farther away than four feet when they speak. A person who moves inside your comfort zone while speaking may be from a different culture or may want to conduct the conversation on a more intimate level.

Eye contact is a powerful communicator, and looking directly into someone's eyes can signal strong interest. When combined with facial expressions such as knit eyebrows or a tense jaw, direct eye contact can mean anger or aggression. If someone is sexually attracted to you, he or she may attempt to hold your gaze for a longer time. Eyes are excellent indicators of emotions, and a smile that does not extend to the eyes may seem false. Pupils dilate when a person encounters something that he or she finds attractive or interesting, making the eye seem larger and darker.

Nonverbal Communication and Elections

Nonverbal communication has influenced how politicians have been perceived by the public. In his previous career as an actor, President Ronald Reagan was trained to use body language to portray specific emotions and attitudes. He used these skills effectively as a politician and became known as "the great communicator." Many people who disagreed with his political positions voted for him anyway because they felt an emotional connection to him. During a presidential debate in 1960, John F. Kennedy appeared more rested than Richard Nixon, which contributed to perceptions that Kennedy won the debate.

Physical attractiveness is an important attribute in politics, since good-looking people are sometimes believed to be friendlier and more accessible. Attractiveness can be managed to some extent with hairstyle, weight control, dress, or makeup. However, height is also a factor. Taller political candidates often seem to command more respect than those who are shorter, and this may sometimes be a factor that helps them receive more votes. According to the *Christian Science Monitor*, between 1789 and 2008 the taller candidate won 58 percent of U.S. presidential elections.

Studies have shown that people with dilated pupils are often considered more approachable and kind than those with smaller pupils.

Facial expressions communicate a vast array of emotions that can enhance verbal communication. In most cases they support the spoken message while adding emotional information, such as enthusiasm, fear, urgency, or hesitation on the part of the speaker. Sometimes, however, body language may conflict directly with spoken words. For example, a frown or grimace while saying "I love you" can send the opposite message. Even very slight micro-expressions that last for less than a second can indicate that a person is not being truthful. You may unconsciously register a fleeting smile or smirk and come away from a conversation questioning the other person's sincerity. This reaction is often referred to as a gut feeling, or intuition. People tend to trust nonverbal communication more than speech, and if there is a mismatch between the two, a listener is likely to believe the body language over the words.

How Can Nonverbal Communication Make a Difference in the Workplace?

Everyone in a workplace, from a job applicant to a business owner, continually projects and receives nonverbal communication. These signals can affect how employees are perceived by their managers and fellow workers, how employees respond to their supervisors, how clients feel about employees, or whether an applicant gets a job.

During a job interview, the interviewer will assess a prospective employee for attributes such as competence, honesty, and reliability. Nonverbal cues such as good eye contact and a relaxed posture can convey these positive qualities. On the other hand, fidgeting, poor eye contact, slouching, or nail biting can give a negative impression. These nonverbal signals can cost an applicant the job, even if he or she gives all the right answers.

Current employees are also judged by their body language. People with hairstyles or dress that are not in keeping with a particular business culture may not be taken seriously or may be seen as disrespectful. Workplace customs also dictate behaviors such as how loudly people speak, how they sit at their desks, or who speaks at meetings. In general, people with more power are more likely to maintain direct eye contact, interrupt while other people are speaking, or use touch to communicate, such as a pat on the back.

Supervisors usually have a larger office space than their employees, which is a type of nonverbal communication that furthers the impression of power. Those who use body-language signals such as an open, relaxed posture or a smiling facial expression foster a positive work environment, which can improve productivity. Supervisors who turn or lean away during a conversation, or who fail to make eye contact, send a negative message and can make employees feel undervalued.

When businesspeople deal with clients, their nonverbal communication can influence the success of the encounter. Dress, hairstyle, tone of voice, posture, and other aspects of body language send messages to the client about competence and trustworthiness. Nonverbal communication can also provide clues as to how a meeting is going. Clients who use gestures such as folded arms, poor eye contact, fidgeting, or moving farther away may be signaling that they are not satisfied with a presentation or offer.

What Role Does Nonverbal Communication Play in Criminal Justice?

While justice is said to be blind, body language can influence lawyers, juries, judges, and even criminals, since it gives information that is not available through words alone. While nonverbal communication is not effective at determining whether someone is lying, in some cases it can still be more accurate than chance. It works best in situations in which a person's typical body language can be compared to changes in gestures, posture, or voice. Lawyers try to observe prospective jurors for such changes when asking questions to determine their attitudes about race, sentencing, crime, or other issues related to a trial. They may look for signs of nervousness such as increased blinking, lack of eye contact, shifting in a seat, or shrugging. While these body language traits may not always be accurate indicators, they often influence decisions as to who is selected to sit on a jury.

Nonverbal communication is also at work during a trial. Lawyers use eye contact, gestures, and other body language to try to sway jurors. Consciously or unconsciously, jurors observe body language throughout a trial, watching not only the witnesses but others in the courtroom. They may make judgments based on how lawyers talk to their clients and question the witnesses, how spectators in the gallery react to testimony or rulings from the judge, or whether a person on the stand seems nervous. Even judges, who try to be impartial, can give away their opinions with facial expressions or postures. This factor can be particularly influential, since people often adopt the opinions of those in positions of authority. The way people dress in the courtroom may also influence jurors.

Body language can even play a part in determining who is victimized by crime. Studies show that muggers and other criminals are more likely to attack people who walk slowly or appear to be weak, old, or feeble. People who wear obvious jewelry or fine clothing can also be likely targets. Police observe body language when they question suspects and witnesses. However, they are typically no better than an average person at detecting when someone is lying.

How Does Nonverbal Communication Affect Relationships?

Body language plays a powerful role in families, among friends, and in intimate relationships. The first communication between people who become romantically involved is often nonverbal, and body language cues can give hints about when a relationship is breaking down.

From birth, infants need close physical touch to thrive. Being held communicates security, warmth, and love. Small children use touch to explore their world, and they use body language to communicate with each other before they can speak. They receive body-language signals from parents and others, such as smiles and postures that show attention. Teenagers often use elements of nonverbal communication such as eccentric dress or hairstyles, eye rolling, or slouching to test their limits. Children whose parents or caregivers consistently project negative body language, such as angry or rejecting facial expressions or poor eye contact, may grow up with emotional problems.

Friends often become very good at reading each other's body language and may even subconsciously imitate it. Two people who cross their legs or rest their chin in their hands in the same way, an action known as mirroring, communicate agreement and camaraderie. In romantic relationships, eye contact signals interest and is part of flirting, and it may be followed by smiles, laughing, or touching the person's hand or arm.

Couples in an established relationship continue to watch each other's body language for clues about things like mood and health. People who have been together for a long time may adopt mannerisms and speaking patterns similar to those of their partners. They may become very attuned to even slight nonverbal communications in each other and may be able to pick up unspoken messages. For example, a raised eyebrow might be enough for one partner to communicate to the other that it's time to leave a party.

Can Nonverbal Communication Affect Health?

Beginning early in life, many aspects of health are influenced by nonverbal communication. When infants are frequently held and touched by caregivers who smile and speak in soothing tones, they are calmer, sleep better, and cry less. Children who are deprived of close physical contact, such as babies who spend their early years in institutions, have higher levels of stress hormones and lower levels of oxytocin and other hormones that are linked to positive emotions and social bonding. They may grow up unable to form normal attachments with others.

For adults, body language is an important aspect of health care. Doctors observe nonverbal cues in their patients to help diagnose illnesses. For example, tremors, rigid muscles, or a shuffling walk can point to certain types of dementia (a progressive condition marked by deteriorated cognitive functioning). Lack of facial expressions or a posture that angles away from others can mean that a patient is depressed. Breathing patterns and guarding postures that indicate pain can also be clues to illness. Patients interpret nonverbal communications from their doctors, such as eye contact or smiling, to make judgments about whether to trust them. This factor can help determine how well a patient follows a treatment.

Can My Nonverbal Communication Betray What I'm Really Feeling?

Nonverbal communication cannot always help you determine whether or not a person is being truthful. Books and other publications offer lists of body language cues, such as increased blinking, dilated pupils, crossed arms, glances to the left or right, speech errors, or rising vocal pitch, that can show when someone is lying. However, while these nonverbal communications can signal deception, they may also result from anxiety, impatience, or physical discomfort, and people who cross their arms may simply be cold. People can train themselves to avoid these nonverbal cues in order to appear truthful. Aside from a few experts and researchers who are trained to identify split-second micro-expressions, the typical success rate for detecting lies is about 50 percent.

While lies are difficult to identify, your body language can give away your emotions and attitudes if your nonverbal communication conflicts with what you say. For example, talking to one person while continuously looking across the room at someone else may betray a lack of interest in the conversation you are having. Parents who say that they are not angry may give away their true feelings if they hunch their shoulders, cross their arms, or speak loudly. Poker players try to conceal their reactions to being dealt a good or bad card, but they may have unconscious "tells" such as narrowed eyes or a change in posture.

Active or Reflective Listening

What Is Active Listening?

Active, or reflective, listening is a communication technique that seeks to increase understanding between a speaker and a listener. The goal of active listening is to establish the clear communication of ideas and feelings and eliminate misunderstanding. Rather than listening passively or distractedly, an active listener pays close attention to what another person is saying without interrupting. He or she then verbally summarizes the key points of the speaker's message to ensure that they both agree on what was said. Once the speaker has succeeded in getting his or her point across, the roles reverse and the speaker becomes the listener.

The process of active listening demonstrates respect and consideration for the person speaking, which helps establish trust between the speaker and the listener. An active listener focuses solely on understanding the speaker's ideas and feelings without reacting or passing judgment. The listener need not agree with the other person's point of view but should indicate full comprehension of the intended message. Active listening asks that you set aside your need to respond or assert your own ideas in favor of clearly understanding what another person is saying, knowing that you will be given the same consideration when it is your turn to speak.

Active listening is a formal skill that needs to be learned and practiced. It is not something that most people do automatically, although once learned it is good practice in almost all circumstances. Sometimes a neutral third party, such as a family therapist, supervisor, or professional mediator, leads the process, but active listening can also be achieved by any two willing individuals who commit to the techniques and procedures involved.

How Does Active Listening Work?

Empathy, suspension of judgment, undivided attention, and summarizing are central to successful active listening. The process can be conducted formally, with a mediator helping to guide the participants through the various stages, or it can be done informally by following the appropriate steps for good active listening. The goal is to facilitate better communication without the usual obstacles to understanding, such as heated emotions or distracted half-listening. Both participants should listen to each other in turn without any interruptions, remaining fully focused on the other person when it is his or her turn to speak.

Active listening works best when the two parties sit facing each other at a reasonably close distance, and they should be in an isolated location with as few distractions as possible. A private enclosed space is best, such as a room with a closed door, especially if this room can be shut off from outside interruptions. The parties speak in turns, with one person speaking first while the other listens intently without responding to what is being said. The speaker should stick to a single subject in order to keep the discussion focused. Full eye contact between speaker and listener is important.

© IQONCEPT/ SHUTTERSTOCK.COM.

As a listener, you should not interrupt the speaker, but you can offer subtle acknowledgments that signal comprehension, such as nodding or quietly saying "I see" or "Go on." It is important for you to withhold any judgment while the speaker is talking and to avoid giving nonverbal clues that might indicate disagreement. You do not have to be in complete agreement with what is being said, but indicating disagreement in any way can distract the speaker and impede communication.

The goal is for the listener to give full, undivided attention to the speaker. You should avoid thinking about what to say next or how to respond or whether what the speaker is saying is even correct. Instead, focus on understanding what is being said. The point is for you to try to empathize with the speaker as well as possible and see things from his or her point of view.

Once the speaker finishes talking, you should summarize what he or she just said. Summarizing serves two functions. It lets the speaker know how well you understood what was said, and it also allows room for clarification if the summary does not accurately reflect the main point that the speaker was trying to make. It may be helpful if you use phrases such as "I heard you say" or "This is what I feel you meant by".

Case Study: Kyle Practices Active Listening

Kyle, the manager of a chain of electronics stores, is known to friends and family as extraverted and talkative, always ready to jump into any conversation, share an anecdote, or offer an opinion. Never a loner, Kyle feels best spending time with other people. He also considers the best part of his job to be his interactions with colleagues at work.

Recently, at a performance review, his boss informed him that a considerable number of Kyle's subordinates felt that he ignored their opinions, talked over them in conversations, and glanced around distractedly while they were talking. Kyle was genuinely surprised. He thought that he had friendly and communicative relationships with other people at work. However, based on the performance review, he acknowledged that he needed to work on his listening skills. With the encouragement of his supervisor, Kyle studied "active listening."

He now practices active listening when having conversations with people at work. Instead of talking over them or jumping into the conversation to share his own ideas, Kyle listens quietly and receptively, nodding to demonstrate that he is listening and summarizing what he has heard once they finish speaking. At first, it was hard for Kyle to change his conversational style, but, with practice, he has become better at allowing others the time and space to speak freely—without his interference. Kyle senses that he is creating better working relationships with his employees now that he talks less and listens more as they have been coming to him more often to discuss their questions and concerns and to share ideas.

The speaker can make corrections or clarifications as needed until he or she feels fully understood. The speaker and listener then switch roles and the process plays out this way, back and forth, until both people have clarified their points and have been fully heard and understood by the other.

In What Types of Situations Is Active Listening Used?

While anyone who learns the techniques can practice them in any listening situation, the process is typically used in situations where people have difficulty communicating their needs and ideas clearly. It is common for people who live or work in close contact to develop habits of listening and reacting to each other that are based on what they expect the other person to say or do rather than on what is actually said or done. Active listening provides a way to break through these assumptions and allow constructive communication to happen.

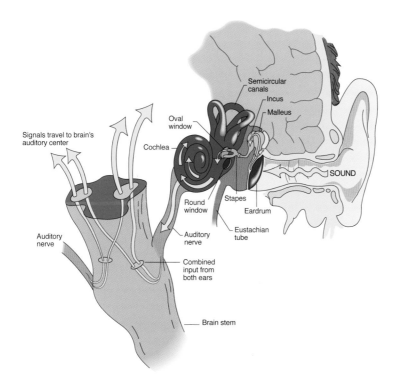

Semicircular
canals
Incus
Malleus
Oval
window
Cochlea
Signals travel to brain's
auditory center
SOUND
Round
window
Stapes
Eardrum
Auditory
nerve
Auditory
nerve
Eustachian
tube
Combined
input from
both ears
Brain stem

The ear can get words to your brain, how your brain processes the words is active listening.
DIAGRAM BY HANS & CASSIDY, © GALE GROUP.

In couples or family therapy, active listening takes place in the presence of a therapist or counselor who guides the process. Sometimes people tune out what other family members are saying because they think they know what is coming next. For example, children who expect their parents to reprimand them may only hear criticism, or parents who expect a certain attitude from teenagers may believe that they hear it in their child's tone. Active listening cuts through these expectations by requiring full attention while listening and restating the message and the listener has shown a clear understanding of what the speaker has said.

Active listening also plays a role in conflict resolution, especially in cases of divorce. It is common for people to send attorneys to speak on their behalf in lawsuits or contract negotiations, but it is usually best for the people involved to talk to each other directly whenever possible. No matter how well prepared lawyers are, they are still in a position of interpreting their clients' needs second hand. When two people who are fully engaged and committed to the process speak directly to each other using active listening techniques, there is less room for misinterpretation.

Active listening can also be useful in resolving workplace issues. Miscommunication or lack of understanding between coworkers can lead to resentment and hurt feelings that impair the employees' ability to work together effectively. Active listening helps reverse these trends and can sometimes even prevent them from happening in the first place. Whether facilitated by a supervisor or manager or implemented among peers, active listening techniques can create greater understanding and empathy among coworkers, which can make them more likely to work cooperatively as a team.

What Are Some Examples of Active Listening?

Imagine that a coworker is unexpectedly rude to you or seems insensitive to your needs. You might be hurt, or you might become angry and begin to dislike that person. However, through the application of active listening, you have an opportunity to explain clearly how you feel about your coworker's behavior, while he or she has a chance to explain and maybe even apologize. You might learn that your coworker was going through a difficult time at home or that he or she was under extraordinary pressure on the job and oblivious to the insulting behavior. Not only do you come to know more about that person's situation, but he or she might appreciate your willingness to listen. In this way, a situation that had the potential to be a major problem can be channeled into mutual understanding.

Sometimes people do not communicate with those they are close to because they fear the other person's reaction. Rather than saying, for example, "It really hurts my feelings when you come home late without calling ahead," a partner might say nothing at all in order to avoid conflict, but the hurt feelings remain and can lead to resentment. If the partners actively listen to each other, however, they can fully explain how they feel, and this can help avoid any hurt feelings.

A difference in power between groups, such as between students and teachers, can impede communication. Those with less power may feel that they have no influence over the decisions of the person in charge. For instance, a group of students who have studied for a test find that it covers topics that were not included in the required studying material. Afterward, they feel upset because they believe that the test was unfairly difficult. They will probably complain among themselves, but the teacher might never find out what they really think. However, if the teacher were willing to use active listening techniques, the students could air their grievances, and the teacher could explain the decisions behind the construction of the test. If the students were fairly heard, the teacher may consider amending the test questions in the future, or perhaps the students might gain a better understanding of the teacher's testing philosophy and could prepare for exams more effectively in the future.

What Are the Benefits of Active Listening?

Active listening improves relationships and promotes goodwill by allowing people to demonstrate their ability to speak and listen purposefully and attentively. If someone does not listen to you or undervalues what you have to say, you may feel slighted. But the opposite may be true when someone takes the time to listen and understand you. Your closest friends are almost always the people you can talk openly with and who listen carefully to what you have to say. Those qualities help create the bonds of friendship. The practice of active listening, even among people who are not friends, can establish a professional connection that may make them more willing to cooperate with one another.

Active listening also helps you express greater empathy toward others, since it requires setting aside your own needs for the purpose of understanding someone else's. Because it involves withholding judgment, active listening provides a safe environment for people to express themselves. When people speak candidly about their concerns, it can make them feel vulnerable, especially if they admit a mistake or a weakness. However, listening actively requires that you do not judge or evaluate what the speaker says, only that you focus on clearly understanding it. The intimacy created by open sharing of ideas and feelings can improve relationships, whether at home, school, or work.

Body Language

What Is Body Language?

Body language is a collective term that refers to the various physical and visual cues people use to communicate ideas or emotions. Sometimes body language is used in conjunction with speech to underscore what is being said, as when people move their hands and arms while talking. It can also be used by itself to send a message, as with a shrug of the shoulders or a wag of the finger. Body language encompasses a wide range of physical movements, including facial expressions, posture, gestures, touch, and bodily proximity.

Despite the emphasis that is placed on the spoken word, more than half of what we communicate to others is through body language alone. Furthermore, people tend to give more credence to nonverbal cues than to spoken ones. Most of us have probably asked people how they are doing and had them reply, "I'm fine." However, if they say, "I'm fine," but their slumped shoulders and lack of eye contact suggest otherwise, are they fine or not? It is hard to know with absolute certainty. Most people consider a verbal response to be a cover for a deeper truth revealed by that person's demeanor.

Since each person's body language is unique and develops over many years to become second nature, it can be difficult to change without conscious effort, just like any habit. For this reason, body language can be a more accurate sign of how a person is feeling than words. It is much easier to casually say, "I'm fine," when we are not than it is to mask the underlying posture or facial expressions connected with being upset.

Body language can be either intentional or unintentional. When we are conscious of it, we can use it to our advantage by adding emphasis to what we say or reinforcing our ideas. However, when we are unaware of it, we can send mixed messages or even contradict our spoken words. Imagine a man nodding his head in agreement while at the same time

This man's body language clearly shows what's on his mind. © PATHDOC/ SHUTTERSTOCK.COM.

saying, "No." In such a case, the spoken message is contradicted by the nonverbal message, which hinders clear communication.

What Are Some Different Types of Body Language?

Facial expressions are the most easily recognized form of body language. Smiling, for example, says a lot about your mood before any words are spoken. Movement of the eyes, eyebrows, eyelids, and lips all send subtle nonverbal signals. While they can be used alone, facial expressions are usually modifiers that emphasize or amend what is being said. A wink might indicate that you are not being as serious as you sound, for example. Eye contact, or lack thereof, also sends signals about confidence and attentiveness, both on the part of the speaker and the listener.

The History of Body Language as a Science

Most people have at least some awareness of the role that body language plays in communication. The study of body language, however, is a relatively new science. One of the earliest thinkers to consider the importance of body language was English philosopher and scientist Francis Bacon (1561–1626). In his 1605 book *Of the Proficience and Advancement of Learning, Divine and Human*, he notes that the works of classical philosophers such as Aristotle (384–322 bce) contain no discussion of the role that gestures play in conveying emotion. Despite Bacon's insistence that significant political and business advantages could be gained by deducing a person's state of mind through body language, more than two centuries would pass before significant advances were made in the study. Indeed, the next major advance did not come until 1872, when English naturalist Charles Darwin (1809–82) published *The Expressions of the Emotions in Man and Animals*. The book describes Darwin's observations of nonverbal cues across species and concludes that some aspects of nonverbal communication are inborn.

Darwin's studies provided the foundation for the modern study of body language, which began to emerge in its present form in the 1960s. Among the best-known studies of body language are those by Paul Ekman (1934–). Ekman began studying nonverbal communication in the 1950s and began carrying out studies funded by the National Institute of Mental Health in 1963. He is best known for his studies of the relationship between facial expression and emotion, which have had a wide influence on both his field of study and popular culture. Due to the work of pioneers such as Ekman, body language is the subject of a wide range of scientific texts as well as popular self-help books.

Gestures, mainly of the arms and hands, are another way people communicate nonverbally. Waving good-bye is a clear hand signal, as is the "thumbs-up" sign, which indicates agreement or positive reinforcement. People gesticulate, or move their hands as they talk, in order to clarify what they mean. When giving directions to a place, most people will supplement their words by a gesture like pointing. Such gestures are not required to convey something, but they help emphasize the words by pairing them with visual cues.

Body posture also sends strong nonverbal signals. Standing upright with your shoulders back and head held high conveys confidence, while slumped shoulders and an averted gaze suggests the opposite. Facing someone squarely during a conversation indicates engagement, whereas standing sidelong or leaning casually at a right angle might suggest disinterest or distractedness. Good posture can also show respect, as when students sit upright in class rather than slumping in their chairs.

Touch and proximity are two forms of body language that typically indicate intimacy. People tend to have the most physical contact with and stand nearest to those they know intimately well, such as a romantic partner or family member. In these relationships personal space is reduced to almost nothing. Outside of these small groups, touching becomes less common, to the point where a handshake might be the only acceptable way for two strangers to make physical contact at first.

It is important to consider that body language is no more universal than any other form of communication and that different cultures send the same message in varying ways. Greeting customs differ widely from country to country and include shaking hands, kissing cheeks, or bowing at the waist. Each of these gestures employs a certain amount of proximity and touch, and someone expecting to be bowed to might be embarrassed by the idea of kissing someone else's cheek. When interacting with people from other countries or cultures, it is a good idea to learn what is customary for them and make adjustments in order to avoid awkwardness.

What Messages Are Communicated through Body Language?

Messages conveyed through body language do not possess the same level of detail or complexity that spoken language does. It would be difficult to explain a high-level math problem through gestures and facial expressions alone. However, body language successfully communicates emotional states or intentions, often more forcefully than words do. A boy hopping around frantically while cradling his hand conveys more about the pain he is in than if he simply says, "Wow, that hurts!" Furthermore, someone running at you with raised, clenched fists clearly shows aggression regardless of what that person might be saying.

People's body language often betrays their true feelings because it is automatic, or done instinctively. A woman seated next to you on a plane might tell you that she is not nervous, but if you observe that she is tightly gripping the armrest, you probably would conclude otherwise. It is much rarer for people to "lie" with their bodies than with their words, in part because body language happens subconsciously.

There is usually a direct connection between what we feel and how we act. Eating sour food might make us pucker, while hearing a sudden noise can make us jump in surprise. We do not usually plan these behaviors in advance. Therefore, body language is a visible sign of how we are reacting to our environment. Learning not to react by keeping our body language in check takes practice. Poker players train themselves to hide their emotions from fellow players. New players will often reveal a good or bad hand by spontaneously showing delight or disappointment, but seasoned players learn to mask these emotions.

Body language also allows for indirect communication when bluntness would be uncomfortable or risky. When two people flirt with each another, they may not come out and say, "I find you attractive," but the way they use their bodies in each other's presence can indicate mutual attraction more subtly. Standing close to someone, smiling, facing the person squarely while listening, and using gentle touches all indicate unspoken attraction.

Our body language says a lot about who we are, what we are thinking, and how we feel. A confident person often exhibits body confidence: standing with upright posture, shaking hands firmly, touching people when appropriate, and leaning in close to converse. A shy person, in contrast, might face slightly away from other people, refrain from touching others, and avoid eye contact. These personal traits are revealed more through body language than verbal communication.

What Are Some Techniques for Using Body Language Effectively?

Being able to use body language effectively begins with increased awareness of it. For most of us, body language is an afterthought, something that happens automatically. However, as with any habit, it can be changed over time with effort and practice. Being mindful of your own body is similar to focusing on your breathing. Most of the time we breathe without thinking about it, but once our attention is focused on the act, we can change the rate and size of our breaths with ease.

After making note of your own body language, ask yourself what messages you are sending with it. If you avoid eye contact, what does this say to other people? You may be an engaged listener, but will other people think so if you never look them in the eye? If you view yourself as a happy person but do not smile much, will other people believe you to be happy? It is helpful to understand that your true self is not always accurately reflected in your physical conduct.

The process of self-awareness can be distracting and time consuming, so it is best to change small things at first. When you stand, what do you do with your hands? Are they in your pockets, at your sides, or perhaps clasped behind your back? Do you make firm eye contact or avoid someone else's gaze? Once you make a habit of noticing these things, it becomes easier to maintain constant awareness. This, in turn, will help you decide which new body habits you want to adopt.

When you have advance notice of some kind of formal interaction, such as a job interview, plan ahead for how you want to be perceived. Confidence is important in job interviews, so practice firm handshakes and establishing eye contact ahead of time. If you usually have a slumped seated posture, practice sitting upright with your feet firmly on the floor. Even if these behaviors do not feel natural, they will help reinforce what you hope to convey with your words. If you avoid eye contact while telling a prospective employer that you are confident you can do the job, you weaken your message.

What Is the Relationship between Body Language and Emotion?

An underlying connection often exists between how we feel and how we behave. We cower in fear or smile when we are happy not because we plan to but because our bodies instinctively react in certain ways. Biting your fingernails is a habit that indicates nervousness.

It might seem to be a given that what people think or feel is revealed through their behavior, and for the most part this is true. Consider the body language of people in victorious circumstances, such as a football player who has just scored a touchdown, a runner who is first across the finish line, or a politician who has won an election. These victors typically raise their hands high over their heads in celebration. It is an almost universal reaction to winning.

Research suggests, however, that certain poses create corresponding feelings rather than vice versa. For example, a confident body posture can lead to feelings of confidence, or a powerful stance can lead to feelings of power. A real-world application of this is to stand with your arms raised and head held high, like an athlete who has just won a race, for two minutes before heading into a job interview or any other situation where you need to feel successful. The theory is that this winning pose in itself will help to create feelings of success and self-assuredness.

Projecting and Interpreting Nonverbal Cues and Signals

When Do People Send and Receive Nonverbal Communications?

People exchange nonverbal cues and signals during every encounter, whether they mean to or not. Even at a distance, we make judgments about people based on their nonverbal communication, or body language. For example, someone with a slow, halting walk may be seen as old, submissive, or feeble, while a person who strides with an erect posture seems positive and confident. In a conversation, a person who leans in and maintains eye contact seems interested, while someone who crosses his or her arms and looks away seems to want to be somewhere else.

Nonverbal communication can be obvious or subtle, such as a fleeting change in facial expression. Either way, nearly everyone incorporates even the smallest cues and signals into their assessments of people and situations. Most people are experts at interpreting body language, and if it conflicts with a spoken message, they will often believe the nonverbal communication over the words.

You cannot avoid sending nonverbal signals. Even a blank expression and a neutral posture convey messages, if only that you are uninterested. In addition, people may interpret your nonverbal communications differently depending on their own experiences and preconceptions. However, you can use your body language to enhance your communication. You can also learn to be better at reading nonverbal signals and cues in others.

Do Men and Women Differ in Their Nonverbal Communications?

Men and women use similar nonverbal communications, including smiles, frowns, angry voices, and nearly all other elements of body language that are recognized across genders and cultures. Still, there are

Being aware of nonverbal clues, whether one-on-one or in a large group like this one, can help you hone your communication to the others' receptiveness. © RAWPIXEL/ SHUTTERSTOCK.COM.

differences. Women generally use body language more than men, especially facial expressions. They also gesture more often and are more likely than men to look at the other person in a conversation. When women are talking with other women, they stand closer and use touch more often than men do when talking to other men.

Women are also better at reading body language. This is true regarding facial expressions, posture, gestures, and eye contact. On the other hand, men are better at detecting potential opponents and communicating in large groups. In fact, women's typical nonverbal communication patterns can work against them in a business setting. Women are less likely to speak up at meetings, particularly if it involves interrupting another speaker. And when women speak firmly they are often seen as aggressive and domineering instead of authoritative.

In both social and work situations, men and women can learn to use nonverbal communications to their benefit. Experts suggest that women in business may do better if they speak up at meetings with an even tone of voice, even if it means interrupting. Standing to speak gives women a nonverbal advantage. Men can improve their work success if they smile more often, increase eye contact, and avoid speaking in a loud or angry tone. Men and women in social situations may benefit from being aware of gender differences in body language and watching for miscommunications.

How Can I Use Nonverbal Communication in My Personal Life?

Body language is often the first way people communicate, especially in romantic relationships. Eye contact, smiling and laughing, changes in posture, and brief touches can be part of what is commonly known as flirting. These nonverbal cues send the message of interest and may lead to dating and longer-term relationships. It is important to gauge the other person's level of interest before offering more intimate nonverbal signals such as hugging, hand holding, or kissing. Sending these messages too early can alienate someone you are interested in. Men, especially, tend to read sexual meaning into body language that may have another meaning.

When you interact with a friend or family member, that person will be familiar with your nonverbal communications. If you have fallen into exchanges that seem negative and unproductive, you may be able to break out of these ruts by adopting body language that sends new messages. Avoid gestures such as crossing your arms, putting your hands on your hips, or turning away. Instead, try maintaining good eye contact, sitting or standing with an open, relaxed position, leaning slightly toward the other person, and briefly touching his or her arm or shoulder. These nonverbal communications indicate interest and involvement in the conversation.

Children are experts at reading body language, and you can use it to improve communications with them. With small children, get down to their level by sitting on a chair or the floor. Mimicking kids' gestures, such as pointing or waving, reinforces their learning processes and helps them feel confident. Infants who see smiling faces and are touched gently and frequently are more likely to feel secure. Older children respond to adults who listen without interrupting, smile genuinely, and avoid negative expressions such as scowls or smirks.

Blue-collar workers: *People who perform manual or physical labor, often for an hourly wage.*

Can Nonverbal Signals Help Me Succeed at My Job?

Body language is essential to succeeding at work, starting with the job interview. From *blue-collar* employment to executive positions, it is important to make a good first impression, and one important factor is your clothing. Dress neatly and in keeping with the company's typical style.

Maintain good eye contact without staring, and try not to fidget. Smiling and nodding convey interest and agreement, but limit them to appropriate moments. Sit straight and avoid crossing your legs.

As an employee, your body language communicates your status and can affect your job success. Business suits signal higher rank for both men and women. Depending on the workplace, too much jewelry, excessive perfume, and very high heels for women may send negative signals. In some jobs, men can appear disrespectful if they dress too casually or let their hair get too long. Both men and women do better if they are careful about touching others in the workplace, limiting touch to pats on the back or arm. Employees may increase their chances for success if they project confidence with a direct gaze, an erect posture, and appropriate smiles.

Supervisors can use nonverbal communication to build collaboration in their organization. An open, face-to-face posture and good eye contact can help, along with an open office door when possible. At meetings, try using a round table so people feel more equal. Watch for signals that someone would like to speak, such as someone raising a hand, and invite that person to contribute.

In negotiating sales or deals, a number of nonverbal signals can help. Buyers may be able to gain power by maintaining a closed posture with crossed arms and a neutral facial expression. Sellers should offer friendly cues such as smiles and good eye contact but avoid excessive laughing or wild hand gestures. People who are close to agreeing on a deal will often nod, lean forward, and open their palms. Dilated pupils may also signal that the person is satisfied with the terms.

What Are Some Specific Situations Where I Should Be Aware of Nonverbal Cues and Signals?

In addition to personal and business relationships, there are a number of other situations in which you can benefit from observing body language. This is especially important when you interact with people who are in positions of power or have influence over some aspect of your life.

For example, physicians and other caregivers can be important to your health and well-being. It is essential that you have a trusting relationship and communicate well. When you meet a medical professional for the first time, watch for signs that he or she is giving you complete attention. That can include eye contact, nodding at appropriate times, and a posture directed toward you. Caregivers often must take notes during your office visit, which may interfere with your assessment of them. However, you may still be able to determine the level of interest in your health. Also, be aware of your own body language and try to project a willingness to listen.

If you have contact with people in law enforcement, notice that police officers typically have controlled body language meant to communicate power and authority. They stand and walk with an erect posture and keep their facial expressions neutral. Be careful that your own nonverbal communication projects cooperation and not aggression. Keep your voice level and avoid waving your arms or standing too close.

People in public office also may have controlled nonverbal cues, which are scripted to project a specific image. This is especially true during election campaigns, but experts suggest watching candidates when they are not giving speeches or responding to direct questions. For example, during a debate the person not speaking may reveal an attitude or point of view through facial expressions or changing posture. The same can happen during informal events or interviews.

Teachers can have significant impact on students, and it's wise to observe their nonverbal communication to assess their attitude toward students. If you are the student, observe your teacher's body language in the classroom. Watch for cues such as good eye contact with students, varying tone of voice, and whether the teacher laughs, smiles, and has a relaxed posture. These things signal that the teacher is interested and committed to his or her students. If your child is the student, watch for these body language cues during parent-teacher conferences or other meetings. As a student, you can improve the classroom experience by showing your own interest with body language signals such as nodding, leaning forward, or shaking your head if you are confused. This feedback can help the teacher tailor the material to the students.

What Pitfalls Should I Watch for When Interpreting Body Language?

Communication is always two-sided. One person sends a message and the other receives it through his or her own filter of previous experience and preconceptions. Even your mood at the moment can influence how you interpret both verbal and nonverbal communications. Being aware of some common mistakes can help you understand nonverbal messages.

Since men typically use fewer facial expressions than women, they may be seen as unemotional or uncaring. Men are also less observant than women of other people's body language, and they may miss some cues. Both men and women can benefit from considering both verbal and nonverbal communications to get the whole message.

People with certain accents or certain tones of voice are often taken less seriously. Regional accents can elicit stereotypes, and deep voices are considered more authoritative, which puts women at a disadvantage. Cultural stereotypes, such as believing people of a different race or from a different country have certain positive or negative attributes, can also get in the way of communication. Try to be aware of any bias these signals may cause.

Physical attributes such as height and attractiveness are significant benefits when it comes to social and professional success. Experts report that attractive women are thought to be more trustworthy, friendlier, better adjusted, and better educated than their less good-looking counterparts. With men, being handsome is associated with intelligence, good work ethic, mental health, and sexual prowess. Height also plays a part, with taller people more likely to get jobs and be elected than others. Overweight or obese people are often discounted as less capable, and they often miss out on jobs or earn less than people of normal weight. It's wise to look past these features when making judgments about someone.

Other issues that can lead to body language miscues include generalizing from other people (for example, believing someone is kind and caring because he or she looks like a teacher you liked) and not considering context. Someone who has recently been ill or has recently had a bad experience may send misleading nonverbal signals.

How Emotions and Stress Impact Nonverbal Communications

Do Our Emotions Change Our Nonverbal Communications?

Emotions are reflected in all types of nonverbal communication, also known as body language, that begin as early as childhood. These emotional signals happen both consciously and unconsciously, and they can convey feelings that children do not have the words to express. For example, infants show their emotions with behaviors such as crying, kicking, and arching their backs when they are upset. Older children who are fearful of new people or experiences may turn away, hide their faces, or cry. Babies and children also reveal their emotions in their facial expressions, smiling when they are happy or interested and frowning or scowling when they are angry or frustrated. Parents easily read these signals long before their children are able to speak.

The emotional swings of adolescence can yield more complex body language. Stressed teenagers may have blank or angry facial expressions, or they may seem nervous and fidgety. They may try to assert their independence with unusual dress or hairstyles or by projecting contempt with a slouching posture and minimal eye contact. Sarcastic eye rolls are another way teens communicate without language. Anxiety about fitting in is common in this age group, and teens in social situations may have a closed posture with tightly folded arms or wear their hair to cover part of their face.

Adults also show a wide variety of emotional body language in their postures, gestures, and tone of voice. Facial expressions are usually the most important conveyors of emotion, and experts have identified seven that are recognized across all cultures and races: fear, anger, joy or happiness, sadness, disgust, surprise, and contempt. Even people who are blind from birth exhibit these expressions, which are thought to be universal and inherited.

Does My Stress Show in My Body Language?

Many people face stress every day from the demands of work, finances, and family. Our bodies recognize stress as a threat and react with stress *hormones* that cause what is known as the flight-or-fight response. With this response, your heart rate and breathing increase and your blood pressure rises, making you more alert. Glucose floods into your blood, giving you more energy. These changes prepare you to act quickly to avoid danger, by jumping out of the way of an oncoming car, for example. When an immediate threat is over, the stress hormones dissipate, and the fight-or-flight response goes away.

This same response can happen from everyday stressors such as conflicts with your spouse or children, problems at work, or even being caught in traffic. Giving a speech, asking for a raise, or interviewing for a job can also bring about the fight-or-flight response. With chronic stress, the stress hormones can linger and eventually cause health problems.

The symptoms of stress can be disturbing and embarrassing, especially if they occur when you need to appear calm and professional. For example, for many people public speaking brings about sweating, shakiness, hyperventilation, and rapid heartbeat. Since the fight-or-flight response suppresses the digestive system, nausea may be a symptom. You may also find it difficult to think clearly. Stressful situations involving family and friends can elicit the same symptoms.

Many of these stress symptoms are easily visible, so people may notice your shaking hands or sweaty forehead. The excess energy generated by the fight-or-flight response can also give you away by leading you to pace, bounce your leg or foot, talk too fast, or bite your nails.

It is fairly obvious from their stances that this couple is having some sort of conflict.
© PETRENKO ANDRIY/ SHUTTERSTOCK.COM.

Hormones: *Chemicals produced by the body's glands that regulate various bodily functions, such as growth.*

Nonverbal Communication in the Digital Age

Reading other people's emotions and nonverbal communication can improve communication and help you better understand what another person may be thinking. However, according to scientists at the University of California Los Angeles, our increasingly digital world is contributing to a lack of awareness about nonverbal communication. Senior researcher Yalda Uhis noted in a press release for the university that "you can't learn nonverbal emotional cues from a screen the way you can learn it from face-to-face communication."

Because so much of our interactions with others has become digital—texting, e-mailing, instant messaging, even playing video games—Uhis recommends practicing face-to-face communication to avoid "losing important social skills." It is important to spend some time away from whatever electronic device you use most. Rather than sending a quick e-mail to a colleague at work, walk down the hall to his or her office to deliver the message. If you can't meet face-to-face with someone because of distance, try Skype or another video conferencing software that allows you to see the person. These interactions will allow you to read the other person's body language and facial expressions, increasing the level of communication between the two of you.

Can My Nonverbal Communication Give Away Emotions That I'd Rather Hide?

There are many situations in which people choose to conceal emotions. For example, you may want to avoid showing anger or frustration during a business meeting, hide disappointment about a forgotten date, or fake delight over an unwanted gift. However, it can be difficult to conceal your true emotions.

For one thing, other people will believe what they see (your body language) over what you say. Someone who sees you limp, for example, will likely not believe you when you say your leg feels fine. Also, it's hard to control all aspects of your body language at the same time. You may be able to smile and sit up straight during an interview, but if you bounce your foot or fidget with your hands, your nervousness will probably be apparent.

People are also good at recognizing insincere smiles, since they don't include the small muscles around the eyes. In addition, you may give yourself away with micro expressions. These fleeting facial expressions last a fraction of a second, but they can betray your true emotion. Though people are often not conscious of seeing micro expressions, they may get a gut feeling that you are being less than honest.

When your body language gives away the emotions or state of mind you would like to hide, it is known as leakage. Leakage often happens from unconscious actions such as tightly crossed arms, a slouching posture, or lack of eye contact. Standing with your feet or body pointed away from the person you are talking with can reveal that you would rather be somewhere else. And nonverbal communications such as uncombed hair or messy clothing can show disrespect or that you are too stressed to be organized.

Can People Misinterpret Emotional Body Language?

While leakage can give away your true emotions, it can also lead to confusion. This can happen if someone bases a judgment about your emotions on a small sample of your nonverbal communications. For example, someone with tightly folded arms and lowered chin may not be hostile but simple trying to stay warm. And your frown and rigid posture at a business meeting might stem from an unrelated situation. Not knowing the context of your body language could cause someone to believe you are angry or unreceptive to the subject of the meeting.

Cultural differences can also cause people to misinterpret emotional body language. In some Asian cultures it is considered bad behavior to express emotions overtly. When an Asian person smiles, it often does not mean he or she is happy; instead, it could be a cover-up for embarrassment. Hand gestures are common in all cultures but can mean different things. Even nodding your head, which means agreement in most societies, means "no" in some countries, including parts of Bulgaria and Greece.

Even seemingly obvious nonverbal signals can sometimes be misinterpreted. Facial expressions are usually the best indicator of a person's emotions. However, when the emotion is extreme it can be difficult to read. For example, the facial expressions for exhilaration and agony can be similar and hard to distinguish without other clues. Body language, such as excited arm pumps after winning a game or sagging shoulders after losing, can reveal true emotions. However, without the other clues, these extreme facial expressions are likely to be misread.

How Can I Use My Emotional Body Language to My Best Advantage?

Emotional body language plays a significant role in work, social, and family relationships. Being aware of potential problems and working toward good communication can help you in all these areas. Start by thinking about your unintentional communications.

Anxiety: *An abnormal and overwhelming sense of worry and fear that is often accompanied by physical reaction.*

Nearly everyone gives away, or "leaks," emotions they don't want to, and you may not be able to avoid it. In fact, your nonverbal communications are likely to convey your true feelings and may give you insights into your own emotions. But if *anxiety* or nervousness are overpowering messages you would rather not send, you may be able adjust your body language. People who depend on communication in their professions, such as politicians or lecturers, sometimes videotape themselves to analyze their body language. This can also work for people preparing for job interviews or other important events.

Even without a video, you can watch yourself for emotional leaks and learn to use positive body language. In business, nonverbal cues can tell a client that you are anxious or bored or that you are uncertain about a deal or relationship. You may be able to replace negative gestures such as stiff or hunched shoulders, poor eye contact, and feet and body pointed away from the other person with more positive ones. For example, an open, relaxed posture, appropriate smiles, a level voice, and a firm handshake can be reassuring. Friends and family also respond better to nonverbal communications that project openness, calm, and interest.

You can also use nonverbal communication to build trust and win approval with a technique called mirroring. This happens when people adopt a similar body position, tone of voice, gestures, and facial expressions. People who are emotionally close often do this unconsciously, but you can also do it on purpose to show support or connection. Mirroring facial expressions during a conversation makes you seem caring, friendly, and even attractive. In general, mirroring others makes them feel you are sympathetic and understanding. Mirroring can backfire, however, if it is overdone. In that case it can seem like you are ridiculing the person. And mirroring the body language of someone in a position of power, such as a supervisor, can make you seem arrogant and disrespectful.

People who find it difficult to manage their body language may benefit from another technique. Studies show that using specific postures, gestures, and expressions can actually change your mood. For example, standing straight and putting your hands on your hips can make you feel confident, opening your hands palm forward can make you more welcoming and receptive, and smiling can make you feel happier. Sitting up straight in a meeting shows that you are engaged, and the simple gesture of steepling your hands (placing your fingertips together) communicates confidence and can even make you feel more confident yourself. These sincere emotions may pave the way for more positive nonverbal communications.

The other side of emotional body language is reading the messages that other people send. Emotional body language is usually unconscious and sincere, and it is important not to base your judgments on isolated gestures or expressions. But you may be able to pick up clues that a person's emotions are not in line with their intended communications. Watch for inconsistencies between words and body language, such as "I'd be happy to" from someone who frowns, tucks in his or her chin, and looks away. Body language can also contradict itself. For example, scratching the head or tilting it sideways, biting a lip, or knitting the eyebrows can indicate confusion, even if the person says, "I understand."

Are There Ways I Can Keep Stress out of My Nonverbal Communications?

While moderate stress can energize and motivate people, too much stress can be damaging. It can interfere with concentration and lead to poor judgment and bad decisions. At work, body language that reveals stress can give a negative impression, suggesting that you may be too distracted to do your job properly. In sales or contract negotiations, revealing stress through body language can result in a poor outcome.

People who are stressed may also damage family and social relationships by showing frustrated, angry body language. This can happen even if your stress comes from something unrelated to your friends or family. Ongoing stress can even affect your health because stress hormones continue to circulate in your body, keeping your blood pressure high and putting you at risk for digestive problems, heart disease, trouble sleeping, and other problems.

Techniques for modifying emotional leakage can also help you avoid conveying stress in your body language. But the best method may be to reduce your stress. Strategies such as getting plenty of exercise, keeping regular sleep times, and practicing relaxation techniques can help. So can prioritizing your activities and letting some go if necessary. People with a lot of stress in their lives may also benefit from seeing a counselor or therapist.

For More Information

BOOKS

Andersen, Peter A. *The Complete Idiot's Guide to Body Language*. New York: Alpha Books, 2004.

Durré, Linnda. *Surviving the Toxic Workplace: Protect Yourself against Coworkers, Bosses, and Work Environments That Poison Your Day*. New York: McGraw-Hill, 2010.

Goman, Carol Kinsey. *The Silent Language of Leaders*. San Francisco: Jossey-Bass, 2011.

Hoppe, Michael H. *Active Listening: Improve Your Ability to Listen and Lead*. Greensboro, NC: Center for Creative Leadership, 2006.

Pease, Allan, and Barbara Pease. *The Definitive Book of Body Language*. New York: Bantam Dell, 2004.

Reiman, Tonya. *The Power of Body Language*. New York: Pocket Books, 2007.

Webster, Richard. *Body Language: Quick and Easy*. Woodbury, MN: Llewellyn Publications, 2014.

PERIODICALS

Harmon, Katherine. "How Important Is Physical Contact with Your Infant?" *Scientific American*, May 6, 2010. This article can also be found online at http://www.scientificamerican.com/article/infant-touch/.

Hoffman, Janet Lee, and Andres Weiner. "The Juror as Audience: The Impact of Non-Verbal Communication at Trial." *Oregon State Bar Litigation Journal*, Fall 2013.

Scott, David. "GOP Debate: Does Height Matter in Presidential Politics?" *Christian Science Monitor*, October 18, 2011. This article can also be found online at http://www.csmonitor.com/Science/2011/1018/GOP-Debate-Does-height-matter-in-presidential-politics.

Whitbourne, Susan Krauss. "The Ultimate Guide to Body Language." *Psychology Today*, June 30, 2012. This article can also be found online at http://www.psychologytoday.com/blog/fulfillment-any-age/201206/the-ultimate-guide-body-language.

WEBSITES

"Active Listening." *U.S. Department of State*. http://www.state.gov/m/a/os/65759.htm (accessed December 14, 2014).

Hanna, Julia. "Power Posing: Fake It Until You Make It." *Harvard Business School*. http://hbswk.hbs.edu/item/6461.html (accessed December 29, 2014).

"The Impact of Nonverbal Communication on a Child's Development." *Global Post*. http://everydaylife.globalpost.com/impact-nonverbal-communication-childs-development-1751 (accessed December 14, 2014).

"It's Not Only Words That Influence Doctor-Patient Relationships." *Robert Wood Johnson Foundation*. http://www.rwjf.org/en/about-rwjf/newsroom/newsroom-content/2011/11/its-not-only-words-that-influence-doctor-patient-relationships.html (accessed December 14, 2014).

Keller, Jared. "Can Body Language Predict Elections?" *Atlantic*. http://www.theatlantic.com/politics/archive/2010/10/can-body-language-predict-elections/65424/ (accessed December 14, 2014).

Kelly, Morgan. "Don't Read My Lips! Body Language Trumps the Face for Conveying Intense Emotions." *Princeton University*. http://www.princeton.edu/main/news/archive/S35/82/65G58/ (accessed December 14, 2014).

Rugsaken, Kris. "Body Speaks: Body Language around the World." *National Academic Advising Association*. http://www.nacada.ksu.edu/Resources/Clearinghouse/View-Articles/body-speaks.aspx(accessed December 14, 2014).

Schwartz, Leslie Contreras. "Nonverbal Communication with Workplace Interactions." *Houston Chronicle*. http://smallbusiness.chron.com/nonverbal-communication-workplace-interactions-844.html (accessed December 14, 2014).

"10 Nonverbal Cues That Convey Confidence at Work." *Forbes*. http://www.forbes.com/sites/jacquelynsmith/2013/03/11/10-nonverbal-cues-that-convey-confid/ (accessed December 14, 2014).

"Understanding Jurors' Nonverbal Communication." *American Bar Association*. http://www.americanbar.org/publications/gpsolo_ereport/2012/august_2012/understanding_jurors_nonverbal_communication.html (accessed December 14, 2014).

Written and Graphic Communication

What Does the Word *Audience* Mean in Terms of Writing?

Although the word *audience* is usually defined as those who watch or listen to a performance, your reading audience includes all those who may read what you write. Most writing is aimed, consciously or not, at a particular audience. Novels may be intended for young adult readers or mystery fans; magazine articles may be directed toward those who love to cook or have a specific problem. Some work-related writing may be targeted at clients or customers, some may be used to explain policies or procedures to coworkers, and some may be produced to inform your supervisor about the progress of your work. Even the most personal journal writing can be said to have an audience of at least one, since you are writing for yourself.

Your writing can benefit significantly from considering your audience before you begin to put your thoughts on paper. Even in the case of your journal, it can be helpful to reflect on who you are trying to reach.

When preparing a presentation, it is best to know who it is you are presenting to and what is the best way to approach them. © QUINKY/ SHUTTERSTOCK.COM.

If you recognize that your aim is solely to release your emotions in the moment, you may feel that you can write freely, with no thought that anyone else will ever see the text. If you intend your journal to be a record of your life that you may reread to recall your experiences, you may wish to structure it for that purpose, even though you do not expect to have readers other than yourself. If you hope one day to publish your memoirs, your reading audience will be much broader, and you are likely to plan your writing according to your understanding of the interests of future readers.

How Is a Reading Audience Different from a Listening Audience?

One of the major differences between reading and listening audiences is feedback. When you speak or perform before a live audience, you are likely to receive an instant response that may help you adjust your delivery. Applause, laughter, yawning, and nodding or shaking of the head are examples of audience responses. While you may receive feedback from your reading audience, it generally comes only after your written work is complete and often long afterward. In many cases, you may receive feedback from very few of the people who read your work. However, imagining your audience and fine-tuning your work to better communicate with your readers is part of the art and skill of writing.

Body language: *The gestures, movements, and mannerisms by which a person communicates with others, including facial expressions, tone of voice, and posture.*

Another difference between a reading audience and other types of audiences is that they cannot see you or hear you. Because you are unable to use the tone and volume of your voice or employ the visual cues of *body language* to communicate, you must be especially attentive to the use of language and tone in your writing. Your target audience must learn everything they need to know about your topic from your words and phrasing. In most cases, they will not be able to raise their hands and ask questions when you have been unclear. It is therefore very important to consider you audience's level of vocabulary, expertise, and sensitivity when you write and to choose words and frame sentences carefully to communicate with them most clearly. For example, since you cannot indicate humor with a laugh or smile, you must use word choice to indicate when you are joking.

What Kinds of Different Reading Audiences Are There?

The types of reading audiences are as varied as the types of individuals you may encounter. As mentioned above, in the business world you may write for clients, coworkers, or supervisors, each of whom represents a different type of audience, each requiring a different approach. Within these business groupings, you may encounter audiences who know very little about the topic you are writing about, as well as experts who are highly informed on your topic.

Other important features that describe differing reading audiences are age, gender, and ethnicity. Your vocabulary, sentence arrangement, and reference points may vary depending on whether your work is addressing children, teenagers, or grandparents. Similarly, if you want your work to be relevant to both men and women or people of all cultures, ensure that your language is inclusive and that you avoid assumptions that are culturally limiting.

Another important factor that distinguishes different reading audiences is attitude. In general, you may find yourself most often writing for a fairly neutral audience consisting of those who have not made up their minds about your topic and are interested enough to read what you have to say. At times, however, you may be called upon to write for a hostile audience whose members already disagree with you. This may occur when you are writing a proposal to change a work policy or if you write about a political issue. It is important to identify a potentially hostile audience so that you can imagine the objections they may raise and make your writing more persuasive. On the other hand, you may encounter receptive audiences who are predisposed to agree with you. On the surface, these may seem like the easiest audiences to write for, but you may feel limited by their point of view or intimidated by the challenge of living up to their interest.

How Can I Get to Know My Audience?

The first step in getting to know your potential reading audience is to spend time thinking about what you are writing and who will be reading it. In the case of business writing, you may know exactly who will read your work. Even in that case, however, consider the possibility that your work could have a larger circulation than originally intended. If you are asked to write a report for your supervisor, you may wish to plan ahead so that the same report is appropriate for the board of directors as well. You may then be able to save your company time and expense by suggesting that your supervisor forward your report rather than creating a new one.

For other types of writing, you will need to first decide who you are trying to reach. You may come to understand that you have more than one audience. For example, if you are a student writing a paper for a class, your primary audience is the teacher who will give you your grade. However, you may plan to publish your paper after the class is over. In that case, your audience may include other scholars in your field or others with similar interests. Similarly, if you are a creative writer, you have the opportunity to decide which audience you want to address. Who will be most interested in your work? Who do you want to influence or reveal yourself to? Perhaps they are people much like you who will empathize with your experience, or perhaps they are very different and you hope your writing will build bridges.

Once you determine who your intended audience is, you may wish to do some research in order to learn about the needs and desires of your readers. This research may be in the form of reading other popular works directed at the same audience. In business or school, it may mean reading other papers or reports that have gotten a positive reception or a good grade. For journalistic writing, such as that for newspapers and magazines, it may mean reading (and reading about) the periodicals in which you hope to be published to become familiar with their audience's interests. If you are a creative writer, you may want to become well-read in your genre in order to become familiar with popular trends. If they are available, reader reviews of other works can help you tune in to the attitudes and concerns of your audience.

How Should My Writing Reflect My Understanding of My Audience?

As a writer, your main tool is language, or the words you use and the way you structure them into sentences and paragraphs. Though you will undoubtedly choose words that appeal to you in your writing, it is important to also give serious consideration to your audience when deciding what language to use. Your vocabulary should be interesting and varied but appropriate for the audience you are trying to reach.

For example, if you are writing an explanation of a scientific process for a popular magazine, you may use common terms rather than technical ones and simplify complex details. If you write about the same process in a report for a scientific conference, your work may be considered unprofessional if you do not use technical terms and acronyms or annoying if you offer too much explanation of things that are commonly understood in the field.

Similarly, your sentence structure and format will be different depending on whether you are writing for a formal business or academic audience or an informal audience of contemporaries who share the same hobby. In general, long and complex sentences should be reserved for scholarly or technical papers, while a direct, clear style is more appropriate for business readers. A casual, chatty structure may be the best way to capture the interest of an informal audience. If you are writing a practical article or a business report, you may wish to use bullets, lists, graphs, and other aids to help illustrate your point with fewer words. This shows respect for your audience's time and indicates your understanding of which facts are most important for them to know.

Tone in writing is the expression of your attitude and emotion toward the subject of your composition and toward your audience. Tone may be expressed through words, sentence structure, and punctuation and is extremely important in developing communication with your readers. An informal tone can seem welcoming or rude, depending on the reading audience. Likewise, a formal tone can seem respectful or stiff, depending on the context. An aggressive tone may be appropriate if you are trying to arouse support from those who agree with you, but it may alienate those who are neutral or hostile. Short sentences punctuated with exclamation points may be rousing in a pamphlet handed out to sympathetic labor union members seeking political change but alienating in a letter to a newspaper about the same issue.

It is especially important to avoid a demeaning tone when trying to reach young or old audiences. Using words such as *spunky* or *feisty* when describing old people or attempting to insert modern slang such as "whassup?" into your writing may cause your audience to dismiss it as out of touch and disrespectful. If you are not a member of the audience you are trying to reach, the best way to communicate with them is to use a frank and courteous tone and to address them as human beings rather than members of a special group. The same is true when writing for children. While you should choose age-appropriate vocabulary, trying to adopt a childlike tone is likely to seem condescending.

Your audience may also influence your decision of how to publish or present your writing. A report for a business audience may be taken more seriously, for example, if it is professionally bound before presentation, while a family Christmas letter may gain a more positive reception if it is printed on colorful paper and includes photographs. If you write for a youthful audience, you may wish to explore the use of social media and web publishing to reach a wider range of readers.

Personal vs. Professional Writing: Letters, E-mails, Memos, and Texts

What Are the Differences between Personal and Professional Writing?

You may use many of the same skills in both personal and professional writing. However, there are a number of important differences between the two types of communication. Much of the skill of writing lies in the ability to understand who your readers will be. Another important element of written communication is voice, or the writing style that will enable you to communicate with them most effectively.

Before writing anything, whether a brief personal text or a long business report, you should spend time considering your audience, what they expect from you, and what you would like to tell them. In much of your personal writing, you will be communicating with people you know, such as friends or family members, so you may not need to observe formal rules of writing structure. However, for a business or academic audience, you will need to write clearly and present the information effectively in order to gain a good reception.

Professional and personal communications require very different writing styles. In personal writing you can be more casual and reveal your personality. In professional writing you should use a pleasant, neutral voice that conveys your business competency. While you can be friendly in a work e-mail, it is wise to leave out personal details. For example, it may be completely appropriate to describe your experience at the doctor's office in a personal letter or e-mail, but professional communication should only include information that is relevant to work issues.

How Has Letter Writing Changed over Time?

Before the invention of the telephone and, later, e-mail, most long-distance personal correspondence was conducted through letters.

Not only does the tone and formality differentiate between personal and professional written communications, so does the color of the paper. © EKATERINA MINAEVA/ SHUTTERSTOCK.COM.

Although the telephone was invented during the late 1800s, for several decades it was generally reserved for emergencies and special occasions. Personal letters were the primary way to communicate with friends and family who were separated by distance, and they remained popular through the end of the twentieth century. While numerous fast and easy forms of electronic communication are available in the early twenty-first century, a handwritten letter can still sometimes be a warm and personal means of conveying news or greetings to someone you know.

Businesses use letters for normal day-to-day communications, but letters can also be used for more official purposes, such as when a written record of a communication is necessary. For example, sometimes an official notice to leave a rented office or apartment must be delivered from a landlord to a tenant by a certain date. A letter may also be used to give more authority to a communication or to lend a personal touch to a business message.

What Should I Know about Writing Personal Letters?

There are a number of occasions when a personal letter may be appropriate. You may wish to write letters to friends and relatives on special occasions, thank-you notes for gifts or acts of kindness, or sympathy notes to those facing difficult times. Even if you usually communicate by phone, text, or e-mail, knowing how to craft an effective personal letter is a valuable skill.

Letters may be formal or informal depending on how well you know the recipient. A warm, conversational tone is generally suitable for a personal letter, although it is best to reserve familiarity, abbreviations, and slang for letters to close friends. You should make an effort to use correct grammar and spelling, and if you are used to the abbreviated communication of e-mail or text messages, you may need to pay extra attention to your wording to ensure that it is correct and readable.

Unless you are writing a close friend, it may be helpful to compose a draft of your letter ahead of time so that you can gather your thoughts

E-mail Subject Headings

Many people don't realize that an e-mail subject heading is an important component of the entire message. Good headings tell the recipient what the e-mail contains before it is opened, allowing him or her to decide whether or not to read it. Busy professionals receive between 20 and 200 messages per day, so a clear, concise subject heading that summarizes your message is crucial. Here are some tips for writing an effective one.

- Don't leave the subject heading line blank. This ensures your message will not be read immediately if at all. It can also convey arrogance by suggesting all communication from you should be read without question.

- Avoid words like *Important, 911,* or *Read Immediately*. Ask yourself whether this information is only important to you or if it's also critical for the recipient. Instead, include a brief summary such as "Important: All Time Cards Must Be Turned in by Thursday." This makes it clear why the e-mail should be read immediately.

- Don't use the phrase "Quick question." If the question truly is brief, summarize it in the subject line. For example, "Do we still need volunteers for the fundraiser?" is clearer and increases the likelihood of a prompt response.

By using the subject line to provide the recipient with a clear idea of your message, you will increase the chances that your e-mail will be read in a timely manner.

and correct mistakes. You can then copy your letter onto stationary or a card, making an effort to write neatly and legibly. It is generally best to write a personal letter by hand, but if you are insecure about your handwriting, a typed and printed letter can also be acceptable. A number of etiquette websites, such as Emily Post (http://www.emilypost.com), provide suggestions for personal letter writing.

What Should I Know about Writing Business Letters?

Although much of your work communication may occur through e-mail, a number of situations in your professional or personal life may require you to write business letters. These may include cover letters to accompany a *résumé* when you are seeking a job or important communications that require a written record, such as notice to a bank that you are closing an account. Business letters should be polite in tone, and they should get to the point quickly and be written in a clear, professional style. Bullet points or lists may help you organize your letter's content.

Résumé: *A document providing a detailed description of a person's previous work experience, educational background, and relevant job skills.*

Business letters generally have a more formal structure than personal correspondence. When writing a letter to a company, you should do some research to learn the name of the correct recipient and address your letter to that person. Your name and address should appear in the upper-right-hand corner. The recipient's name and address should be written on the left-hand side of the paper, slightly below your address, and the date should be placed under the recipient's address. The letter should begin with a formal greeting, such as "Dear Mr. Jones," and the closing should be formal as well, ending with "Sincerely" and your full name, for example.

Unlike personal letters, business letters should almost always be typed, and this allows you to take advantage of computer programs that check spelling and grammar. However, your signature should always be handwritten, followed by your name in print. Many word-processing programs offer templates, or patterns, for writing various types of letters.

What Is a Memo?

Abbreviated from the word *memorandum*, a memo is a short note that is used to communicate about a specific issue or to help you or someone else remember an important point. Memos are usually used for communication within a business or an organization, and they are more frequently circulated on paper than by electronic means.

Business memos are often used to summarize the results of a meeting, to bring up a problem, or to spread the word about an upcoming event. Some companies use special forms for writing memos. These may be passed around to the appropriate recipients, who will then initial them after reading in order to provide a record that the memo has been received.

What Should I Know about Writing Memos?

As with all writing, your first step in creating a memo should be to consider your audience. Memos are most efficient when they are delivered to the appropriate recipients, and they should not be sent to those to whom they do not apply. You can use your judgment to determine whether the information you want to convey is suitable for the memo format. Confidential or sensitive information should not be transmitted through a memo, since it is not a private form of communication.

If your workplace does not provide memo forms, you should structure your memo for ease of reading. At the top, you should create a heading that clearly lists all recipients as well as your name as the sender. You should then add the date and a concise description of the subject. It is best to use one simple font throughout, and you should be sparing in your use of emphatic formatting, such as bold type and all capital letters, as it can make the tone seem too strong. You do not want to give your coworkers the impression that you are shouting at them.

You should spend some time thinking about the subject of your memo. Even in a brief communication, you can frame your suggestion, announcement, or problem in persuasive language, using an introduction to present your topic, a paragraph or two to explain the situation further, and a conclusion in which you may offer a solution or suggestion. You should use polite language throughout and close by thanking your colleagues for their support or help with the issue. If you are new to writing memos, you may wish to ask a coworker for feedback before sending your memo to its recipients.

What Should I Know about Personal and Business E-mails?

E-mail is a form of written communication that is transmitted among computers, either through a network or over the Internet. E-mail messages may contain attachments, such as documents and photographs, and they may be addressed to one or many individuals or groups. E-mails are transmitted much more quickly than postal mail and have become a standard form of both personal and professional correspondence.

Many of the rules of effective communication in letters, such as attention to audience and tone, also apply to e-mail. The increased speed of e-mail transmission frequently invites a more economical style of writing than that used for traditional letters. However, you should take care to avoid being so concise that you sound abrupt or short. A warm tone can be conveyed in a personal e-mail with a few friendly words or a warm closing. Likewise, a cordial closing to a business e-mail can demonstrate consideration and help build strong business relationships. It is best to keep your tone calm and respectful and, as in memos, avoid the use of all capitals or other formatting that may suggest an angry tone.

E-mail is particularly useful because of its efficiency. While a chatty e-mail to a friend may be an appropriate way to maintain connections, e-mail can also be useful for brief, practical messages or for logistical arrangements such as setting up a meeting. You should make an effort to respond to e-mail correspondence promptly and clearly. If an e-mail is addressed to a group, you should be sure to direct your reply to all members of that group by clicking the "reply all" option. The "CC" (carbon copy) option will show the names and addresses of other recipients. If you want to protect the privacy of those receiving your e-mail, you can use the "BCC" (blind carbon copy) option to hide that information.

What Should I Know about Personal and Business Texts?

Texting, also called text messaging or short message service (SMS), is the process of sending and receiving written messages with your cell phone. Texting has become increasingly popular in the early twenty-first century, especially among young people, who may text far more often than they converse by telephone. Many use a special texting jargon made up of certain abbreviations for words and phrases that are widely understood. A number of websites provide glossaries of common texting shorthand that can help you in deciphering and composing informal personal text messages.

Texting is a convenient and efficient way to send and receive brief messages. In your personal life, text messages can help you communicate regularly with family and friends in a way that may be less intrusive than telephone calls. Texting has become increasingly common in the workplace as well. It is sometimes used in everyday communication with coworkers, and it can be an efficient way to set up a meeting, confirm the delivery of a shipment, or announce a new product or service. Some businesses also use texts for advertising purposes.

Text messaging is an even more concise medium than e-mail. When writing texts, it is best to keep your message brief and to the point. Though you may use slang and texting jargon in your personal communications, you should avoid using it in any professional context. You should use direct, simple phrasing in order to make your meaning as clear as possible and always proofread texts carefully before sending. Many phones have auto-correct programs that make texting more efficient by suggesting common words before they are completely spelled out. While these programs can be useful, they frequently make errors that can make texts difficult to understand.

You should observe proper etiquette when texting for personal or business reasons and avoid texting while in the company of others, at a meeting, or when doing so will endanger yourself or others. On the job, you should avoid sending texts to your coworkers or clients too frequently. Because you are not face to face, it may be easy for friendly texts to cross the line into inappropriate behavior.

Professional Writing for Publication

How Is Writing for Publication Different from Unpublished Writing?

There are numerous types of personal and professional writing that are never intended for publication. For example, most people's personal journals will never be published, which allows them to write with complete freedom. You may express your feelings, organize your thoughts, or make sense of life events without worrying how other people may interpret your words. Writing works that will be read by others requires more thought and planning. Even when writing a letter to one individual, you must consider who will be reading your work and how you can best express yourself so that your audience will understand your meaning.

This is true of most business writing, which is usually created for other readers and must be written with care and clarity. In order to become an effective business writer, you must assess your audience and choose your words, tone, structure, and content to interest that audience. For example, an informal style may be perceived as disrespectful and sloppy when used in a report to your superiors, while too formal a tone in an office e-mail may alienate your coworkers.

These same skills are the foundation of writing for publication. If you wish to have your writing published, you will have several levels of reading audiences to consider, including the publisher, editor, and reader. Though your work is primarily addressed to the reader, in order to have your writing published so that you can reach the reader, you must learn and implement the standards of both publishers and editors.

What Work Situations Might Call for Me to Publish My Writing?

Even if you have never had the ambition to become a published writer, your career may require you to write for publication. For example, most academics are required to publish articles or books about their field of study on a regular basis. If you have a job in a field other than higher education or research, you may still be asked to write a report about a meeting or work project for a company or trade journal. Or you may be tasked with helping to launch a new program by writing an article for a local newspaper or magazine.

Other reasons to publish include wanting to explain or clarify specific parts of your company's work in order to increase public safety or attracting young people to enter your field. You could also use publishing to advance your career by writing about experiences you have had or suggestions for improvement in the industry. Similarly, writing a review of an industry publication may be a good way to express your ideas and gain the notice of your superiors or important people outside of your company. Having your writing published can be a valuable addition to your *résumé*.

When writing for publication, you may have to tailor your personal style to meet the publication's guidelines.
© KARRAMBA PRODUCTION/
SHUTTERSTOCK.COM.

Résumé: *A document providing a detailed description of a person's previous work experience, educational background, and relevant job skills.*

What Is Freelance Writing?

Freelance writers are self-employed writers who generally work on specific projects rather than being hired as employees. Freelancers may work for one publication or publisher or for several, and they may work on assignment or come up with their own ideas for articles, which they then attempt to sell to publishers. Freelancers usually work on a contract basis, meaning that they are hired to complete a particular project and are paid once that project is completed. Writers who freelance are often treated as owners of their own business and may have to register with the state accordingly. They are paid under the rules for contract labor and are required to pay self-employment tax on their income tax returns.

Freelance writing has both benefits and challenges. As a freelancer, you will usually have more independence than traditional employment typically affords. Although some employers may require freelancers to put in regular hours at the workplace, many freelance writers work from home and may set their own hours. Freelancing may be an excellent choice if you are unable to commit to a full-time job or you want to have time to pursue personal writing projects.

However, because freelancers are self-employed, this type of career may be insecure and usually lacks traditional benefits such as health insurance and paid time off. If you work as a freelance writer, promoting yourself and finding paying work will be an important part of your job, and you may face periods of unpaid unemployment between projects. There are a number of websites, such as Freelance Writing (http://www.freelancewriting.com/) and the Write Life (http://thewritelife.com/), that offer resources for aspiring freelancers.

How Do I Get My Writing Published?

The first step in having your writing published is identifying what kind of publisher might be interested in your work. If you are a novelist, this may mean researching publishing houses that have produced works in your genre. If you write nonfiction articles, you should investigate journals, newspapers, or other publications that publish works on your subject. For example, if you wish to write about the conservation of natural resources, you might seek out publications that appeal to environmentalists, hikers, campers, hunters, and those with liberal political ideology. When examining potential publishers, you should ask such questions as: What kinds of writing do they publish?; What is the general tone and professional level of their publications?; and Who are their readers?

First, you must determine if the publisher considers unsolicited manuscripts. If it does, then you must follow the publisher's guidelines for submissions in writing your proposal or query letter. Most publishers are not interested in receiving copies of completed books or articles, and some prefer to communicate only with literary agents rather than writers.

Of those publishers who do accept queries from writers, they will want a concise description of your proposed project and a persuasive argument about why they should publish it. Your query letter and proposal should be a demonstration of your writing skill as well as a clear explanation of the work you have written or are planning to write. You should discuss what your writing will add to the existing body of work on your subject, why you think it will interest readers, and why you are qualified to write it. If you have completed a novel or another type of book, your proposal may include an excerpt of several chapters, but you should only include a sample if the publisher's guidelines ask for it. Many magazine publishers prefer to receive a detailed explanation of the idea for an article before it is written so that they can request that the final product reflect their own philosophy and priorities.

What Is a Blog?

Getting your writing published can be a long and frustrating process, as there are many more writers than publishers. However, the advent of web or Internet publishing has made it possible for almost anyone to become a published author. If you are intimidated by the world of professional publishing, you may want to present your writing first in the form of a weblog, more commonly known as a blog. Blogs are personal websites that allow the creator to post regular entries, or articles, about a variety of subjects. You can create a blog about any topic that interests you, such as travel, cooking, home repair, or current events. You can also release a novel in installments or publish short stories on a blog.

Starting a blog is a fairly simple process. Websites such as WordPress (https://wordpress.com/) and the Blog Builders (http://www .theblogbuilders.com/) offer free websites for bloggers and provide simple instructions for setup. Once you have established your blog and begun publishing, you can work to publicize your blog. Once again, it is important to identify your reading audience before deciding whether to promote your blog among your friends, coworkers, and on social media. A blog can give you an opportunity to improve your writing skills, get feedback, and create a body of work that may help you promote yourself to a print publisher.

What Does an Editor Do?

Editors correct, polish, and improve a writer's work and ensure that it matches the publisher's guidelines and philosophy. They may work with writers to brainstorm ideas, target an audience, make revisions, and generally prepare a manuscript for publication. Editors may make corrections themselves or return a manuscript with suggested changes for the author to make.

As a writer, you may work with various types of editors. The editor in chief of a publication supervises the staff of editors and writers and is in charge of the overall content of the publication. Managing editors are usually responsible for individual sections of a publication and often make assignments to writers. Developmental editors can help you see and address larger issues such as content or pacing problems. Copy editors correct factual, grammatical, and typographical errors in manuscripts and are responsible for ensuring that the writing meets the publisher's standards and guidelines.

What Do I Need to Know about Working with an Editor?

When working with an editor, it is important to maintain high standards of professionalism and courtesy. It is never pleasant for writers to receive criticism or correction of their work, but keep in mind that the editor's job is to make your work better. An editor can be a valuable resource for improving your writing and making it more marketable. Do not hesitate to ask your editor for suggestions or advice if you feel bogged down or confused when you are writing.

Make a strong effort not to respond to editorial criticism defensively. Instead, work to maintain an attitude of openness and appreciativeness, and recognize that your editor may know more than you do about the intent and readership of the publication for which you are writing. It may help to view your editor's criticism as an attempt to help you become a better writer. Respond to corrections in a positive and friendly manner and always thank your editors for their work on your piece. If you strongly disagree with a suggested change, you may respectfully make your case to your editor. However, choose carefully which editorial suggestions to challenge, as you do not want to get a reputation for being a difficult writer.

What Does Copyright Mean?

All writers should have at least some familiarity with copyright. Copyright is legal protection of your written, musical, or artistic work that bars other people from publishing or otherwise using your creation without your permission. Copyright automatically applies to any original written work you create as soon as it exists in manuscript form, and you can indicate that your work is copyrighted by placing the word copyright or the copyright symbol (©) next to your name at the end of the manuscript. Though it is not legally required, you may want to pay a small fee to register your copyright with the United States Copyright Office (http://copyright.gov/). Registering your copyright may help you prove ownership of your writing if legal challenges arise.

Although U.S. law provides for the creators of artistic works to retain ownership and control of their creations, in some cases you may not be allowed to copyright your work. Some employers of freelance writers require that their employees sign contracts designating their writing as "work for hire." This means that the employer retains ownership of all work created on the job. If you are a writer under a work for hire contract, you do not have a copyright on your work. Your employers may use or republish the work as they wish without your permission or any additional payment.

Posting on Social Networks

What Is Social Media?

Social media is a term used to describe a variety of websites that allow people to make connections and exchange information. While traditional forms of media, such as newspapers and television, are created by professionals and distributed to consumers, the content of social media is created by the numerous individuals who use social media sites, most of whom are not media professionals. Some social media sites are broadly inclusive, such as Facebook (http://www.facebook.com) and Friendster (http://www.friendster.com), which allow users to communicate with wide networks of friends and family. Others may be dedicated to a specific area of interest. These include PatientsLikeMe (http://www.patientslikeme.com), which allows users to share information about medical conditions and health care; IT Central Station (http://www.itcentralstation.com), directed toward those who work in the information technology industry; and Catmoji (http://catmoji.com), where cat lovers can share pictures and videos.

Some critics express concern that social media sites encourage only superficial connections. However, as modern lives have become increasingly busy and the daily use of personal electronic devices has expanded, a growing number of people have found social networking to be an efficient way of staying in touch with family and friends. This increasing popularity has led business leaders to view social media websites as an effective means of reaching a wide audience to advertise their products and services. By the 2010s *public relations* for many businesses included a presence on social media sites such as Facebook, Twitter (https://twitter.com), and YouTube (http://www.youtube.com).

Public relations: *The practice of building and maintaining an organization or individual's relationship with the public.*

How Long Has Social Media Been Around?

Social media represents the modern evolution of a human need to communicate that began with the development of speech and writing and continued through the invention of the postal system. As technology progressed, the telegraph and telephone made instant communication over long distances readily available, and radio and television introduced the possibility of communicating with an increasingly large number of people. When computers were developed during the twentieth century, it was only natural that one of their primary uses would be to facilitate and expand communication.

During the late 1960s, scientists created a network of computers that allowed rapid communication worldwide. This network, called the Internet, soon became a vital means of communication as e-mail and instant messaging were introduced. By the 1970s computer users began to gather on networks called bulletin board systems (BBS) to exchange information on a wide variety of subjects. They could use e-mail to communicate with people they knew, but a BBS allowed them to meet and chat electronically with people they did not know. The World Wide Web, launched during the early 1990s with the development of the hypertext transfer protocol (HTTP), greatly increased the ability of computers to communicate with one another and allowed more efficient Internet browsing.

Both businesses and consumers are using social media for information sharing and networking. You can even access your favorite social media sites on your smartphone. © TWIN DESIGN/SHUTTERSTOCK. COM.

In the late 1990s the first social media websites began to appear. SixDegrees.com, launched in the United States in 1997, allowed users to create profiles that included personal details, such as schools, work, and friends. The British website Friends Reunited (http://www .friendreunited.com), which reconnects former schoolmates, appeared in 1999, followed by Friendster and MySpace (https://myspace.com) in the early 2000s. In 2005 YouTube created a space where anyone could post a video to be viewed on the Internet, and in 2006 Twitter introduced the idea of "microblogging," or the broadcasting of very short messages. By 2008 Facebook had become one of the most widely used sites for sharing information and pictures with friends.

What Is Facebook?

Founded in 2004, Facebook began as a networking website for students at Harvard University in Cambridge, Massachusetts, where it quickly became a popular way for users to connect and share information.

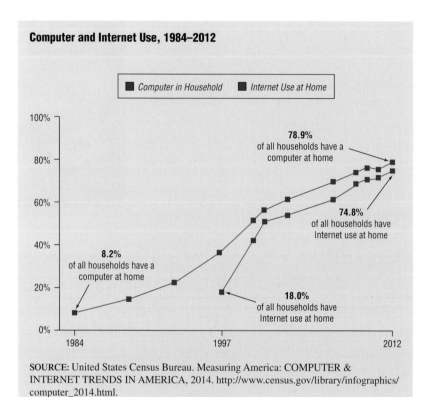

Computer and Internet Use, 1984–2012

■ Computer in Household ■ Internet Use at Home

78.9%
of all households have a
computer at home

8.2%
of all households have a
computer at home

74.8%
of all households have
Internet use at home

18.0%
of all households have
Internet use at home

1984   1997   2012

The presence of computers in the home and the use of the Internet has grown exponentially since 1984. ILLUSTRATION BY LUMINA DATAMATICS LTD. © 2015 CENGAGE LEARNING.

SOURCE: United States Census Bureau. Measuring America: COMPUTER & INTERNET TRENDS IN AMERICA, 2014. http://www.census.gov/library/infographics/computer_2014.html.

In 2005 the site's user base expanded to a number of colleges and universities, and by 2006 anyone over the age of 13 could create a Facebook profile. In September 2014 Facebook reported over 1.3 billion active users each month. Adults, teenagers, and business executives have all found Facebook to be a useful forum for easy and efficient communication with a large group of people. Facebook has become so popular that terms such as *facebooking*, to describe communicating through the site, have entered common usage.

Facebook users create a page where they can post personal information, such as their profession, place of employment, and schools attended. Users may update their page as often as they want, inserting information about daily activities and photographs that they would like to share with family and friends. Readers may start a conversation by writing a comment in response to a post that interests them or by simply clicking "Like." These comments will be viewed by other friends who visit the page, and they may continue the conversation with their own comments. Users also have the option of communicating through private messages.

Facebook users can create special "fan pages" to publicize events or causes or to share a special interest or hobby. While users can limit viewers of their personal sites to friends, fan pages can be viewed by anyone. Many businesses create Facebook fan pages in order to take advantage of the site's wide popularity for marketing their products or services.

What Do I Need to Know about Communicating on Facebook?

Facebook users create a profile page by going to the site and filling out the "Sign Up" form. The form asks for such personal details as name, e-mail address or mobile telephone number, birth date, and gender. Through your e-mail or mobile number you will receive a confirmation link or code that allows you to continue. Once you click the link, the Facebook site will provide instructions for personalizing your page with photographs, graphics, and your own thoughts and comments.

Using the "Find Friends" application, you can locate people you know who have Facebook accounts and ask them to connect with you. Facebook may also suggest friends for you based on connections you have in common. You may wish to put some thought into whom you choose to accept as a friend on Facebook. Even though you may receive a large number of friend suggestions and requests, you should probably not "friend" anyone whom you do not know personally. Unless you intend to use your Facebook page chiefly for professional contacts, it may be unwise to connect with employers or other supervisory acquaintances, such as teachers.

You may post on Facebook as often or as seldom as you wish, although you should try to avoid posting too frequently. Posts should generally be written in the friendly tone of a personal letter but should be kept brief and to the point. While it is socially acceptable to use Facebook to communicate distressing news, in general you should make an effort to present an upbeat voice and try not to allow your posts to become lists of daily complaints. You can spark an interesting discussion by asking a provocative question or writing your thoughts about a current event, but you should do your best to encourage positive interaction by keeping your own tone constructive and courteous.

If negative comments are made in response to one of your posts, you may want to respond to them privately. If you feel that one of your Facebook friends is behaving in a hostile manner, you can block his or her posts or "unfriend" that person in order to stop receiving unwanted communications.

What Is Twitter?

Twitter is a website that allows users to share brief comments, photographs, web links, or videos. Messages sent on Twitter are called "tweets" and must be no more than 140 characters in length. Tweets may be read on a computer, tablet, or mobile phone and are generally received in "real time," or as soon as they are sent. Twitter is often called a microblog website. Blogs, or weblogs, are personal websites that allow the creator to post regular entries about a variety of subjects. On Twitter, users may post miniature versions of blogs to update friends and followers about their daily lives, comment about an event in the news, or join an ongoing conversation on a current topic. Tweets may be public, in which case they may be viewed by anyone who logs onto the Twitter website, but they may also be protected, meaning that readers must be approved by the account holder. You may "follow," or subscribe to, the Twitter accounts of others in order to be notified when they post tweets.

Twitter posts have become recognized internationally as an important way for those involved in a newsworthy situation, such as a natural disaster, a war, or a political demonstration, to communicate directly with the public about their experiences. Actors and other celebrities often use Twitter as a personal way to keep in daily touch with their fans. Businesses have also begun to make significant use of Twitter to publicize special offers or new products, as well as to keep their company name in the public consciousness.

What Do I Need to Know about Communicating on Twitter?

You can set up a Twitter account quickly and easily by going to the website, entering your name and e-mail address, and choosing a username and password. The website will then ask you to define your interests and will offer you the opportunity to follow numerous Twitter accounts related to subjects you choose. After setting up a profile page, you may begin reading tweets that interest you and sending tweets of your own. If you choose to follow another account, any tweet sent by that user will automatically appear on your page.

Brevity and clarity are the most important factors in using Twitter. Because tweets are limited in length, they present a special challenge to the writer. In order to streamline your message, you may want to eliminate extra words, such as *the*, and use numbers and symbols whenever possible. However, you should take care that you do not use so many abbreviations that your tweet becomes difficult to understand. If you include web links in your tweet, websites such as TinyURL (http://tinyurl.com) and Bitly (http://bitly.com) can help you find the shortest workable version of your link.

One important way in which tweets are organized is through the use of hashtags. Hashtags are subject terms in social media posts that make it easier to search for popular themes. They are designated by placing a # sign immediately before a word or phrase. For example, you might launch a discussion of breakfast beverages by tweeting, "I sure love my #latteinthemorning!" When the tweet is posted, "#latteinthemorning" will appear as a link that your readers may click in order to read posts on the same subject or post a tweet that contributes to the conversation. If a hashtag subject becomes popular and draws numerous contributors, it is said to be "trending." Hashtags can provide an interesting and useful way to navigate Twitter posts, but you should be careful not to overuse them. Inserting more than two can interfere with your message and annoy your readers.

How Can I Use Social Media in My Personal and Professional Life?

Social media can be a satisfying way to maintain contact with others. These may include your intimate circle, distant family members, old school friends, or coworkers. The most important thing to remember when communicating through Facebook, Twitter, and similar services is that social media sites are public in nature. Though it may seem that your posts will only be seen by trusted friends, inappropriate photographs and comments may cause you future embarrassment or even legal problems if they are viewed by a former spouse, a client, or a potential employer. Before using social media, you should make sure that you have installed appropriate privacy settings. Even with the highest privacy levels installed, you should take care never to post information that you do not wish to be made public.

Social media is also proving to be an effective business tool. Creating a Facebook or Twitter account for your business may help you publicize it and build your customer base. However, simply having a social media account will not automatically help your company if you do not maintain and update your page with useful tips, fresh information, and attractive offers to encourage customers to "like" the page and check it frequently. In organizing content for your social media presence, it may help for you to set specific goals for your outreach efforts, such as boosting one month's profits. You also may find it useful to set aside some time each day for composing tweets or updating your business Facebook page in order to keep your followers' interest.

Communicating through Graphics

What Is Visual Communication?

Visual communication is the use of images to share, illustrate, or reinforce ideas. The images and symbols left by the earliest people on ancient cave walls and rock faces provide evidence that visual communication has long been an important part of human interactions. Even the development of alphabets and written language can be viewed as part of the human desire to make ideas visible.

Visual communication generally involves the use of visual aids to capture an audience's attention and help listeners understand and remember the ideas being expressed. These visual aids may include writing, pictures, graphs, charts, maps, and other images. They may also include a presenter's *body language*, facial expressions, and movements.

Whether you are aware of it or not, you are surrounded by visual communication. Advertising logos, books, traffic signs, and the screens of computers, tablets, and mobile phones are all examples of visual communication. A number of colleges and universities have instituted visual communication departments in which graphic designers, advertisers, publishers, visual artists, and art directors for film and television can learn visual communication principles to use in their work. Even if you do not work in the field of art or communication, you may find that understanding how to use visual aids will improve your ability to communicate effectively with clients and coworkers.

Body language: *The gestures, movements, and mannerisms by which a person communicates with others, including facial expressions, tone of voice, and posture.*

How Is Visual Communication Different from Verbal and Written Communication?

Verbal, or spoken, communication and written communication both use words, phrases, and sentences to express ideas. Visual communication, on the other hand, uses images to express ideas. Though all can be effective ways to communicate, many experts agree that the human brain

Different types of charts and graphs can be used for different purposes. Seen here are a simple comparison, a pie chart, a line chart, and a bar chart. © KIROVKAT/ SHUTTERSTOCK.COM.

responds more quickly to images than to words. This may be because the use of oral and written language is relatively new in human development, while images have been used since ancient times. For whatever reason, most people first think in images, then they translate those images into words. The old saying "A picture is worth a thousand words" expresses the idea that your brain can process visual information much more rapidly and clearly than it processes language.

The fast pace of electronic media, such as television and the Internet, has greatly increased the use of visual communication. Some people fear that this expanded reliance on images will lead to reduced verbal and written skills. However, others believe that images often provide a more efficient and effective means of communication than words do and that a combination of images and text can help an audience maintain interest and retain information. Images can also quickly convey emotional content, a fact often exploited by advertisers and creators of political propaganda. Images may bypass the logical parts of your brain to ignite an emotional reaction, and some people have used this to manipulate public opinion, as well as government and business decisions.

The Politics of Emoticons

Emoticons, a type of graphic communication, have become widely used in text messages on smartphones, in e-mails, and on social media exchanges. Apple's iPhone, for instance, offers a wide variety of round and yellow smiley faces, covering the spectrum of human emotions, from happiness to anger to sadness, among other emoticons such as images for food, hand symbols, faces, animals, plants, clothing, and electronics. In lieu of typing out entire messages, many users use emoticons to quickly and effectively express themselves. A quick glance over Apple's emoticon offerings, however, shows that the majority of the face and hand symbols portray white people—not people of color.

Beginning in roughly 2011, some iPhone users began to decry this lack of diversity on social media sites such as Twitter and Facebook, as well as in the news. In August 2013 Megan Neal wrote about the lack of emoticon diversity in her article "The Petition to Make Emoji Less Racist" for *Motherboard*, a news website. She noted that emoticons often depict white people in privileged positions. "Some white emojis," she argued, "such as the image of the police officer, appear to hold positions of power, emphasizing the idea that minorities do not commonly occupy skilled jobs like these. In addition, the blonde princess [emoticon] represents that only pure and royal whites can obtain power." In March 2014 Apple acknowledged the lack of emoticon diversity and promised to remedy the situation.

While images may be good at eliciting a strong and immediate reaction, text may be more useful for explaining complex ideas.

What Is a Graphic?

In visual communication, a graphic is an image. Photographs, drawings, and symbols are all examples of graphic images. When used as a descriptive term, a graphic is generally related to visual art. Graphic designers use colors, typefaces, shapes, and image or art placements to communicate through print or online publications and advertisements. Graphic novels are like long comic books, composed entirely of pictures and dialogue.

As you learn to incorporate images into your written communications, you will most likely be working with computer graphics. These are images found through websites or created by computer programs. A number of sophisticated programs are available to help you create computer graphics for your specific needs. The Mashable website (http://mashable.com/2007/10/27/graphics-toolbox/) provides a list of dozens of free programs for creating customized computer graphics.

What Are Some Different Types of Graphics I Can Use?

There are a wide variety of graphics that can be used to complement or replace text in your written communications. Some of these, such as clip art and word art, may be available as a feature of your word processing program. Clip art describes a broad range of nonphotographic images that may be copied and pasted into a document to highlight a point or illustrate an idea. Word art is text that is modified with colors, outlines, shadows, or shaping to appear more decorative or eye-catching.

Graphs and charts can help readers or listeners understand complex ideas by condensing large amounts of information into easily under-stood images. Graphs are used to show the relationship between two or more sets of numbers, such as the profit earned over a period of time or the way workers divide their time during a shift. Common types of graphs are the line graph, which connects points along a single line; the bar graph, which uses rectangles of varying heights to compare data; and the circle graph or pie chart, which uses sections (or slices) of a circle to show percentages of a whole amount. Tables are graphics that present information in easily readable rows and columns. Some charts may use images or symbols to graphically demonstrate the information being presented.

Diagrams and maps are other types of popular graphics that may be used as visual aids. Diagrams are simple drawings that explain how things work or what they are composed of. Maps represent a physical space, such as a city, a country, or the interior of a building. Photographs are another valuable graphic tool for enlivening both personal and business documents. Because they provide accurate images of real people, places, and things, photographs can personalize a presentation or document and make it more intimate and convincing.

How Can I Use Graphics to Improve My Communication?

Graphics can be used in any situation in which you wish to improve your effectiveness in presenting information to an audience. In an oral presentation, you can insert graphics through the use of a presentation program, such as Microsoft PowerPoint, or by using a slide projector or overhead projector. You may even draw your own charts and graphs on a blackboard, white board, flip chart, or a large pad of paper set on a stand. If you are confident and fairly skilled at freehand drawing, a graphic created in front of your audience as you speak can provide entertainment and interest as well as highlighting valuable information.

In written presentations, inserting explanatory graphics can help break up long passages of text and provide a clear illustration of the facts you have written. Although graphics can add visual appeal to a text, don't go overboard. Too much clip art can give a cluttered look, while too many graphs and tables can overwhelm your readers. In business writing, take care to use tasteful clip art rather than cartoonish or corny images.

Before inserting graphics, consider your written work as a whole. Who is your audience? In an informal party invitation, lots of color and graphic art can be festive, while too much color can make a business report appear unprofessional. Outline the major points of your writing, and decide what kind of graphics will help you convey the most important information to your reader. For example, an appropriate clip art image can help set the tone at the beginning of a piece of writing or set off a special section, such as "Worker Responsibilities" or "Frequently Asked Questions."

Details of company finances may be clarified by the insertion of a graph showing profits and losses. A description of a manufacturing process might be accompanied by a diagram that illustrates the procedure. However, do not attempt to cram too much information into a single graphic. You do not want your reader to strain to understand the graphic. If you are explaining a complex concept, it may help to use several diagrams, graphs, or tables to illustrate your ideas.

How Can I Find Graphics to Use in My Communications?

As mentioned above, some graphics, such as clip art and word art, may be available on the word processing program that comes with your computer. Learning to use these is a good way to become familiar with the use of graphics. A number of websites, including *For Dummies* (http://www.dummies.com/how-to/content/how-to-insert-a-clip-art-into-a-word-2013-document.html), offer clear instructions for inserting clip art into your documents. However, word processing software comes with a limited number of choices. You can find many online sources that offer a much wider choice of clip art. Some, such as *Openclipart* (https:// openclipart.org), are free, while others, such as *clipart.com* (http://www. clipart.com), charge a subscription fee.

Your word processing or presentation program will also allow you to insert photographs into your documents. You can use personal photos already stored on your computer, or you can use a scanner to digitize paper photos, such as old family snapshots and other historical pictures. Many websites offer access to stock photos, which you can download for a nominal fee or for free. The *SiteBuilderReport* website (http:// www.sitebuilderreport.com/blog/where-the-best-designers-go-to-find-photos-and-graphics) provides a list of free sources for photos and other graphic images.

To use photos most effectively, you may have to edit your image to fit the space or to highlight the most important content. Your word processing program may have some photo-editing capability, but in order to edit your photographs more easily and professionally, you may need to purchase photo-editing software. Free editing software is available online through sites such as *Pixlr Editor* (http://apps.pixlr.com/ editor/) and *Picasa* (http://picasa.google.com/).

If you need more sophisticated or personalized graphics, such as a chart or graph that shows your company's sales over the course of a month or a diagram demonstrating a new procedure being instituted at your workplace, software is available to help you create graphics. Shawn McClain's article "How to Build a Graph on Google Docs," available on the *Houston Chronicle* website (http://smallbusiness.chron.com/ build-graph-google-docs-28522.html), offers instructions for creating a personalized graph using Google's free word processing website. Other sites, such as *Excel Easy* (http://www.excel-easy.com/data-analysis/charts. html) provide tutorials to help you use spreadsheet programs such as Microsoft Excel to create individualized charts and graphs.

For More Information

BOOKS

Isaacs, Florence. *Business Notes: Writing Personal Notes That Build Professional Relationships*. New York: Clarkson Potter, 1998.

Jamieson, Harry G. *Visual Communication: More than Meets the Eye*. Chicago: University of Chicago Press, 2007.

Nightingale, Virginia. *The Handbook of Media Audiences*. Malden, MA: Wiley-Blackwell, 2013.

Webb, Christina. *Writing for Publication*. Hoboken, NJ: Wiley-Blackwell, 2009.

PERIODICALS

"Publishing Contracts 101 (Protect Your Work)." *Writer's Digest*, September 2009. This article is also available online at http://www.writersdigest.com/writing-articles/by-writing-goal/get-published-sell-my-work/publishing-contracts-101.

WEBSITES

Donston-Miller, Debra. "Ten Social Networks for Special Interests." *Information Week*. January 8, 2013. http://www.networkcomputing.com/networking/10-social-networks-for-special-interests/d/d-id/1108080?page_number=1 (accessed December 2, 2014).

Gault, Kevin. "Punch up Your Writing with Graphics." *whitepapersource*. http://www.whitepapersource.com/writing/punch-up-your-writing-with-graphics/ (accessed December 10, 2014).

Guerena, Elisia. "How to Craft the Perfect Text Message." *Mobile Commons*. July 9, 2014. https://www.mobilecommons.com/blog/2014/07/how-to-craft-the-perfect-text-message/ (accessed November 18, 2014).

Gurnett, Kelly. "Nine Online Gold Mines for Finding Paid Freelance Writing Jobs." *The Write Life*. September 23, 2103. http://thewritelife.com/find-freelance-writing-jobs/ (accessed December 1, 2014).

McClain, Shawn. "How to Build a Graph on Google Docs." *Houston Chronicle*. http://smallbusiness.chron.com/build-graph-google-docs-28522.html (accessed December 10, 2014).

Neal, Megan. "The Petition to Make Emoji Less Racist." *Motherboard*. August 23, 2013. http://motherboard.vice.com/blog/the-petition-to-make-emoji-less-racist (accessed January 7, 2015).

Parker, Joey. "What Does Apple Think about the Lack of Diversity in Their Emojis? We Have Their Response." *MTV*. March 25, 2014. http://act.mtv.com/posts/apple-responds-to-lack-of-diversity-in-emojis/ (accessed January 7, 2015).

Rising, Lori Anne. "How Influential Writers Engage Their Audience." *Ragan's PR Daily*. March 12, 2014. http://www.prdaily.com/Main/Articles/How_influential_writers_engage_their_audience_16183.aspx (accessed November 13, 2014).

Shore, Jake. "Differences between Academic and Personal Writing in English." *Seattle PI*. http://education.seattlepi.com/differences-between-academic-personal-writing-english-1540.html (accessed November 18, 2014).

"Social Network." *Computer Hope*. http://www.computerhope.com/jargon/s/socinetw.htm (accessed December 2, 2014).

Teten, David. "How to Write a Memo That People Will Actually Read." *Forbes*. August 1, 2013. http://www.forbes.com/sites/davidteten/2013/08/01/

how-to-write-a-memo-that-people-will-actually-read/ (accessed November 13, 2014).

Wray, Amanda. "What to Think about When Writing for a Particular Audience." *Writing Commons*. http://writingcommons.org/open-text/writing-processes/think-rhetorically/711-what-to-think-about-when-writing-for-a-particular-audience (accessed November 13, 2014).

"Writing the Basic Business Letter." *Purdue University Online Writing Lab*. https://owl.english.purdue.edu/owl/resource/653/01/ (accessed November 18, 2014).

Organizational, Problem-Solving and Decision-Making, and Conflict Resolution Skills

Overview: Organizational, Problem-Solving and Decision-Making, and Conflict Resolution Skills

What Are the First Steps of Effective Organizing in the Workplace?

While every project is unique, there are some common steps that apply to the process of organizing a work project. If you will be leading a group project, you should start by allowing enough time for the planning phase. The amount of initial planning you will need will be based on the project's size, time line, and complexity, but most projects will require some amount of thoughtful planning before you begin the actual work.

When the group meets for the first time, team members should establish some ground rules. Some of these rules may seem like common sense, but the group should still discuss them before the project begins. For example, all members should agree to speak respectfully, listen attentively, participate actively, and be timely and responsible. If a project involves sensitive issues, there may be a need for an agreement among group members to keep certain information confidential. It may be useful for you to keep a list of the rules on hand as a reminder each time the group meets. You should also consider establishing a process for problem solving in case any conflicts arise.

Once the rules have been set, make sure that everyone understands and agrees to the details of the project, including goals and objectives, priorities, how resources will be used, and a time line for accomplishing tasks. Knowing your goals and objectives can help you guide the group to a successful outcome. A focus on defining and keeping to goals and objectives is sometimes called goal-oriented organization (GOO). This approach allows the team's goals to drive the project.

As the leader of the group, you should delegate responsibilities by assigning tasks to the other members. You might start by considering whether specific roles should be handled by certain group members and

You can get a number of apps for your smartphone that can help with organization and decision-making. © BLOOMUA/ SHUTTERSTOCK.COM.

whether particular jobs should be assigned to an individual, a small group, or the whole team. Some people may have particular skills that are best suited for specific responsibilities. You should also decide who will take care of official communication, either within the group or with external parties or media. Even assigning small tasks, such as who will be in charge of bringing coffee, can help the group function more smoothly.

Once the work begins, however, things do not always go as planned. It is likely that at some point you will have to make changes to any rules you establish. The work may proceed more quickly than planned, or the team may run into unforeseen conflicts, so the best approach is often to expect the unexpected. You should do your best to achieve a balance that allows you to stay the course and remain flexible.

How Can I Successfully Delegate Tasks?

Delegating tasks is an essential part of organizing. The most effective organizers consider which individuals are best suited to particular tasks. A person may have skills that are directly related to the work at hand, but some team members may also have transferable skills that may be useful to the group. For example, while a graphic artist would naturally seem to be the ideal choice for creating artwork, a father of six children might be an expert at managing a tight budget.

You should always be clear about the specific results that you want from the group. Make sure that any necessary resources or materials are available, and keep the lines of communication open for any questions or concerns that may come up while the work is underway. Assessing the work styles of individual team members can help you determine what kinds of support they may need from you. Some people work best with just the basics and may simply need to know what you want and when you need it in order to accomplish their tasks. For such relatively independent workers, allowing them the opportunity to be creative and take care of the tasks in their own way may be the best approach. Other workers may need support along the way or may prefer to have very specific directions. As you learn the different work styles of various group members, you can adjust your management style accordingly.

Sometimes you may find it challenging to give up control, delegate work, and allow other people to take responsibility for parts of the project, but you will be able to accomplish more by doing so. If you are less overwhelmed, it will be easier for you to focus on the big picture. Additionally, allowing workers the freedom to use their creativity may inspire them to contribute more to the work. They may have a greater sense of commitment to the project if they feel that their work is valued.

What Is an Organizational System?

While individuals in the group may work well at specific tasks, looking at a project as a system can help you to assess how effectively all of the parts are functioning together. If you are able to observe the overall patterns, you will be able to be more proactive and avoid potential problems. The use of a system can also help you understand the root causes of problems so that you can integrate solutions into the project.

Groups are often organized according to certain structural systems. A hierarchical structure resembles a pyramid with layers built on top of one another. The higher the layer, the fewer the number of people involved. People who are higher on the pyramid have more power and manage the people directly below them, while the person on the top has the most power. In a flat structure, one person is in charge, and that person manages everyone. Individuals are assigned specific tasks but do not make decisions or manage other group members. A divisional structure assigns work to small groups, or divisions, that work somewhat independently. Each division is in charge of one or more tasks but also reports to the head of the group. Some people use formal systems such as these, while others may prefer to create a system that is more specifically suited to their group or project.

How Do I Make Necessary Decisions?

Decision making is an essential organizing skill. To approach an issue that requires a decision, you should begin by thinking about your goals and objectives and what might be the best way to achieve them. As you consider alternatives, you can weigh the pros and cons of each option. However, you should be careful to avoid getting bogged down in too many alternatives. If you spend too much time looking for perfection, you may not be able to come to a decision. There is no absolute right or wrong way to go about the process, but you should try to determine the most effective approach for the task and the people involved.

Some group structures require leaders to make decisions independently, while others involve some or all members of a group in the decision-making process. There are positives and negatives for each method. If your team's members are more directly involved, it is more likely that they will be committed to the decision. However, involving others in decision making can also cause the process to take longer than it otherwise might, since the group may need time to come to an agreement. Some groups make decisions by consensus, a model in which everyone must agree on some or all outcomes. In some cases, you, as leader, might make all of the critical decisions, while in others you might only make those that are incidental. Most groups use a range of decision-making methods, depending on what they feel is best for a particular task.

There are many tools available that can help with the decision-making process. In a decision matrix analysis, all of the options are listed in rows on a table and all factors that require consideration are listed in columns. Each option is paired with its associated factors in order to create scores that can help determine which option is best. In another method, called SWOT analysis, each option is considered for its strengths, weaknesses, opportunities, and threats.

How Can Problems Be Avoided?

Even with the most detailed planning, the most cooperative group, and the best leadership, problems can and often do occur. However, while they may sometimes be stressful at first, not all problems are negative. In some situations, you may be able to view them as opportunities for refining your work.

The first rule in problem solving is to be proactive. As your group begins work on the project, you can lead a discussion about potential problems that might occur and how the members want to deal with them. You may not be able to anticipate specific problems, but you can create a general process for addressing them. For example, you can decide whether such issues should be brought to the whole group immediately or whether you should address them first. You can then decide whether or not the group as a whole should address the issue.

The problems that can occur during the course of a project may vary widely. Some may be small, such as the print shop running out of the color of paper you decided to use for a flyer, while others may be larger, such as a lack of sufficient funding. Even having more funds than expected can be problematic if it means that new decisions about allocating funds will have to be made, although most group leaders would likely welcome that type of problem.

What Are Some Useful Methods for Addressing Problems?

Some problems may be purely logistical. For example, one group member may not be available to give a talk on a particular day. Other problems can be more complex. If you have a shortage of funds, it can impact many parts of a project. You may need to adjust the amount of funding allocated for each task or eliminate certain activities. To address any problem, no matter its size, you should start by clearly defining it. You should also determine whether it needs to be dealt with immediately or if it can be set aside for a while.

Depending on the scope of the problem, you may need to involve particular people or the entire group in the process of finding a solution. Once you decide which members should be included in this process, they can discuss alternative solutions to the problem and the consequences of each option. For example, if it is a funding issue for an event, can a small amount of money be cut from each part of the project, or should an entire part of the project be cut? To get a better sense of all of the pieces of a complex problem, it can be useful to create a representative diagram of the problem and its implications. You can also have a *brainstorming* session within the group to stimulate creative solutions.

Brainstorming: *A group session where employees contribute their ideas for solving a problem or meeting a company objective without fear of retribution or ridicule.*

When looking for a solution to a problem, it is important to think about short- and long-term needs. A group member may be able to give a talk once, but if she has to do it every week for two months, will she have time for her other tasks? For complex problems or sensitive issues, you can employ decision-making tools such as SWOT or a decision matrix analysis. Once you have decided how to approach the plan, you should be clear and specific about the action that should be taken. It may help to set up a time to check in with the group to make sure that the solution is working. If it is not working effectively, it may need more tweaking or attention.

Getting to the root cause of a problem can help you avoid a similar problem in the future. If the group member is unable to give a talk because of a temporary illness, a one-time substitute would be an adequate solution. However, if she declines to give the talk because of conflicts with others in the group, a short-term solution may not be the answer. In this case another solution, such as shifting the responsibilities of group members, might prevent the issue from recurring. An effective process for solving one problem can be used as a starting point for solving others. It can also build trust among group members and give them confidence about their ability to work together.

What Can I Do If There Is a Conflict Between People?

Conflicts may occur between people for a variety of reasons. Individual group members may differ not only in their opinions but also in the manner in which they go about their work. Groups may experience conflicts when members have different values or come from cultural backgrounds where there are different assumptions about relationships, teamwork, or how a task should be approached. These differences may be clear from the beginning, or they may come up later while the work is in progress. If a group is dealing with particularly sensitive issues, such differences can be more pronounced and emotions may be more intense.

Some people may try to avoid conflict by remaining quiet rather than discussing their thoughts or feelings of disagreement. For some incidental matters, avoiding conflict can be practical. If, for example, you think it would be better to bind a report with three staples instead of two, engaging the full group in a discussion about this might not be a good use of time. In most cases, however, avoiding conflict is an ineffective means of dealing with a situation. Small conflicts can become larger if people suppress their ideas and feelings. Those who continually avoid conflict may disengage from the work of the project or may even become openly angry or emotional.

Like problems, conflicts are not necessarily negative. They can help clarify priorities, and resolving them can build trust as the group members get to know one another better and learn to respect and appreciate their differences. Conflicts can also energize people. When group participants feel passionate about an issue, they are likely to be more engaged and enthusiastic. However, these situations can be problematic if they are not handled effectively. If members of the group are allowed to behave inappropriately or disrespectfully, or if emotions get out of control, the work may slow down or stop if the conflict is not resolved.

What Are Some Effective Tools for Conflict Resolution?

Before working together, your group should decide how they would prefer to handle conflict, since the middle of a conflict is usually not the best time to try to figure out a process for resolution. Then, when a conflict arises, you should have the group review the agreement on how to solve it. It can also be useful for members to review other agreements that they have made, such as those concerning goals and objectives and any general ground rules that they have established. Depending on the situation, it may be useful for everyone to discuss the reasons why the group was formed in the first place, especially if some or all individuals are particularly committed to its purpose. If all participants are clear on the group's established rules, the reasons they joined the group, and what they are ultimately trying to accomplish, this may help lend overall perspective and direction to the problem-solving process.

Clarity is essential for the successful resolution of conflicts. If the entire group is participating in the process, you should make sure that everyone, not just those directly involved in the conflict, has the opportunity to state what he or she believes the conflict is about. Each person should be listened to and affirmed. It may be necessary for you to set limits on how long each person may speak. After you have defined the conflict, it can be helpful for the team to take a short break to think about what has been said and, if emotions are high, to have some quiet calming space. If the group is a large one, sometimes breaking up into smaller groups can make it easier for members to discuss possible resolutions, which they can then bring back to the larger group.

Once those on all the sides of the conflict have had a chance to express their viewpoints, the next step is to seek resolutions. Sometimes, just letting the group talk through the conflict may be enough. In other situations, you may need to consider numerous solutions before the team can find one to settle on. You should encourage team members to compromise, keep the goals in mind, and work collaboratively. Reminding them of ways in which other conflicts have been resolved may give them confidence that can help them come to an agreement. Depending on the issue at hand, the team may need to "agree to disagree," as long as this imperfect resolution does not prevent the group from making progress toward achieving its goals.

Sometimes it can be challenging to move forward from a conflict, especially if emotions run high or the conflict has created a lot of stress. Problem-solving tools are available to help groups move forward when they are stuck. It can be useful to break the conflict down into smaller parts. Some people use the metaphorical image of a parking lot, where certain parts of an issue can be "parked" so that they can be addressed later, while the group can move on and deal with the parts of the conflict that can be resolved. Try to get people to think creatively, and encourage all ideas. Even if they do not seem feasible, they may still inspire the solution that the group is looking for.

If a conflict is between two or three people and cannot be resolved within the group, it may be necessary for you to work with those people outside the group. At some point, you might also decide to bring in someone who can be more impartial, such as an outside mediator who is professionally trained in conflict resolution. With good planning, a clear structure, and open communication, conflicts and problems can be turned into opportunities for your group to work more effectively.

For More Information

BOOKS

Dale Carnegie Training. *The 5 Essential People Skills: How to Assert Yourself, Listen to Others, and Resolve Conflicts.* New York: Simon and Schuster, 2009.

Kallet, Michael. *Think Smarter: Critical Thinking to Improve Problem-Solving and Decision-Making Skills.* New York: Wiley, 2014.

Robbins, Stephen P., and Tim Judge. *Essentials of Organizational Behavior.* 13th ed. Upper Saddle Hill, NJ: Prentice Hall, 2015.

PERIODICALS

Duffy, Jill. "Get Organized: Tips and Tools for Managing a Project." *PC,* January 21, 2013. This article can also be found online at http://www.pcmag .com/article2/0,2817,2414461,00.asp.

Tytel, Mallary. "Thoughtful Decision Making." *Bloomberg Business,* November 11, 2006. This article can also be found online at http://www.bloomberg .com/bw/stories/2006-11-11/thoughtful-decision-making.

WEBSITES

Cardinal, Rosalind. "Managing Conflict at Work." *Huffington Post.* January 12, 2015. http://www.huffingtonpost.com/rosalind-cardinal/managing-conflict-at-work_b_6446928.html (accessed January 28, 2015).

Cochran, Craig. "Six Problem-Solving Fundamentals." *Quality Digest.* http://
www.qualitydigest.com/sept02/articles/02_article.shtml (accessed January
27, 2015).

Creel, Ramona. "Project Management Plan: Five Steps to Organizing and Managing Any Project." *SMEAD.* http://www.smead.com/hot-topics/project-
management-plan-1371.asp (accessed January 28, 2015).

Goodrich, Ryan. "SWOT Analysis: Examples, Templates and Definition." *Business News Daily.* January 1, 2015. http://www.businessnewsdaily.com/4245-
swot-analysis.html (accessed January 28, 2015).

"How to Organize Project Teams for on Time, on Budget Results." *ITtoolkit.
com.* http://www.ittoolkit.com/how-to-it/projects/organize-project-teams
.html (accessed January 27, 2015).

Nickols, Fred. "Ten Tips for Beefing Up Your Problem-Solving Tool Box." *Distance Consulting LLC.* 2012. http://www.nickols.us/ten_tips.htm (accessed
January 27, 2015).

"Principles of Conflict Resolution." *U.S. Geological Survey.* http://www
.usgs.gov/humancapital/cm/documents/principlesofconflictresolution.pdf
(accessed January 28, 2015).

Getting Organized and Project Management Skills

Why Is It So Important to Be Organized When Beginning a Project?

Organization is often the key to successful completion of a project, whether in school, at home, or in the office. Similar to a traveler using a map to navigate to an unfamiliar place or a novice chef following a recipe to prepare a new dish, organization involves outlining a strategy by which to arrive at the desired final outcome. Every day, in every walk of life, people tackle new projects that require a plan of action. A homeowner works to declutter a basement. A student writes a research paper. A manager prepares his or her department's quarterly review. All of these people must approach their projects in an organized fashion to ensure that tasks are completed properly and by a particular deadline.

Being organized at the outset of a project saves time and eliminates stress in the long run. As a first step it is a good idea to be certain an individual tapped for a project has the skills needed to complete the undertaking. For example, a person with very basic computer skills may

not be the right fit for a website design project. Knowing the skills and materials a project will require ahead of time will make the task feel less daunting or overwhelming.

Other skills needed to organize projects include keeping track of progress, identifying and solving any problems that may arise during the process, and addressing issues quickly in order to keep things moving forward. Organized individuals know how to make lists, do research, meet due dates, manage their time well, communicate with their teammates or instructor, carefully record important information, and keep their work space neat and clean.

Working in an office environment sometimes calls for prioritizing many competing activities and multitasking when necessary. © HONZA HRUBY/ SHUTTERSTOCK.COM.

Why Are Lists So Helpful When Completing a Project?

Lists detail the essential building blocks for a particular undertaking. For example, a recipe begins with a list of necessary ingredients, and a piece of furniture that requires assembly comes with a list of every part that should be included in the box. When you start a project, it is helpful to make a list of the resources you need to complete it. This inventory will give you an idea of what you already have and what you still need to acquire. Unless you have all of the resources needed to complete a project at the beginning, it will be riddled with numerous starts and stops, wasting your time and that of everyone working with you.

In addition to an ingredients list, a recipe also includes a numbered list of steps that must be followed. Similarly, you should begin a project by listing the necessary steps, arranged in a logical order. Making a step-by-step list that breaks the project into smaller, more manageable pieces and helps you to prioritize tasks. This also helps you see how far the project has progressed and where it still needs to go. For example, writers commonly list their ideas in outlines that guide them as they work. Although some outlines are very formal, with main topics and subtopics, others are more basic and may include a simple numbered list of ideas in the order in which the writer intends to discuss them. Some computer programs, such as Microsoft Outlook, can be used to create to-do lists. You can note the range of dates for working on tasks and create pop-up notices reminding you what tasks are due each day, week, or month. Without such lists or outlines, tasks may be forgotten, the project could meander without ever reaching its goal, or the finished product might seem more confusing than necessary.

When Is Research Necessary?

After you take an inventory of resources at the start of a project, you might discover that you do not know or have everything you need. You can then do research in order to find information or to acquire whatever you are lacking. Several Internet search engines, including Google, Yahoo!, and Bing, have become very popular with people researching a variety of subjects and items, whether they are students seeking information for class papers, workers looking for financial statistics, or Cyber Monday shoppers hunting down the right gifts for everyone on their gift-giving lists. Libraries are also useful places to find information contained in certain printed resources, such as books, encyclopedias, and subscription databases or periodicals.

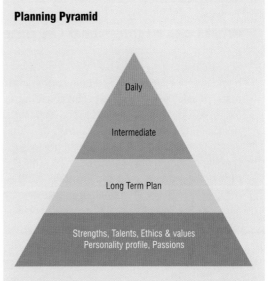

Planning Pyramid

Daily

Intermediate

Long Term Plan

Strengths, Talents, Ethics & values
Personality profile, Passions

SOURCE: U.S. Department of State. "Planning—Daily, Intermediate, and Long Term." [online] from http://www.state.gov/m/a/os/64938.htm.

Personal job and career goals can range in length from daily to very long term. The foundation of your goals should be in line with your own personal strengths, talents, ethics, values, personality profile, and individual passions. ILLUSTRATION BY LUMINA DATAMATICS LTD. © 2015 CENGAGE LEARNING.

There are times when people themselves are the most valuable sources of information. In such cases, you may need to conduct surveys or interview individuals in person. Investigative reporters frequently interview those involved in a newsworthy event. Similarly, corporations developing new products will survey focus groups to get feedback on those products. Historians writing books and filmmakers producing documentaries will find that they must interview those personally involved in historical events in order to tell the whole story. The ability to fill in the blanks through research is a skill that is highly valued by many employers and organizations.

How Can a Calendar Help?

Calendars are an important part of everyday life. They can be an invaluable tool for completing projects, whether at home, work, or school. You can use a calendar to schedule meetings and deadlines and to track progress.

What Does a Professional Organizer Do?

Because organizing projects at work and at home is both challenging and time consuming, many people have turned to professional organizers for help. According to the National Association of Professional Organizers (NAPO), you may want to hire a professional organizer for help making a physical space or an aspect of your life more ordered and effective. NAPO-certified organizers are trained professionals and have the specialized skills needed to deal with the unique needs of their clients. Some specialize in specific clientele, such as people with attention deficit disorder (ADD) or those who struggle with chronic disorganization (CD). Professional organizers do everything from helping a client organize a messy desk to helping a large company organize its office space. Rates for professional organizers depend on a variety of factors, including their experience level and geographic location.

A variety of different calendar formats exist, including paper, electronic, year-at-a-glance, month-at-a-glance, week-at-a-glance, and daily agendas.

The calendar available with Microsoft Outlook, which includes a to-do list feature, enables individuals not only to note an activity or meeting occurring on a particular day but also to record details about the event and set a pop-up reminder. Some people find it helpful to use project management software, including Outlook and other computer, tablet, and smart phone applications, because it sends everyone involved in a project an e-mail reminding them of an upcoming due date. Being able to use these various calendars and programs is a valuable skill that can improve efficiency and help a project go smoothly.

What Does It Mean to Manage Time during a Project?

When attempting a project, it is important to develop good time-management skills, starting with understanding how long you have to complete the project and how much time you should devote to each step in order to meet deadlines. Life is full of distractions that could derail the progress of a project. Those who work at home are often distracted by the need to do laundry, walk the dog, or do other types of house-work. Those who work at the office might be distracted by an incoming e-mail that pops up on computer as they work. Meanwhile, just about anyone can be distracted by alerts on their cell phones, tempting them to stop what they are doing to respond. All these distractions can prevent a project from being completed on time.

The more complex the project, the more complicated it will be to manage the time needed to complete it. For example, contractors building a house must coordinate the crew laying the concrete foundation with those hired to erect the frame of the house; install the wiring, plumbing, and dry wall; paint the interior; attach the aluminum siding to the exterior; and so on. If any of those crews is delayed, the entire project could come to a halt. In contrast, it is much easier to control the progress of a project attempted by a single person, especially if that person can focus on the work and tune out distractions. That kind of self-discipline can pay off in the end, perhaps with an A from your teacher, a raise from your boss, or good word of mouth that draws more customers to your business.

Why Is Good Communication Essential during a Project?

Whether you are working on a project alone or with a group of people, good communication skills are essential. Group members need to check in with classmates or coworkers to report on the progress of their portion of the project and to share any challenges they may be facing. When problems arise, other group members may be able to offer solutions, thus enabling the project to move forward. Because everyone is working together, it is important to communicate honestly and offer input so the project is a success.

It is similarly important for an individual doing an assigned project alone to be able to communicate clearly and honestly with a supervisor, teacher, or client as to how the project is progressing. Supervisors and teachers usually encourage such communication because their unique expertise enables them to provide advice and guidance to move the project forward. Problems or challenges with any part of the project need to be communicated clearly in order to obtain the assistance needed. For contractors and clients, two-way communication throughout a project is essential to ensure that the contractor knows exactly what the client wants and delivers it on time and on budget.

Why Are Good Note-Taking Skills Important?

Good note-taking skills are essential for many types of projects. When working with a team, members must be able to record the ideas of their teammates accurately and to keep track of what each person will contribute to the undertaking. In such a situation, good listening skills go hand in hand with good note taking. Group members must hear what others are saying and understand their own responsibilities in order to avoid confusion and the duplication of tasks. If it is necessary to interview others for the project, as reporters and historians often do, it will be important to quote subjects accurately. If the interview is recorded electronically, a careful transcription is often required.

Plagiarize: *To use another person's words or ideas without giving credit to that person.*

When working on a solo project, taking accurate notes of ideas learned in research, measurements taken, or other essential information will keep you in control of the project. A tailor making a suit for a customer will suffer embarrassment and a loss of business if the measurements he takes result in a suit that is too big or too small. A research paper that incorrectly quotes its sources could receive a failing grade or, worse, be suspected of *plagiarism*. Detectives often find that details recorded early in an investigation end up being useful later and enable them to catch the criminal or perpetrator they seek. It is thus very important to develop effective note-taking skills and the powers of observation that go with them.

Does Neatness Count?

When organizing a project, thinking clearly is crucial, and it is often impossible to think clearly in messy surroundings. Keeping your work space neat enables you to apply a certain kind of logic to your project, and that logic will be reflected in the end product. Clutter and confusion will only make it more difficult to find the important tools, information, and equipment needed to complete the project. A mechanic whose tool box and work bench are disorganized, forcing him or her to hunt for every wrench and screwdriver, will take twice as long to fix a car, which will be frustrating for the mechanic and the car owner. A cook whose kitchen is not well organized may not be able to find the essential ingredients or utensils he or she needs to create that special meal.

Neat, organized work spaces have several common characteristics. You may choose to have separate piles of items, arranged in a very particular way, that you consider logical. Another option is to use color-coding systems, whether to distinguish files containing different kinds of information or to identify the pieces that will be assembled to make the final product. Bringing logic and order to your physical work space will help you find what you need quickly and easily, while cluttering a work area with items unrelated to a project can cause confusion and stress.

Developing Organizational Skills

What Are Organizational Skills?

Organizational skills are techniques that people use in order to be more productive and efficient. In the workplace, organizational skills are essential for a number of tasks, including keeping a physical work space such as a desk, stockroom, or computer desktop neat and sensibly arranged so that employees can access needed items quickly. For example, a chef working in a kitchen might rely on an organizational system to keep ingredients separated, fresh, and easy to reach in order to streamline the cooking process. Organizational skills are also essential to managing time effectively at work so that employees can stay focused, productive, and on schedule. A bus driver, for instance, needs to keep track of when to arrive at each stop.

People acquire, practice, and develop organizational skills so that they can perform their jobs more successfully. Having good organizational skills helps you to be more productive, more efficient, and less anxious at work. Furthermore, organizational skills may help you produce work of greater quality, thus earning the respect and trust of your colleagues and supervisors.

What Kinds of Organizational Skills Are There?

Organizational skills can be divided into two basic categories: physical and mental. Physical organizational skills are those that can be done in your place of work. Mental organizational skills are those that involve organizing one's thoughts, time, and work style.

Many people find it useful to keep their work area organized. For office workers, this can include a desk that is clean and orderly so that all needed items are within reach. For example, you might keep file folders on your desk so that you can access them quickly. You might keep your

People use various methods and tools to help develop and maintain organizational skills. © ATTSETSKI/ SHUTTERSTOCK.COM.

pencils, pens, scissors, paper clips, staples, and other necessary office materials tucked away in a drawer, so as not to clutter the desk. Other organizational strategies may include keeping a dry-erase board above your desk where you can write yourself reminders or messages or a corkboard on which you can pin a calendar, important papers, and notes. When everything you need is easily accessible you spend less time wondering where things are and more time actually working.

Successful workers often find mental organization useful as well. For example, if you have an important deadline looming in a month, you might organize your workdays and weeks into smaller, more manageable units. This helps to ensure that you meet your deadline and are able to avoid last-minute, sloppy work. An organized mental workspace may also mean scheduling your workday around your energy levels so that you work when you are most efficient, limiting chats with colleagues to conserve work time, focusing on one task at a time, and working through bouts of procrastination (putting things off).

How Do I Develop Organizational Skills?

First identify which area of your work life you would like to organize. It may be appealing to try to work on all of your organizational skills simultaneously, but attempting to tackle too much at once is often ineffective. Instead, pick one organizational skill that you would like to develop. Be as specific and detailed as possible here. Perhaps the skill you would like to improve is time management. If possible, it is advisable to narrow your focus even more. What aspect of time management would you like to develop? Your ability to meet deadlines? Your ability to work efficiently during the day so that you do not have to stay late in the evening? The smaller and clearer your goal, the likelier you are to achieve it.

Once you have identified the organizational skill you would like to develop, ask yourself why it's important to your professional career. This step may require you to analyze your short-term, long-term, and

Organizational Skills Training

If you are struggling to develop your organizational skills, you might want to find out what educational opportunities are available to you. Because organizational skills are central to work life and project management, many schools, companies, and professional organizations offer courses and workshops designed to help participants master them. Courses may range from training on a specific organizational tool, such as a software program or a daily planner, to broader discussions of organizational strategies and other aspects of project management.

If you work for a large organization, stop by your human resources department to see if it offers any training programs that interest you. Check with local community colleges to find out if they offer any courses that fit your needs and your schedule. You may also want contact the local branch of the Department of Workforce Development to see if they can help you find the kind of instruction you need. Although many courses are available online, it is important that you research the reputation and legitimacy of any company offering online training before enrolling.

If you are worried about the cost of these training programs, get creative. If organizational challenges are hampering your work, talk to your manager or human resources department. The company you work for may be willing to cover some or all of the costs of the training. Moreover, if others in your organization are grappling with similar problems, the company may be willing to hire a professional trainer to provide guidance onsite.

personal career goals. Having a definite reason (or even multiple reasons) for developing an organizational skill may help you stay committed to your goal. For instance, you may want to keep a cleaner desk at work. Before you try to develop this organizational skill, consider why having a well-ordered desk is important to you. Perhaps it is because you have a hard time finding items that you need in your desk, which makes you less productive and more distracted at work. This in turn could make you a less valuable employee. Or perhaps you would like to have a clean desk because your supervisor gives you a stern glance every time she walks by your messy desk, and you would like to make a better impression on her so that you can advance in the company. Concrete motives may inspire you to stay committed to developing the organizational skill you have identified.

Next develop a clear plan for achieving the organizational skill you would like to develop. Make a list of all the tasks you will need to accomplish in order to do this. No item is too small to put on your list. For example, in order to meet a deadline that is a few months away, you may need to buy paper clips. Even though this item seems small, put it on the list. After making this list, you will have a clear road map of what needs to be done in order to achieve your goal. Try not to take tackle everything on the list at once. Instead, accomplish one item at a time. This will break a large task, such as organizing a desk, into a more manageable one.

Finally, you will need to prioritize the development of your skill. Developing an organizational skill is not something that happens once every few months or when you have spare time. Rather, it is a daily event. In order to stay organized, you must make time to organize every day, if only for a few minutes. In fact, spending a few minutes organizing each day is a doable goal for most people. A great way to stay on track is to ask a colleague at work to hold you accountable for your actions, or you might even pledge to develop organizational skills together.

What Are the Benefits of Developing Organizational Skills?

There are many benefits to developing organizational skills in the workplace. Chief among these are increased worker efficiency and productivity as well as a higher-quality product. In addition, organizational skills help to reduce stress in the workplace.

 Developing your organizational skills can improve efficiency and productivity at work. You will be able to complete work projects in a given period of time without wasting time, energy, money, or other valuable resources due to organizational problems. For example, a combination of physical and mental organization will limit the amount of time you spend looking for copy paper in the stockroom or mindlessly surfing the Internet. Again, the goal of developing your organizational skills is simply to do your job better.

Another benefit of developing your organizational skills is the quality of your work. What "quality" means in your workplace may be different from another workplace. In general, however, quality refers to the idea that a product is made as well as possible. Since less time will be lost dealing with a disorganized physical or mental workspace, you will have more time and energy to focus on the work at hand.

In addition to improving the quality of your work, developing organizational skills may help you advance professionally in your workplace. For instance, your supervisor may notice your superior organizational skills and promote you to a higher position. Another positive is that developing workplace organizational skills may lead to less stress at work. Not being organized can contribute to lack of focus, misdirection, and wasted time, all of which can cause *anxiety*. Eliminating such issues may provide real relief.

Anxiety: *An abnormal and overwhelming sense of worry and fear that is often accompanied by physical reaction.*

Finally, it is important to remember that organization should occur as part of a larger goal, such as increasing worker productivity or making a workspace easier to use. Organization for the sake of organization may be a waste of valuable time that could otherwise be spent working.

How Can I Use Internet Technology and Smartphone Applications to Help Me Stay Organized?

Thanks to the advent of the Internet, smartphone applications (often called "apps"), and other technology, there are many tools available to help you develop physical and mental organizational skills. These services can be useful because they remind you to stay organized, keep you accountable, and remove some of the tedious "busy work" inherent in organizing.

If you have a hard time organizing your receipts, business cards, and other miscellaneous papers on your desk, a website called Shoeboxed (https://www.shoeboxed.com/) can help you simplify and streamline your filing system. For instance, if you need to save receipts at work for reimbursement and tax purposes, Shoeboxed allows you to store them safely online. If taking photos and uploading receipts sounds too complicated or time consuming, the app provides you with prepaid shipping envelopes. Just drop the envelope in the mail, and a Shoeboxed staffer will upload your important documents.

If you spend a considerable amount of time at your computer and have trouble being productive during the workday, RescueTime (https://www.rescuetime.com/) may be especially helpful. The app monitors how you spend your time on the computer. At the end of the day, it provides a detailed report of your activities. You can see right away if valuable work time is being squandered on social media, news websites, or other sites that distract you. You can also program RescueTime to alert you when you've spent a specific amount of time on a certain task. This may be helpful if, for example, you are trying to reduce the amount of time you spend checking e-mail. The app can also block sites that are time-wasters.

Applying Organizational Skills to Manage Projects

How Can Organizational Skills Help in Managing Projects?

Organizational skills are techniques that people use to develop and maintain orderly physical and mental workspaces. When managing a project at work, most people find it helpful to have organizational skills. Organizational skills allow whatever project you are working on to remain focused and streamlined, as well as productive and efficient. In order to keep a project on budget and on deadline, behind-the-scenes organization is crucial. In addition, the organizational skills applied to a project will help it be of the highest quality possible.

Orderly workspaces are important because they tend to improve worker efficiency and productivity, ensure higher-quality products, and create a less stressful office environment. It is important to remember, however, that applying organizational skills to projects is not a goal in and of itself. Rather, it is a tool that workers use in order to achieve desired results. There are a number of other secondary benefits as well, including employee satisfaction, customer satisfaction, and a reduction of stress for everyone involved with the project.

Applying organizational skills to projects you are managing is something you can do even if you are not the project manager. Any project, small or large, can be improved by sound organizational practices.

What Is Project Management in the Workplace?

Project management is an umbrella term that encompasses many different activities in the workplace. In general, project management refers to the act of directing, supervising, and completing a time-sensitive or long-term assignment that involves a variety of stakeholders. For example, a project manager at a publishing company might supervise every step of a book's publication; a project manager at a software company might direct the development of a new computer program; and a general contractor at a building company might oversee the construction of a home. Successful project managers tend to have excellent planning, communication, supervisory, and budgeting skills. It is also beneficial for them to be flexible and possess a variety of backup plans. Even the most carefully planned projects likely will experience unforeseen obstacles.

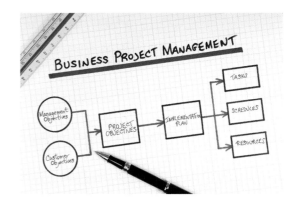

Project management, when done correctly, is a carefully planned and organized effort to achieve specific goals within a specified timeline. © FOTOLUMINATE LLC/SHUTTERSTOCK.COM.

In general, project managers supervise employees who are a part of their project team. If you are a member of a project team, you will also need to manage your own personal projects. Since you will be working on one aspect of a larger project, your personal undertakings will be smaller and more manageable than a project manager's. Nevertheless, you can apply the same organizational skills to your own work that a project manager would to a large project, just on a smaller scale.

Students in high school, college, and graduate school also have to manage projects, such as group assignments, presentations, and research papers. Although some organizational skills used by project managers in the workplace, such as budget management, are not applicable to students' endeavors, other qualities, such as time and workspace management, are quite useful.

What Organizational Skills Can I Apply to Manage Projects?

In order to effectively manage projects, a number of organizational skills must be used, including time management and workspace, budget, and communication skills. If you do not yet possess these skills, it is possible to develop them while you are managing a project. Indeed, successful project managers see every endeavor as an opportunity to improve their organizational skills through on-the-job learning.

Another technique of successful project managers is asking for help when needed. Are you subpar at keeping an orderly workspace or communicating regularly with clients? Asking a colleague who has these skills for help may ultimately improve the quality of your project.

How Do I Organize a Project Timeline?

Since most projects are time sensitive, you as the manager must be able to organize time effectively. In particular, you are responsible for determining the start and finish dates of the project. This is not as simple as picking dates off the calendar. Instead, determining a project's start and finish dates requires substantial forethought, such as asking yourself if you have the resources to accomplish the task in a certain amount of time. For instance, you may need to hire more people to complete a project in two months, or you may have to extend the length of the project to four months if you do not have the resources to expand your staff. Depending on your industry, start and finish dates might depend on outside factors such as material availability. A general contractor, for example, may need to budget extra time for acquiring a specific type of marble for a stairwell. You may want to discuss your start and finish dates with a supervisor or another project manager to determine if your timeline is reasonable.

After you have set the start and end dates of a project, you should create a calendar that outlines interim deadlines. An important part of organization is breaking up large chunks of time into manageable units. For example, a woman who is opening a coffee shop might have set deadlines for acquiring outside funding by December 1, locating and renting a suitable space by January 1, renovating the space by February 1, hiring employees by February 15, and opening for business by March 1. Due to unforeseen factors, such as shipping delays or a financial partner backing out at the last minute, it is normal not to meet every interim deadline. Nevertheless, the very act of developing such deadlines and trying to adhere to them helps to keep your project moving forward.

How Do I Organize a Project Workspace?

A well-arranged workspace will allow you and other employees to complete tasks without becoming distracted by disarray. In an office environment, ensuring an organized setup might mean that the stock room is arranged in the simplest way possible. Or it might mean asking the information technology (IT) expert to make sure all computers, copiers, scanners, and other often-used electronics are running smoothly so that time will not be lost to mechanical failures. Organizing your workspace at the start of the project will help guarantee that you and your team can focus solely on the issues at hand.

Throughout a project, make sure that the maintenance of the workspace remains a priority. You might spend 10 minutes each morning, for instance, tidying your desk, which will help to improve your productivity throughout the day. You may also want to ask team members to handle key essential office organizational tasks each week.

If your office is prone to wind up in disarray, it might be worthwhile to hire a full-time or part-time office assistant to keep everything in order. This will allow you and your project team to focus on efficiently completing your work instead of cleaning the office.

How Do I Organize a Project Budget?

Creating a budget is another key organizational task for a project manager. A budget is a financial plan that takes into account the amount of money that you plan to spend and receive during a given period. As a project manager, your goal is to bring the project in either on or under budget. A project that runs over budget generally is not considered wholly successful, even if it is of high quality.

As a project moves forward, part of your job is to continuously assess the budget. Locating, formatting, and then analyzing the financial data will help you identify areas where you are under budget or over budget. Once you have identified the areas where the project is draining more money than expected, you can take the necessary action, such as transferring money to where it is needed most or revising the budget to account for the added expenditures. It is also wise to keep your team members abreast of the budget. That way they can take personal responsibility for the money spent on their parts of the project.

How Do I Organize Communication with My Project Team?

On most projects, there are a number of stakeholders who have a vested interest in succeeding. Within a workplace, they tend to be the project managers themselves, project team members, and higher management (such as vice presidents, chief executive officers, or owners). Productive working relationships are built on solid communication between partners. In fact, according to the Society for Human Resource Management, worker satisfaction greatly depends on feelings of good communication between colleagues. Fundamentally, effective communication helps all the stakeholders feel necessary and involved. These positive feelings encourage the stakeholders to work diligently and well together. This, in turn, increases the likelihood of a higher-quality outcome to the project.

 When planning and budgeting for a project, you may find it helpful to determine a framework for communicating regularly with your project team. Many project managers conduct weekly or biweekly meetings to assess the status of each member's progress, to give members new information, and to remind everyone of goals. Determine what you want each meeting to accomplish, whether it is camaraderie or better communication. These meetings will likely translate to long-term success. Make sure, however, that meetings do not waste valuable time.

For the sake of efficiency, designate a note-taker for these meetings so that you can maintain accurate project records. You may also want to check in individually with team members every few weeks. This can be done through e-mail, instant messaging, or in person. The goal here is to determine how much progress the person is making, identify and solve any issues, and develop a good working relationship.

Different Organizational Systems

What Is an Organizational System?

Organizational systems enable people to keep track of their affairs. Bills must be paid on time, doctor visits must be scheduled, and other important tasks must be completed, all while you try to maintain a social life. As you gain experience in the workplace and rise to a higher position, responsibilities increase, and your job becomes more complex. An inability to find the right system to manage each aspect of your life can cause confusion, stress, and failure. Many people are familiar with the anxiety that comes from losing track of an important document, booking two meetings at the same time, or forgetting to pay a bill. With a good organizational system, you can avoid such missteps.

Regardless of whether you have low-tech or high-tech preferences, organizational systems can be used to improve your productivity, manage your projects and financial affairs, and secure important personal and company information. Electronic devices, including computers, smart phones, and tablets, help to organize a person's life in countless ways. Finding the right systems for your particular purposes will bring order to your life and assist you in reaching your goals more effectively.

What Systems Help with Scheduling?

A calendar or digital tracker that enables you to sort out your appointments, meetings, and events can relieve stress and increase efficiency. You may choose to write each appointment or event on a wall calendar or in a daily or weekly appointment book. The type of calendar you use will depend on the number of different tasks you have to schedule. Smart phones are equipped with calendars where you can note appointments and set alerts to remind you of upcoming events. The goal is to make sure that you keep appointments and do not accidentally overbook yourself.

Research filing systems are just one method of an organizational system for keeping and finding records. © GIBLEHO/ SHUTTERSTOCK.COM.

A number of mobile phone applications (apps) and computer programs also make it easier to schedule both your professional and personal lives. A ticket tracker such as Bluetail enables companies to schedule tickets or service appointments and assign personnel to the various tasks. Online schedulers such as Doodle and Vyte.in provide platforms for meeting or party attendees to vote on convenient event days and times. These schedulers often sync with your personal calendar to alert you to potential conflicts. Apps such as NeedToMeet allow invitees to see each other's calendars and work around everyone's schedules. For more basic digital scheduling, Microsoft Outlook has a function for you to select a meeting time and invite attendees, who will find the event added to their Outlook calendars when they accept.

How Can You Become More Productive?

When you are productive, you feel, and often actually are, more successful. Productive people are able to multitask, balancing projects at home, in the community, and at the office. The more efficient these people are, the more projects they complete. However, to be that productive, you have to employ an organizational system, one with tools that fit your needs. A formal outline or a simple list of project tasks or ideas is a good way to start. Then notes or drafts can be gathered or produced on separate notepads or in notebooks. The notes for each project can be stored in separate folders, with perhaps a different color folder for each project. If you prefer, make your project notes on index cards, perhaps with colorful sticky tabs to flag specific tasks or ideas for easy searching and organizing. Finally, an easy-to-use calendar helps with scheduling tasks and keeping track of deadlines along the way.

Spreadsheet: *A document that stores data in a grid of horizontal rows and vertical columns.*

Numerous computer programs are geared toward improving productivity, such as the Microsoft Office suite. It allows you to write documents, send e-mails, produce slides and graphics, and create *spreadsheets*. Systems designed to prioritize projects and help you multitask, such as IBM Verse, are also available, while note-taking software, including OneNote and Evernote, allow you to quickly and easily save and organize information found on the Internet.

Chronic Disorganization

Chronic disorganization (CD) is an inability to stay organized and is often accompanied by dissatisfaction or distress. People with CD often felt either physically or emotionally deprived as children. They also may struggle to keep track of time and experience anxiety whenever they try to get their lives in order. Unlike hoarding, CD is not considered to be an official disorder by mental health professionals.

Temporary disorganization due to a busy work schedule or personal stress does not constitute CD. Rather, it is a long-term problem that seems to grow worse over time. The Institute for Challenging Disorganization specializes in helping people identify their disorganization issues and address them successfully. It provides helpful fact sheets regarding disorganization, quizzes to help people determine their levels of disorganization, and lists of professional organizers who are certified to assist people with CD.

What Are the Best Ways to Organize Your Documents?

As you become more productive, you often amass more documents. Thus, it becomes necessary to develop one or more filing systems for your documents, whether with an online product or a good old-fashioned filing cabinet. Those who prefer to keep printouts of documents, e-mails, and articles for easy reading and future reference can develop a filing system in which papers are stored in separate folders, organized alphabetically or by subject or date. Regular maintenance of those files is important. Since the material likely will take up a good deal of physical space in filing cabinets or storage bins, you must review it periodically in order to discard what is no longer needed.

Filing systems on desktop computers and laptops have a lot of memory, allowing users to create folders, subfolders, and even sub-subfolders. If you are lacking in physical space, this is a good way to operate. And as long as those folders are organized in a way that is logical to you, you will be able to access information quickly. External computer hard drives are removable devices that enable users to back up their electronic documents so that they can be stored in a secure place. For group projects, wikis are very useful, as they allow multiple users to collaborate by posting documents, meeting transcripts, and project notes to a shared site and then permit anyone in the group to modify the content. Many individuals and businesses also opt for cloud-based storage providers, such as OneDrive, Dropbox, or Google Docs, where content is stored on the Internet in a password-protected location with abundant space as well as access for multiple users.

What Systems Can Help to Organize Group Projects?

Group, or team, projects enable collaborators to contribute their own unique skills while being enriched by the abilities and knowledge of others. To organize team members effectively and produce a quality project, you must communicate clearly and ensure that everyone meets deadlines. Effective project managers maintain accurate lists of what each team member is doing, as well as records of project expenses and calendars showing the due dates of various tasks. The lists can be recorded on paper by hand or by using different types of computer tools, such as the Microsoft Office suite. A cloud-based storage system gives group members the ability to deposit and retrieve documents in a shared location and to synchronize several different types of devices.

Software for project management is also a handy organizing tool. Programs such as Basecamp, Teamwork.com, Microsoft Project, and Mavenlink keep pertinent project information centrally located. These systems chart every aspect of a project, including who is involved, what their assignments are and when they are due, relevant documents and resources, and important messages from team members. Additionally, automatic e-mail reminders can be sent to team members as the due dates for their assignments approach.

What Systems Help to Organize Finances?

Everyone wants to achieve at least a degree of financial success. To do so, you must employ a system that effectively organizes your finances. Every bank account holder receives a paper transaction register, where each deposit, withdrawal, and paid bill can be recorded. If you write down your transactions faithfully, such registers are a handy way to control your spending, provided your math is correct. However, such registers do not make it easy to pinpoint how you are spending your money and where you need to budget better.

This is another area where software is enormously helpful, whether your finances are complex or relatively simple. One of the most popular programs is Quicken, which gathers all your data in one place, keeps your accounts balanced, and lets you quickly and easily see where your money is going. Other programs, such as Mint.com and Betterment, use similar systems to show spending habits and provide assistance in budgeting and investing.

How Can You Keep Your Money and Information Safe?

With computer hacking emerging as a serious problem in the early twenty-first century, security and information management are more important than ever. The right security system might be cloud based or simply a reliable piece of hardware. It really does not matter as long as your money and information are safe and easily accessible to you. Computer security systems such as McAfee and Norton AntiVirus scan every website you visit and block sites that could be dangerous to your computer. In addition, password managers, including 1Password, Keeper, and RoboForm, help you to devise unique passwords that are less vulnerable to hackers. It is also important to back up your files, either via a cloud-storage provider or an external hard drive, so that nothing is lost if your digital files are somehow corrupted or deleted.

For those who rely instead on an extensive paper filing system, it is essential to have a shredder to dispose of outdated documents that might contain personal or sensitive information, such as Social Security and bank or credit card account numbers. Depending on where your file cabinet is located, you might also want one that locks. Some people opt to store important papers in a safe with a combination lock.

What Are the Best Ways to Organize Your Household?

Many people underestimate the complexity of managing a household. Luckily, systems exist that can help you in this regard. Some of the most basic, easy-to-adopt organizational systems require little more than a pencil and paper. Anyone can buy or create a calendar, hang it on the wall, and record important appointments and events. A to-do list can be written and tacked to the refrigerator, right next to the grocery list. A blackboard assigning chores to each family member might be hung in a high-traffic part of the house, while the latest bills can be stored in a desk or dedicated container. Those are all tried-and-true low-tech systems that people have employed in order to run their personal lives.

You can also download one of the many family-management apps to your smart phone or tablet. For example, Cozi allows you to enter important events and appointments in a calendar, create various types of to-do and shopping lists, and plan meals for the week. Such software typically enables several family members to sync their devices so that everyone knows exactly what is happening in the household. Using and consulting such apps can become part of the family's daily routine, helping the household operate more smoothly.

For More Information

BOOKS

Hallowell, Ned. *Driven to Distraction at Work: How to Focus and Be More Productive*. Cambridge, MA: Harvard Business Review Press, 2015.

Kondo, Marie. *The Life-Changing Magic of Tidying Up: The Japanese Art of Decluttering and Organizing*. Berkeley, CA: Ten Speed Press, 2014.

Leist, Laura. *Eliminate the Chaos at Work: 25 Techniques to Increase Productivity*. Hoboken, NJ: Wiley, 2011.

Levitin, Daniel J. *The Organized Mind: Thinking Straight in the Age of Information Overload*. New York: Dutton, 2014.

Schmidt, Terry. *Strategic Project Management Made Simple: Practical Tools for Leaders and Teams*. Hoboken, NJ: Wiley, 2009.

Sova, Dawn B. *Getting Organized at Work*. New York: Learning Express, 1998.

PERIODICALS

Allen, David. "When Office Technology Overwhelms, Get Organized." *New York Times*, March 18, 2012, BU1. This article is also available online at http://www.nytimes.com/2012/03/18/business/when-office-technology-overwhelms-get-organized.html?pagewanted=all&_r=0.

Fallows, James. "How You'll Get Organized." *Atlantic*, July/August 2014. This article is also available online at http://www.theatlantic.com/magazine/archive/2014/07/how-youll-get-organized/372295/.

WEBSITES

Carter, Sherrie Bourg. "Eight Easy Organizational Tips to Increase Your Productivity at Work." *Psychology Today*. September 18, 2011. https://www.psychologytoday.com/blog/high-octane-women/201109/8-easy-organizational-tips-increase-your-productivity-work (accessed February 3, 2015).

DuPont, Paula. "The 16 Best Meeting Scheduler Apps and Tools." *Zapier*. https://zapier.com/blog/best-meeting-scheduler-apps/ (accessed January 8, 2015).

"Getting Organized at Work." *Rice University Human Resources.* http://people. rice.edu/uploadedFiles/People/TEAMS/Getting%20Organized%20at%20 Work.pdf (accessed February 3, 2015).

Gralla, Preston. "OneNote vs. Evernote: A Personal Take on Two Great Note-Taking Apps." *Computerworld.* http://www.computerworld.com/ article/2488890/desktop-apps/onenote-vs-evernote-a-personal-take-on-two- great-note-taking-apps.html (accessed January 8, 2015).

Hastings, Rebecca R. "SHRM: Job Security Is No Longer Top Driver of Sat- isfaction." *Society of Human Resource Management.* http://www.shrm.org/ hrdisciplines/employeerelations/articles/pages/shrm-job-security-is-no- longer-top-driver-of-satisfaction.aspx (accessed January 15, 2015).

Hatcher, Diane. "Are You Chronically Disorganized? Fact Sheet." *Institute for Challenging Disorganization.* https://challengingdisorganization.org/content/ fact-sheets-public-0 (accessed January 29, 2015).

Kooser, Amanda C. "What Does 'Good' Organizational Skills Mean?" *Hous- ton Chronicle.* http://smallbusiness.chron.com/good-organizational-skills- mean-2882.html (accessed January 15 2015).

Parker, Jason. "Take Control of Password Chaos with These Six Password Managers." *CNET Magazine.* http://www.cnet.com/news/best-password- managers/ (accessed January 8, 2015).

"Ten Quick Tips for Getting Organized." *Entrepreneur.* January 11, 2006. http://www.entrepreneur.com/article/82924 (accessed February 3, 2015).

Westland, Jason. "Project Management: Four Ways to Manage Your Budget." *CIO.* http://www.cio.com/article/2406862/project-management/project- management--4-ways-to-manage-your-budget.html (accessed January 15, 2015).

"What Is Project Management?" *Project Management Institute.* http://www .pmi.org/About-Us/About-Us-What-is-Project-Management.aspx (accessed January 15, 2015).

Problem Solving and Decision Making

What Are Problem-Solving Skills?

A problem is a challenge that causes difficulties at work, at school, or in your personal life. Problem-solving skills are techniques that help you determine and apply solutions wherever challenges arise. Problems can be small, large, or somewhere in between. Some will require the thoughtful application of problem-solving skills over an extended period of time. Small issues may have easier solutions and require less attention than larger ones. The best way to solve a problem depends upon the type of situation you are facing.

Since most of us encounter a variety of problems on a regular basis, it is worthwhile to take the time to learn about and develop problem-solving skills. Problem solving is a process that involves several steps. The first step is to identify the source of the problem. Once you have done that, you can come up with a number of possible solutions and choose the best one to implement. Afterward, you may want to reflect on the problem-solving process to evaluate whether you have solved the problem successfully.

PROBLEM
SOLVING
STEPS

When working through a problem, it can be helpful to define your approach and follow specific steps. © KEITH BELL/ SHUTTERSTOCK.COM.

What Are Some Kinds of Problems and Why Do They Happen?

Some problems are expected and planned for, while others may come as surprises. A big problem for one person may be a small problem for another person, or he or she may not see it as any trouble at all. Whether a problem seems large or small is usually dependent upon your preparedness and problem-solving skills. For example, you might get a flat tire while driving a car. Flat tires are a fairly common occurrence, and you can therefore expect that, at some point during your driving career, you will probably have a flat tire. However, since flat tires usually happen unexpectedly, they can cause unwanted setbacks.

Problems occur when events do not happen according to plan. This might mean that you have to do work that you had not initially expected or wanted to do, such as changing a tire by the side of the road. This would be a small problem for someone who knows how to change a tire, but it would be a big problem for someone who does not. However, sometimes the responsibility for solving a problem belongs to someone else. An essential problem-solving skill is the ability to assess whether or not you should involve yourself in finding a solution to the problem.

How Do I Identify a Problem?

To solve a problem, you must identify it correctly. Some problems are obvious, while others are less apparent and require extra work to figure out. It is important to pinpoint the true cause of the problem so that you can effectively resolve the underlying issue rather than just approaching the parts of the problem that may be visible on the surface.

Symptom: *Something that indicates the presence of an illness or bodily disorder.*

For example, physicians deal with medical problems all the time. In order to treat a disease, a physician must discover what the root cause is. If a patient arrives in the physician's office with body aches, fever, respiratory congestion, and fatigue, treating each issue separately will not address the one central problem that is causing the rest. *Symptoms* are often easier to identify than a problem's real cause, but you will know that you have found the source of the problem if it accounts for all the symptoms that are present. In the case of the physician, if he or she gives the patient a flu test and it comes back positive, then the doctor can be fairly confident that the patient's symptoms are all caused by one problem, the flu virus.

How Can I Discover the Cause of a Problem?

It is easy to figure out why some problems happen. Sometimes a car stalls because there is no gas in the tank, or sometimes a shipment cannot be made because a key material is not available. However, some problems are more complex and require careful deliberation. These problems may require the input of others. Sakichi Toyoda, the founder of Toyota Industries, developed a useful system for problem solving. His advice was to ask the question "Why?" five times in order to discover the ultimate reason for a problem. This system, known as the Five Whys, can apply to most problems that you encounter.

For instance, a marketing coordinator at a company might consider the reasons why a recent advertising campaign did not generate new business. "Why?" she might ask herself. "Because I did not put advertisements on television, only on radio." "Why?" "Because I did not have enough in my budget to afford television." "Why?" "Because the CEO would not give me more money for *marketing*, even though I presented a strong case for it." "Why?" "Because he doesn't believe that advertising is important." "Why?" "Because he is used to acquiring clients himself through his sales team, not through advertising." Through this line of inquiry, the marketing coordinator has now identified why she has a problem. Now she can turn her attention to finding a solution.

Marketing: *The process of promoting, selling, and distributing a product or service.*

How Do I Find the Solution to the Problem?

Once you have identified the problem and its root cause, you can then look for one or more ways to solve it. Ideally, a successful solution eliminates the problem entirely. Some solutions may be obvious right away, while others may take more time and energy to discover. Some might even require the help of professionals in order to determine the best possible approach. A key problem-solving skill is the ability to move beyond identification of the problem to the process of finding a solution.

If a good and workable solution does not immediately occur to you, brainstorming is an effective way to generate ideas. A brainstorm is a short, intense period of time in which you apply all of your mental energies to a task that must be accomplished. This activity can be done alone or with a group. You may want to brainstorm solutions to your problem on a piece of paper, jotting down every idea that occurs to you. Don't worry if some of the ideas don't seem very good. If you remain open to any and all possibilities and allow your creativity to flow, you will have a better chance of coming up with the right answer.

Sometimes you may not know whether a solution to the problem exists. In such situations, research may help. You can consult books, articles, websites, or manuals that relate to your problem. Another way to research a problem is to discuss it with other people who may have expertise in a relevant area. This could mean talking to a supervisor, an instructor, or a friend or family member.

Some especially difficult problems may require complex solutions. For these problems, it might be most efficient to call in a professional to find a solution for you. A professional plumber, for example, will be able to find the source of your leak quickly and accurately. Knowing when to delegate the problem to a qualified professional is another key problem-solving skill.

How Do I Choose the Right Solution to the Problem?

If you approach a problem by brainstorming, you might generate a handful of potential solutions. To identify the best one, you should consider what your goals are and what resources you have. For example, if you have a very old computer that needs a new hard drive, you may decide to purchase a new hard drive, or you may decide to purchase a new computer instead. Both options are possible solutions. The path you take depends on a variety of factors unique to you, and another person might choose differently. If the implementation of the solution will require the involvement of other people, it might be a good idea to ask them what they think about your proposed solution and whether they have the time, skills, or resources to help you.

You should do your best to choose a solution that solves the entire problem rather than just one aspect of it. Ideally, the solution should solve the problem for a long time or, if possible, permanently. It is particularly advantageous if the solution is simple and easily implemented and even better if it is also inexpensive and does not require too many resources. The right solution will depend upon what your needs are at the time.

What Should I Do Once I Have Chosen a Solution?

Once you have decided on the best solution to the problem, you should consider the best way implement it. Small problems may be easy to fix, but larger and more complex problems may require a detailed plan of action in order for their solutions to be successful. The type of plan required will be unique to the type of problem you have. It should include a timeline for the solution as well as a way to measure success.

If solving the problem requires the participation of a group, one person can be designated to direct the solution's implementation. Otherwise, the project may get off track or take longer than planned, or it may never be completed at all. The implementation should proceed in a timely fashion, so a timeline that details when each aspect of the solution should occur may be useful. You should also come up with a way to determine whether the solution was a success or a failure. You may decide that the solution will be considered successful if the problem is eliminated. However, even if you do not end up with the outcome you were hoping for, you may also decide that the solution was a success if you developed and matured as a problem solver during the process.

Why Should I Reflect on the Problem-Solving Process?

A helpful way to learn and grow from problem solving is to reflect on it once the process is over. By spending some time contemplating and analyzing the way you solved a problem, you can improve your problem-solving skills, which will help you later in life when you inevitably encounter another difficult situation.

One way to reflect is to write about the problem-solving process in a private journal or, if the problem took place at work, a document on your computer that can easily be referenced and added to. You can also talk to a colleague, friend, family member, or counselor. By writing or talking about the experience, you can figure out what worked well and what did not. Then you will be able to use this knowledge to make similar or different choices in the future.

Developing Problem-Solving Skills

Why Should I Develop Problem-Solving Skills?

Most of us are naturally equipped with basic problem-solving skills. When there is a problem, we tend to seek and then implement a solution. Few of us devote time to consciously develop and improve such skills, however. Problem solving, like any other skill, requires practice over time and mindful effort to improve. Since problems are an ordinary and expected part of everyday life, taking time to develop the way you solve problems is worthwhile.

Brainstorming:
A session where employees either individually or in a group contribute their ideas for solving a problem or meeting a company objective without fear of retribution or ridicule.

Most problems generally require the same basic skills to solve. First, you identify the problem and determine why it is happening. Then you **brainstorm** for possible solutions, choose one, and implement it. Finally, you reflect on the problem-solving process. What these skills look like in practice will vary depending on the problem you are tackling. A firefighter's problem will be different than a professor's, for example. The main purpose of developing problem-solving skills is to allow you to solve problems more effectively, quickly, and easily, whatever your problem may be.

In order to develop any problem-solving skill, it is beneficial to keep an open mind, view problems as learning opportunities, focus on the solution and not the problem, and stay patient. These mental practices will enhance and improve the problem-solving skills you already have, regardless of the type of problem you encounter in the workplace, at home, at school, or in any aspect of your life.

How Do I Develop Problem-Solving Skills?

First decide which mental practice you would like to improve. For instance, would you like to remain open-minded when determining what the problem is? Stay focused on the solution and not the problem when implementing a solution? Stay patient when developing a solution? Choose one mental practice to work on. Trying to tackle all of them at once may be overwhelming. Also consider why you want to develop this mental practice. Is it to become a better job applicant? A stronger student? To simply handle life's curveballs more gracefully? If you're not exactly sure why you want better problem-solving skills, you may not be motivated to develop them through specific mental techniques.

After you have decided which mental practice you would like to work on and why, begin to practice it. Like learning how to play an instrument or write a paper, developing a mental practice takes time and repetition. To remind yourself to practice this skill, it may be helpful to make a note for yourself and place it somewhere that you see often, such as next to the bathroom mirror. You may also want to set a reminder on your phone. As problems arise in your day-to-day life, no matter how small or insignificant, you can apply your chosen mental practice. When you discover that there is a traffic jam on your way to work, for example, you can practice maintaining a positive attitude. When you find yourself brooding over why a problem happened, you can practice focusing on the solution.

When trying to tackle specific problems at the office, it can be helpful to call upon the combined knowledge and expertise of others. This approach can also have the added benefit of allowing you to learn some alternate techniques for problem-solving. © AUREMAR/ SHUTTERSTOCK.COM.

How Do I Keep an Open Mind When Solving Problems?

"Keeping an open mind" is a figure of speech that refers to the concept of creating a mental attitude that is receptive to new ideas, people, and ways of doing things. Keeping an open mind while solving problems means that you are open to and interested in finding unanticipated explanations for why a problem occurred, pursuing a variety of solutions to a problem, or implementing a solution in a new way. The primary benefit of having an open mind when solving problems is that this approach could help you discover solutions that you never considered.

What Is the Difference between Novice and Expert Problem Solvers?

According to Lori Breslow, the author of an essay titled "Transforming Novice Problem Solvers into Experts," the essential difference between novice and expert problem solvers is that experts do not start actively solving a problem as soon as it occurs. Rather, they analyze and consider the problem from multiple angles before they begin working toward a solution. Novices, on the other hand, do not pause before they problem solve. Instead, says Breslow, they "jump right in." Her area of expertise is engineering, an industry that often presents complex problems that require sophisticated mathematical skills to solve. However, Breslow's insights on solving mathematical problems apply to problems that occur in any aspect of life.

What marks an expert problem solver is the person's comfort level with complexity.

An expert problem solver knows that some problems will not have straightforward solutions. The problem-solving process may have moments of confusion or uncertainty, but an expert knows that this is normal and doesn't get too discouraged. Experts also understand that there are many ways to solve a problem, so they are not committed to one way of doing things. They will experiment and be flexible and open-minded in their approach. Experts also have confidence. They believe that they have the power to solve a problem on their own, even if it takes a long time. Novices, conversely, become overwhelmed easily and give up. Another key difference between experts and novices is that after experts solve a problem, they reflect on the problem-solving process, noting what worked well and what didn't. They can then apply this knowledge to future problems.

Especially when solving routine problems, you may think that you already know the cause of the problem or the "right" way to solve it. While having experience with certain problems may help you solve them more effectively, that experience may blind you to alternative ways of problem solving.

An effective method to keeping an open mind when presented with a problem is to take 5 or 10 minutes to pause and think before you dive into the process of solving the problem. During this time frame, sit quietly and let any idea float into your mind, however seemingly unrealistic, impractical, or downright silly it may seem. You can jot down your thoughts on a piece of a paper if you would like, or simply take mental notes. The goal is to be open to every thought that pops up, accepting them with interest and without judgment. After 5 or 10 minutes, consider what has occurred to you. Have you come up with a fresh solution to a problem or a new way to implement the solution?

For example, a restaurant manager may need to keep an open mind when trying to figure out why the kitchen is producing food slowly. The most obvious answer, "The chefs do not have the skills to cook quickly," may be correct. But the problem may be more complex than that. Instead of immediately finding fault with the chefs, the manager could take a few minutes sitting, letting any and all thoughts flow into his mind. During this period of open-minded thinking, he may notice that perhaps the reason why the chefs are slow is because the sous chefs have not done enough preparatory work during the day. The chefs are doing work that is not technically theirs while trying to prepare incoming orders. Or it may occur to the manager that he has never explicitly told the chefs that he wants food prepared in a specific amount of time, so they don't know what is expected of them.

How Do I View Problems as Learning Opportunities?

Since problems can cause a variety of personal, professional, scholastic, or financial setbacks, they are often viewed negatively. In fact, when confronted with a problem, you may feel anxious, ashamed, angry, confused, or any number of other challenging emotions. However, if you change the way you view the very nature of a problem, you may start to see it not as an undesirable situation to be avoided but rather as a chance to learn something new and beneficial. After all, problems are simply indicators that a certain approach or plan of action is no longer working well and that you need to switch course. An advantage of seeing problems as learning opportunities is that you will no longer shrink from problems or feel upset when you deal with them. This means that when you have to solve a problem, emotions such as anger and anxiety will not slow you down or prevent you from thinking clearly and calmly.

To view problems as learning opportunities, ask yourself what you can learn from solving the problem. In the same way you work on the skill of keeping an open mind, pause for a few minutes before you start solving a problem. Consider what you could learn from tackling the problem, taking into account any and all "silver linings." For example, it may occur to you that, through the process of solving a problem, you will learn how to use a new computer program. Knowing exactly what you are going to gain from solving a problem may help you regard problems in a new, more positive light.

Seeing problems as learning opportunities does not mean that you ignore the reality that they can cause significant setbacks. Rather, this approach allows you to also see the potential benefits of the problem. Like changing any pattern of thinking, viewing problems as learning opportunities requires practice.

How Do I Stay Focused on Finding a Solution When Solving Problems?

Although finding out what the root cause of a problem is will help you avoid that problem again, sometimes spending too much time dwelling on what went wrong can get in the way of actually solving the problem and implementing a solution. For people who are inclined to procrastinate, wasting time analyzing why a problem happened may prevent them from actually moving forward. A key aspect of staying focused on the solution is trusting that a solution exists. Especially when addressing large or particularly complex problems, solutions may not seem immediately apparent. Or the solution that you develop may seem extremely difficult or even impossible to execute. Nevertheless, staying focused on the solution will help you take steps in that direction. You can't know that a solution won't work until you try it.

In order to stay focused on the solution, you will need to carefully monitor your thought processes. Anytime you find yourself dwelling on why a problem happened, take one small, concrete action toward a solution. This may mean writing a to-do list, making a phone call, or sending an e-mail. Focusing on the solution does not mean that you will never be able to analyze why a problem occurred. Rather, it means that you do such analysis *after* you've determined a solution and implemented it. Often taking one action will energize you to take another. Before you know it, you'll be on the road to a solution, not stuck in the past.

How Do I Stay Patient When Solving Problems?

When you are struggling with a problem, it is normal to want the problem to be solved as quickly as possible. Often this desire stems from the discomfort of feeling the difficult emotions that can arise when something does not go according to plan. Small problems often have speedy solutions, but larger or more complicated problems often take much longer to solve. Patience is the ability to calmly proceed in the face of discomfort. With patience, you won't needlessly rush the problem-solving process. Instead, you'll problem solve at a comfortable pace, calm and collected.

To stay patient as you work through a problem, breathe deeply and mindfully, take the long view, and acknowledge your emotions. Psychologists and spiritual teachers promote the benefits of deep breathing as a stress-reduction activity. It can have a calming and mellowing effect on the body. As you breathe, it may be helpful to focus on the inhale and exhale, paying attention to how your body is feeling. Another way to develop patience is to take the long view. Imagine yourself in a year, or in even 5 or 10 years from now. Adding a dose of perspective may help you see that the problem is not necessarily that significant.

Finally, an effective way to stay patient is to acknowledge the emotions you are feeling. Are you angry that you have to stay late at work to solve a problem? Are you mad at yourself for letting the problem occur in the first place? Acknowledging and accepting your emotions may, almost without you realizing it, diminish their intensity.

Problem Solving in the Workplace

What Is Problem Solving in the Workplace?

Problems can occur in any aspect of life. How you go about solving a problem will depend on the area of your life in which the problem occurs. For example, how you solve a personal problem at home will likely be different than how you solve a workplace problem at your job.

Most problem solving generally follows a specific time line: identify the problem, determine the cause, brainstorm solutions, implement a solution, and reflect on the problem-solving process. When solving a problem in the workplace, it is important to remember the company's mission, to collaborate effectively with colleagues, and to develop an action plan for implementing a solution. Keeping the company's mission in mind when problem solving will help you cultivate solutions that are in line with the company's goals and values. Collaboration is dependent on employees communicating successfully with each other. Since the solution to a problem in the workplace tends to be complex, an action plan outlines the time line and strategy for implementing the solution. This helps to ensure that the solution will be completed and that there are accountable parties.

What Are Some Examples of Workplace Problems?

The kinds of problem you may encounter at work will be shaped by the industry in which you work. For example, the problems that a small, nonprofit organization face will likely be different than those of a multinational corporation. On the other hand, there are common problems that are found across industries, affecting small and large companies alike.

A major problem that a company may confront is not having financial solvency. This means that the company is not able to bring in enough money to pay for all of its expenses. Another common problem for companies is producing a product that is not uniform or

Some problems in the workplace aren't nearly as complex as in this picture! © ALPHASPIRIT/ SHUTTERSTOCK.COM.

of high quality. Minor but no less important problems include ineffective or malfunctioning infrastructure or interpersonal conflicts between employees.

When you are an employee, your problem-solving role will be determined by your position within the company. When solving a problem, the role of a CEO (chief executive officer) will almost certainly be different than that of an administrative assistant. Company leaders and managers will generally be in charge of identifying the problem and developing a solution. Those in subordinate positions may be in charge of researching causes of the problem and implementing the solution.

Why Is Professionalism Important When Problem Solving in the Workplace?

Unlike problem solving in other areas of your life, it is important to behave professionally in the workplace at all times. Professionalism refers

Chayan Solves a Problem in the Workplace

Chayan is the manager of a Thai restaurant. Occasionally, he reads customer reviews of his restaurant on websites such as Yelp. Although most customers rave about the quality of the food, he has noticed a trend of complaints about how long it takes food to be served. One customer even wrote, "This is my favorite Thai place, but I just can't go back here anymore. It takes forty-five minutes for my food to show up ... even when the restaurant has no other customers!" After reading that review, Chayan vowed to create a kitchen in which food is prepared in a timely manner without sacrificing quality.

Clearly the problem at the restaurant was dishes taking too long to be prepared. But why was the problem happening in the first place? Before developing a solution, Chayan first determined the reasons for this problem. After observing the kitchen for a week, he discovered that food was being cooked slowly for three primary reasons. First, the cooks did not know that cooking food quickly was a priority. Second, they did not have the skills to cook faster. Third, the kitchen was understaffed.

To remedy the problem, Chayan developed a solution with the help of the restaurant owner and main chef. Together, they decided that, since the problem was threefold, it needed three specific solutions. First, the cooks would be informed that dishes must be prepared more quickly. Second, their cooking skills must be improved through training. Third, the restaurant must hire more kitchen staff.

With the assistance of the owner and chef, Chayan wrote an action plan that outlined each step of the solution process. In the action plan, he took into account the resources he would need as well as the possible obstructions to the plan. As the solution was implemented, Chayan monitored its progress.

to a certain code of conduct that you adhere to in the workplace. Ideas of professionalism may differ in different industries. But, in general, professionalism in the workplace refers to a worker's ability to perform his or her job capably, work well with others, and display a positive and motivated attitude. Professionalism also refers to the ability to remain calm, think quickly, and work hard even when under pressure.

Since problems often cause setbacks that require extra work to solve (as well as have the potential to cause emotional reactions such as anger or *anxiety*), it is crucial to stay professional during the problem-solving process. First, maintaining a professional approach will allow you to focus single-mindedly on the problem at hand without becoming distracted or upset. Second, your professionalism will show your colleagues and supervisors that you are a valuable asset to the team.

Anxiety: *An abnormal and overwhelming sense of worry and fear that is often accompanied by physical reaction.*

Why Remember the Company's Mission When Problem-Solving in the Workplace?

When solving problems in the workplace, it is not enough to simply find a solution and implement it. This is because the solution should abide by the company's mission, a concept that guides and drives the company forward. Most companies have mission statements that outline the organization's reason for existing. In addition, the statement may present the company's foundational principles, ethical values, and long-term goals. To find your employer's mission statement, you may want to refer to the company handbook, which is often prefaced with a mission statement. You could also ask your supervisor for the details of the mission statement. By remembering the company's mission when problem solving in the workplace, you can develop a solution to a problem that is in keeping with that mission. It is also wise to review the employee handbook that outlines employer and employee conduct to ensure that the solution is appropriate.

For example, if the solution requires employees to work overtime five days a week, but the employee handbook states that employees may only work overtime three days a week, a new solution that does not require extensive overtime will need to be developed. Alternatively, the policies presented in the employee handbook may need to be altered so that the proposed solution can take place. In general, however, it is best to observe the mission statement and handbook policies because they are designed to keep in mind the health of the company and its employees.

Why Is Collaboration Important When Problem Solving in the Workplace?

Unlike solving personal problems, in which you are the only person affected, problem solving in the workplace typically will require you to work with your colleagues. Collaboration is important for a variety of reasons, including providing the opportunity for employees to share their ideas with each other. Collaboration also includes group *brainstorming*, an activity that may prompt ideas that would not have been thought of individually. Since problems that occur in the workplace may be difficult to solve because they tend to involve a variety of stakeholders, it is valuable to have colleagues work closely together, joining forces to find a viable solution. Moreover, since every employee arrives at the workplace

Brainstorming:
A session where employees either individually or in a group contribute their ideas for solving a problem or meeting a company objective without fear of retribution or ridicule.

with special skills, areas of expertise, and experience, collaboration allows each person to contribute to the problem-solving process.

In practice, collaborating in the workplace may entail workers sitting at the same workstation or meeting room, brainstorming and bouncing ideas off one another. Or it may involve employees working individually and checking in over e-mail, through instant message, or in person. Touching base could occur throughout the day or a few times a week, depending on the workplace and the nature of the problem being solved. Collaboration may also occur informally at the water cooler, during lunch breaks, or any place where employees tend to gather in groups. Collaboration can be facilitated by designing an office that creates workstations where employees can gather. It can also be facilitated by management encouraging employees and rewarding them when they work together to create solutions.

Why Is Communication Important When Problem Solving in the Workplace?

As mentioned above, productive collaboration is a key aspect of problem solving in the workplace. It works best, however, when coworkers are equipped with the skills to successfully share their ideas and to listen and understand the ideas of others. Although collaboration and communication seem similar, workplace communication refers to employees' ability to effectively share with and receive information from each other. It also encompasses how they share information.

There is a variety of technological tools available to facilitate employee communication, including e-mail, instant messaging, and social media. The tools do no good, however, if employees are not encouraged to communicate with each other or are not supported when they do communicate. Good problem-solving emerges from a workplace environment that values the free expression of ideas and values open-mindedness. If employees feel comfortable, supported, and listened to when sharing ideas, they will be more likely to do so frequently and without fear. If an employee is rude or sarcastic, uninterested or bored, dismissive or condescending, there is a higher chance that collaboration may not happen. In general, if you communicate in a way that is well mannered, kind, and respectful, it is likely that your ideas will be heard by others, and the company will be one step closer to solving a problem.

For information to be shared so that a problem can be solved, there needs to be a communication infrastructure within the company. In general, this means that coworkers will need to have access to a company telephone, e-mail, and instant messaging system (if available) so that they can easily and quickly communicate. Distributed workforces may also rely on video conferencing software so that they can communicate face-to-face.

While telephone, e-mail, and instant messaging are excellent ways for employees to contact each other, the potential pitfall is that "information silos" can easily occur. An information silo refers to the idea that specific information is held by a small circle of people to the accidental exclusion of the rest of the group. To avoid information becoming "siloed," and therefore unable to be used by other coworkers, regular team meetings could be held to ensure all information is shared. Online sharing platforms for businesses such as Yammer and Slack may also help make sure information is shared across the company.

Why Is an Action Plan Important When Problem Solving in the Workplace?

When problem solving on your own, it is not always necessary to create a detailed plan for how you will go about implementing a solution. In the workplace, however, creating an action plan is extremely useful. An action plan is a written statement that outlines how a solution will be implemented, who is responsible for each task, and how long the solution should take to implement. An action plan also allows all parties involved to see how a solution will be implemented and takes into account potential roadblocks. A successful action plan should specify exactly which resources will be needed as well as possible obstacles to the completion of the action plan. For each obstacle listed, the action plan should describe a realistic resolution to it. Implementing a solution rarely occurs without a hitch. That's why preparing ahead of time for what might go wrong helps save time and resources. An effective action plan will also provide metrics for how a company will measure the success of the implementation.

During the implementation of the action plan, a leader should periodically monitor progress. Effective monitoring methods depend on the type of problem being solved. In general, however, monitoring methods include team meetings in which employees share their individual progress and employee output is reviewed. An action plan is worthless unless each individual player is performing his or her own unique part. Monitoring allows the designated leader to ensure that this occurs.

Decision-Making Strategies

What Is Decision Making?

Most people make thousands of decisions every day, whether they realize it or not. Weighing your options for what to wear to work, deciding on the best movie to watch over the weekend, or narrowing down candidates for an open position at your job are all examples of decision making. In many cases, you may be unaware of the process that is taking place in your brain when you make a decision. If you are used to making certain decisions regularly, such as what you will eat for lunch each day, then you may be unaware that you are engaging in the decision-making process at all. This is called unconscious decision making.

Decision making consists of several steps. When you are presented with a situation where a decision is necessary, your brain takes into account a number of potential decisions that you could make. After that, your brain will filter, or sort out, the decisions that appear to be most logical and appropriate for the results you are trying to achieve. These steps comprise the decision-making process that you rely on each day.

Why Is Decision Making So Important?

Everyone makes decisions, regardless of their age, occupation, or lifestyle. A doctor decides on the best medicine to prescribe for a patient. A mother creates a grocery list that fits into her weekly shopping budget. A child chooses between playing with toys and reading a book. All of these people make decisions based on the results they want to achieve. You should carefully consider the benefits and drawbacks of your options as you make a decision, or else you may be unhappy with the results or find yourself dealing with unexpected consequences. This is why the decision-making process is so important to your daily life.

When making a decision, whether it directly benefits you or someone else, going through the process step by step will ensure that you have weighed each of your options equally in order to make the best decision possible. People who approach decisions this way are more efficient in their daily personal and professional lives and are able to conduct business more successfully.

How Is Decision Making Related to Problem Solving?

Most people solve at least one problem per day, whether it is a small problem such as changing a broken light bulb or a big problem such as getting a car's damaged tires replaced. In any

Decisions often have many facets to them. Using a good strategy can help with the final outcome.
• WAVEBREAKMEDIA/ SHUTTERSTOCK.COM.

situation, you should use effective decision-making strategies to find a solution that will eliminate the problem and bring about beneficial long-term results. Good decision-making methods can help you avoid jumping to conclusions, which may cause you to address the problem too hastily.

Sometimes you may need additional resources to arrive at the best decision, such as feedback from others or additional time to think about your choices. For example, if you were feeling unfulfilled in your job, it would be better for you to schedule a time to discuss your concerns with your boss rather than simply quitting your job. Without a plan to make your decision in the most productive way possible, you might end up making the wrong decision or causing more serious consequences.

What Are Some Effective Decision-Making Strategies?

After you become aware of an important decision that you need to make, you may realize that you do not know how to arrive at the most effective choice. Strategies such as *brainstorming*, clarifying goals, and using the process of elimination may help. These strategies help you to view the whole decision-making process rather than just one aspect of the problem.

Brainstorming:
A session where employees either individually or in a group contribute their ideas for solving a problem or meeting a company objective without fear of retribution or ridicule.

Brainstorming is an especially effective strategy in situations when more than one person is involved in making the decision. In a group brainstorming session, all members contribute their ideas and opinions to come up with an effective plan of action for solving a problem or completing a project. A brainstorming session will make it more likely that the plan is supported by all group members and that it produces an outcome that benefits everyone.

There may be times when you will be solely responsible for the outcome of a decision. In such cases, clarifying your goals is a good way to start the decision-making process. To do this, you should decide exactly what outcome you want to achieve. For example, you may have a goal of losing weight. To clarify that goal, you could define exactly how many pounds you want to lose. From there, you might use the process of elimination to help you decide what type of exercise routine would work best to help you lose weight. The process of elimination involves either writing down or thinking about all of the possible decisions you could make. If you outline the advantages and disadvantages of each one, you can eliminate decisions from your list that are unsuitable for your goal until you figure out which decision is the best option for you.

Considering the outcomes of your potential decisions is a strategy that can be used in combination with the process of elimination. By deciding what outcomes you would like to see, you can eliminate options that will not yield those outcomes. If you have established that you would like to lose 20 pounds, you might decide that walking three times a week might be more likely to help you achieve this goal than running only once a week. You should take as much time as you need to determine what results you want from your decisions and how these results align with your goals.

How Do Decision-Making Strategies Differ at Work, at School, or in My Personal Life?

Not all decisions are equal. Some decisions will be more or less complex than others, some might occur regularly, and others might only have to be made once. For each type of decision, however, it is important to know which decision-making strategies will work best for each situation. In a work setting, employees use decision making to perform their jobs on a daily basis. Some workplace decisions might be made individually, such as a manager deciding how to assign work to an employee, while decisions among colleagues might be made as a team. When working on a project within a group, it is best if all members who are involved in the project are given a chance to contribute their ideas.

In instances involving your school or personal life, using the right decision-making strategy can help you control the outcome. In such cases, the process of elimination might be especially useful. If you are deciding how many hours to spend studying on the night before an exam, you can consider your options. Studying for one hour might allow you more time to rest before you take the exam, but it might not give you enough time to master the knowledge necessary to get a good grade. Studying for a longer period of time might improve your mastery of the content, but you might be more tired when you take the test. If you decide that it is most important for you to feel prepared, then you can eliminate the option of spending more time resting and devote more time to studying instead. You should carefully assess how each potential outcome will affect the goals you are trying to achieve.

What Are Some Common Flaws in the Decision-Making Process?

Decisions can sometimes result in negative outcomes, and these unwanted results can make decision-making flaws apparent. For example, a student might decide to wake up 10 minutes later for class on Mondays because traffic is usually light on those days. However, an unexpected accident on the highway could make that student late for class. Assumptions are one of the most common flaws in decision making. An assumption, or expectation, that a particular thing will never change can lead you to avoid considering other possible scenarios, which might lead to unexpected results.

Other flaws that sometimes affect the decision-making process can take place when people do not know which decision-making strategy to use for a particular situation. Using a strategy that works best for personal decisions, such as clarifying individual goals, is unlikely to be effective for a group decision since it is not group-based. When considering your decision-making strategy, you should make sure that you are using the right approach for the problem you are trying to solve.

How Can Negotiation Improve the Decision-Making Process?

Negotiation is a form of group discussion in which the members work toward a compromise so that an agreement can be reached. When members of a group are working on a problem together, each person will have his or her own ideas and perspectives to contribute to the task at hand. It is almost impossible to make strategic decisions when two or more people are not in agreement on any aspect of the process. Negotiation helps to eliminate confusion, making it easier for group members to share ideas, communicate, and determine what steps are needed to complete the task.

For example, if the members of a tour group are in disagreement about the order in which they should visit landmarks, it might take three times as long for them to complete a city tour. If they use the process of negotiation within their group, however, every member could have a chance to contribute suggestions about the best order in which they should visit the landmarks, and they might be able to form a plan more quickly and effectively. Although people often have different ideas about how the decision-making process should go, the process functions best when all opinions in a group are given equal consideration. This can help the members of the group achieve their collective goals in a mutually acceptable way.

What If a Decision-Making Strategy Proves Ineffective?

No matter how hard you try, a time may still come when your chosen decision-making strategy proves ineffective. Imagine that a salesperson decides to use process of elimination to decide which return clients to approach, but after a few months his or her sales numbers are down. Although the salesperson had the best intentions, he or she may not have considered all available options, and another idea, such as better marketing techniques, might have done more to increase monthly sales.

The best way to recover from a situation in which a decision-making strategy proves ineffective is to use the outcome of that decision as a lesson to help you adjust your future methods. The quality of every decision will depend on your selection of goals and the resources you have in place that can help you achieve those goals. Learning from an ineffective decision-making strategy can help you make better decisions in the future.

For More Information

BOOKS

Burkus, David. *The Myths of Creativity: The Truth about How Innovative Companies and People Generate Great Ideas.* San Francisco: Jossey-Bass, 2013.

Gray, Dave. *Gamestorming: A Playbook for Innovators, Rulebreakers, and Changemakers.* Sebastopol, CA: O'Reilly Media, 2010.

Jones, Morgan D. *The Thinker's Toolkit: 14 Powerful Techniques for Problem Solving.* New York: Three Rivers, 1998.

Michalko, Michael. *Tinkertoys: A Handbook of Creative Thinking Techniques.* Berkeley, CA: Ten Speed Press, 2010.

Pokras, Sandy. *Problem Solving for Teams: Make Consensus More Achievable.* Rochester, NY: Axzo, 2010.

Watanabe, Ken. *Problem Solving 101: A Simple Book for Smart People.* New York: Portfolio, 2009.

PERIODICALS

Breslow, Lori. "Transforming Novice Problem Solvers into Experts." *Teach Talk* 13, no. 3 (2001). This article is also available online at http://web.mit.edu/tll/tll-library/teach-talk/transforming-novice.html.

Carey, Benedict. "Tracing the Spark of Creative Problem Solving." *New York Times*, December 7, 2010, D2. This article can also be found online at http://www.nytimes.com/2010/12/07/science/07brain.html?pagewanted=all.

WEBSITES

"Ask 'Why' Five Times about Every Matter." *Toyota*. March 2006. http://www.toyota-global.com/company/toyota_traditions/quality/mar_apr_2006.html (accessed January 16, 2015).

Dye, Renee, Olivier Sibony, and Vincent Truong. "Flaws in Strategic Decision Making: McKinsey Global Survey Results." *McKinsey and Company*. January 2009. http://www.mckinsey.com/insights/strategy/flaws_in_strategic_decision_making_mckinsey_global_survey_results (accessed January 7, 2015).

"Five Whys: Getting to the Root of a Problem Quickly." *Mind Tools*. http://www.mindtools.com/pages/article/newTMC_5W.htm (accessed January 21, 2015).

Gallo, Amy. "How to Master a New Skill." *Harvard Business Review*. November 29, 2012. https://hbr.org/2012/11/how-to-master-a-new-skill.html (accessed January 16, 2015).

"Generating Many Radical, Creative Ideas." *MindTools*. http://www.mindtools.com/brainstm.html (accessed January 6, 2015).

Guterman, Jeffrey T. "Problem Solving the Solution-Oriented Way." *Psych Central*. http://psychcentral.com/lib/problem-solving-the-solution-focused-way/00021018 (accessed January 23, 2015).

Kemp, Sid. "Six Tips to Assess Problems, Find Solutions." *Entrepreneur*. June 2, 2009. http://www.entrepreneur.com/article/201986 (accessed January 16, 2015).

Marone, Mark, and Chris Blauth. "Creating a Problem Solving Culture: Exploring Problem Resolution in the Workplace." *Achieve Global*. 2004. http://www.rpi.edu/dept/hr/docs/Creating%20a%20Problem%20Solving%20Culture.pdf (accessed January 27, 2015).

Perry, Susan. "Decision-Making." *BrainFacts.org*. April 9, 2013. http://www.brainfacts.org/sensing-thinking-behaving/awareness-and-attention/articles/2009/decision-making/ (accessed January 4, 2015).

"Problem Solving and Action Planning." *Penn State Extension*. http://extension
.psu.edu/animals/dairy/hr/tools-for-teams/running-an-effective-team-
meeting/problem-solving (accessed January 27, 2015).

Robinson, Joe. "How Positive Thinking Can Make You a Better Problem
Solver." *Entrepreneur*. December 18, 2012. http://www.entrepreneur.com/
article/225170 (accessed January 23, 2015).

"What Is Problem Solving?" *Mind Tools*. http://www.mindtools.com/pages/
article/newTMC_00.htm (accessed January 16, 2015).

Conflict Resolution Skills

What Is Conflict?

Conflict is an active disagreement between two or more individuals or groups. While people disagree all the time about all kinds of things, conflict arises when the disagreement is strong enough to lead the parties involved to feel that their needs are being threatened, hindered, or ignored. Conflict is not always rooted in questions of right and wrong but is often a problem of perception (the way you see or understand something) and can stem from assumptions we make about other people's motives. Someone else's intentional aggression toward us can make us angry, whereas an honest mistake is usually easy to forgive. We might think another driver is being rude or aggressive by cutting us off in traffic, for instance, but maybe that other person simply had a lapse in attention. If we feel slighted, we may get angry at the other person when, really, it was simply a misunderstanding.

Although conflict is a normal part of life, people often see it as something to avoid. This is understandable considering that conflict provokes strong emotions such as anger, resentment, frustration, and disappointment. When managed and resolved productively, however, conflict can

Conflicts can arise in project teams due to differences in values, attitudes, needs, expectations, perceptions, resources, and personalities.
© MAST3R/SHUTTERSTOCK .COM.

lead to a better understanding of ourselves and our relationship to others.

What Are the Different Types of Conflict?

Conflict varies in size from interpersonal to international. It can be as small as two children arguing over a toy or as large as two countries going to war. While the types of conflict are many, they can be broken down into two broad categories, situational and behavioral.

A situational conflict is one in which the parties involved are at odds over an event beyond their control. An example is when two people are vying for the same parking space. Two cars cannot park in one spot, but if both drivers feel that they are entitled to the space, conflict may ensue. Since the fact that there is only one available parking space is no one's fault, people in these types of situations may feel that they are the victims of circumstance.

Situational conflict also occurs when resources are limited and people disagree over how to distribute those resources. In personal relationships, decisions about money are perhaps the most likely to result in conflict. Let's say a couple is saving money for a future goal. One partner wants to use that money to go on vacation, while the other wants to buy a car. If there isn't enough money to allow for both options, conflict can arise. In this case both people agree on the overall goal of saving money, but the decision about how to distribute the money is the source of conflict.

Behavioral conflict, on the other hand, is when a person's conduct or decision making leads to a dispute. This could happen when a teenager comes home long past curfew, for example, or when a person talks loudly on a cell phone during a film in a theater. Both of these potential conflicts happen because of the perception that someone has behaved in a selfish or insensitive manner. But, as mentioned earlier, intent has a lot to do with the severity of the conflict. If the teenager was late because she was studying in the library and lost track of time, or if the person on the phone was calling 911 because of an emergency, the likelihood of conflict is reduced.

Perhaps the most obvious type of behavioral conflict is when one person or group purposefully antagonizes another. This type of conflict is perhaps the most difficult to resolve. In personal relationships a break of trust, as with infidelity or willful abuse, can lead to sustained or permanently unresolved conflict.

What Are Common Causes of Conflict?

Conflict occurs when people are in strong opposition over an idea, activity, or outcome or when they feel that their well-being is being jeopardized, intentionally or not, by the actions of someone else. Often the reason for conflict is people's needs or desires not being met according to their expectations.

In everyday life, and especially in the workplace, conflict arises from misunderstandings, miscommunication, personality clashes, differing values, and competing goals, among other things. Imagine reaching out to shake hands with someone who bows to greet you instead. This "culture clash" could lead to awkwardness or embarrassment, especially if both of you are not well informed about the other's cultural background. Even though both parties would be acting politely and courteously according to their own customs, each might perceive the other's conduct as rude or inappropriate.

Misuse of authority or an imbalance of power can also lead to conflict and is usually accompanied by a sense of unfairness or injustice. This can happen when a teacher favors a particular student or a supervisor treats certain employees differently or plays favorites through extra attention, encouragement, or promotion. Such unequal treatment leads to conflict among subordinates because they feel they are being treated unfairly. Extreme cases can involve unwarranted *discrimination*.

The differing degrees of importance people place on activities can lead to conflict as well. Imagine you and a coworker are asked to work together on a project. For you the project is very important because you are hoping for a promotion, while your partner doesn't have the same motivation. Because the project matters more to you, you will probably work harder on it than your coworker, which might lead to resentment. Conflict is less likely to happen when people have an equal stake in the outcome of a project or task.

Discrimination: *1) Unequal treatment of individuals, usually on the basis of gender, race, age, religion or disability. 2) When one group of workers is treated differently from others in terms of wages paid, employment and promotion opportunities.*

How Does Conflict Develop?

During the time between the conflict's beginning and its resolution there are many ways it can escalate. For one, conflict rooted in disagreement will likely persist until the disagreement is addressed. But addressing conflict necessitates making it public to some degree, either by bringing it to the attention of a manager or other authority figure, which people are often reluctant to do. So the conflict remains and, depending on the behavior of those involved, can get worse.

When left unchecked, conflict will often intensify over time because of the strong emotions it provokes. If someone is hurt, angry, or frustrated, those feelings will continue to build until the conflict is resolved. Unfortunately, resolution can prove difficult when people are not communicating with each other or trust has been broken as a result of the dispute.

The same behavior that resulted in conflict will continue to fuel it unless something or someone intervenes to stop it. In the simplest terms, think of two children arguing over a toy where both have hold of it and refuse to let go. This conflict can lead to yelling, kicking, biting, or hitting as both children try to win the toy for themselves. Even if one child manages to grab the toy from the other, the overall conflict usually continues until someone else, often an adult, puts an end to it. However, even when the object of conflict has been removed, hurt feelings can remain. As a result, since feelings of ill will are typically a direct result of conflict, it can be difficult for people to be rational in such an emotionally charged state. In these cases, stepping away from the situation in order to "cool off" is usually a good idea.

How Can Conflict Impact Work and Relationships?

Conflict is disruptive. At home or in the workplace, unresolved conflict creates disunity and distrust. Communication usually stops between people in conflict, and cooperation and kindness evaporate. Even worse, conflict can spread so people not directly affected can be divided by loyalty to one side or the other and that creates more discord.

Residences, classrooms, and workplaces are all highly interdependent settings and require many people to work together for things to go smoothly. Well-behaved students and courteous teachers facilitate classroom learning, just as cooperative and conscientious employees make for a productive and harmonious work environment. Mutual respect and honesty keep personal relationships strong. But all of that is disrupted in the wake of conflict.

Conflict has a direct effect on productivity as well. Most workplace conflicts are dealt with by managers, and the more time managers spend dealing with conflict between employees the less time they have for the other aspects of their jobs. Coworkers in conflict are often under greater stress and suffer distracting mental anguish, which detracts from their job performance.

In What Ways Can Conflict Be Productive?

Despite the negative opinions people often have about it, conflict can bring to light hidden or previously unknown issues between people. If conflict is handled well, either by the people involved or through mediation by a neutral third party, people can end up learning about their own strengths, weaknesses, and attitudes, as well as those of others. Sometimes it takes a conflict to reveal people's deeply rooted attitudes and biases, but once these are brought to light, people have a clearer idea about the attitudes and points of view of those around them.

Indeed, successfully resolved conflicts can lead to increased trust among individuals, which in turn may foster fellowship and boost morale. Since conflict often arises from misunderstanding, once the conflict is cleared up, what remains may be increased understanding. Anyone who has been in an argument knows the sense of relief that comes with resolving one's differences with someone else. Since conflict brings up heightened emotions, it can also enhance the relationship between two people or groups. We tend to learn more about someone we've been in conflict with than someone with whom we've never disagreed.

Conflict can also be productive by preventing "group think." When people are in opposition, it usually means they have different opinions about an issue or a task. These diverse opinions, when expressed calmly and reasonably, can lead to better decision making in a group setting. People sometimes fail to take into account other points of view because they are accustomed to thinking in one particular way. Someone else's opinion may open up new avenues of action or problem solving for the group.

How Can I Avoid Unnecessary Conflict?

To some degree conflict is unavoidable, but by keeping in mind its under-lying causes, it is possible to anticipate and thereby reduce its impact. It is important to recognize that we can't control how other people react, but we can control our own reactions. If someone says something that angers you, pause and think before replying. This can be difficult, especially if your emotions flare up, but resisting your first impulse will allow you to respond more calmly and rationally.

Another approach is to make an effort to see things from other people's point of view, remembering that not all slights are personal. Try to understand the other person's intent or motives before reacting. If someone is rude to you, consider that they may be under stress and that the rudeness was unintentional. If a person is chronically irritable or confrontational, however, the best option might be to keep contact with this person to a minimum whenever possible.

It helps to present ideas and opinions as suggestions rather than absolutes. Saying to someone, "Your plan will never work," or "That's a stupid idea" will probably make them angry. Try saying instead, "I have a different approach for you to consider." It never hurts to treat people as you would want them to treat you.

Lastly, step back and take the long view of the situation. Conflict might arise over an immediate goal or need, but consider how important it is in the scheme of things. Ask yourself if getting what you want today is more important than working cooperatively and peacefully in the long term. Sidestepping conflict now might mean less stress and greater harmony in the future.

Tips and Techniques for Managing and Resolving Conflict

What Is Conflict Management?

Conflict management is a means of identifying, addressing, and resolving disagreements between people in a fair and efficient manner. The goal of successful conflict management is to settle problems in a way that brings about a constructive and positive outcome for all of those involved, or a so-called *win-win resolution*. Well-managed conflict not only leads to the elimination of negative feelings but also serves to increase trust and goodwill between those who were previously in opposition.

Win-win solution: *A solution providing a good result for everyone involved.*

Conflict can interfere with a person's ability to work with or get along with someone else. It can be particularly disruptive if the parties have a shared history or will continue to have contact in the future, such as in workplaces or within families. If a coworker is rude to you or makes you angry, you will still have to find a way to work with that person unless you quit your job. Conflict resolution among family members is even more important, since familial bonds are not easily broken.

Conflict management cannot succeed without the willingness of the parties to compromise. A compromise occurs when each person agrees to give up some of what he or she wants in favor of easing tension and increasing goodwill. Convincing two parties who are at odds to work together can be difficult, because it is often a lack of ability to compromise that leads to conflict in the first place. However, a compromise is at the heart of any successfully managed conflict.

Communication and understanding are also key to managing conflict. It may be helpful for two people in conflict to talk to each other in the presence of a mediator. A mediator can be a manager, supervisor, teacher, therapist, or trained professional. In cases of disputes between young children, a parent can act as a mediator. In guided mediation, the people involved in the disagreement have a conversation in the presence

There are many different ways to try to resolve conflicts. © MAREKULIASZ/ SHUTTERSTOCK.COM.

of a third party who can remain impartial and help guide the discussion. This process is often preferable to the intervention of authority to decide the outcome of the conflict.

Who Is Responsible for Managing Conflict?

Human resources: *The department in a company that is responsible for hiring and managing employees.*

When conflict arises at work, it is normally dealt with at a managerial or supervisory level, often involving a company's *human resources* department. Many workplaces have guidelines or procedures for managers to follow when conflict occurs between employees. Even if this is not the case, most workplace disputes are settled with the involvement of a manager or supervisor rather than among peers.

When conflict happens on a personal level with a spouse, family member, friend, or neighbor, however, there are no standardized procedures or structures in place to manage it. In a dispute between two neighbors in the same apartment building, for example, a landlord may be able to step in to help resolve differences. In other cases, especially within families, people may need to seek the help of a professional counselor or therapist who can offer unbiased advice and appropriate strategies for reaching agreement.

Ultimately, each participant is responsible for being willing to work toward the resolution of a conflict. In addition to mutual willingness, it is important for each side in a disagreement to try to see things from the

Quick Tips for Conflict Resolution

Despite our best efforts, conflicts sometimes arise between two or more people in a variety of situations. However, there are techniques that can help resolve any kind of conflict.

- Remain calm. Conflicts often begin or escalate because one or both parties are stressed and angry. The key to effectively resolving any issue lies in your ability to remain relaxed and in control of your emotions. Take several deep breaths to keep yourself from becoming emotionally overwhelmed.

- Recognize how you're feeling and why. When you understand why you feel strongly about something, it can help you manage those feelings. If you're angry or sad about something, it's important to admit it. Ignoring your feelings will only impair your attempts to resolve the conflict.

- Pay attention to nonverbal cues. Things like tone of voice, gestures, facial expressions, and posture offer clues to how another person is feeling. Talking loudly and crossing arms in front of his or her body indicate that the person is defensive and doesn't feel safe. You can make him or her feel more at ease by employing a calm tone and a touch on the arm.

- Joke about it. Using humor can help you both avoid conflict and resolve it when it does occur. Expressing your concerns in a humorous way can make a delicate or difficult situation seem less serious and can help lighten any tension. Just make sure that the other person is laughing with you. Never make jokes about them or at their expense.

other's point of view. This does not mean that they will end up in perfect agreement, but each person may come to understand the other and may even come to a degree of self-realization in the process.

What Are Some Strategies for Managing Conflict?

Common conflict management styles include collaborative, compromising, accommodating, competing, and avoidance. Collaborative conflict management seeks to get both parties what they want by finding areas of common ground and encouraging the parties to work together to solve the problem.

As an example of a collaborative approach, imagine that you have to work with a colleague on a big presentation, and while you want to start working on it right away, your partner wants to put it off until the last minute. Rather than arguing about how unfair it is for you to have to do all the work, you might try looking for ways in which you and your colleague can accommodate each other's preferences. If you discover that your partner enjoys public speaking but you do not, you may be able to come to an agreement that he or she will handle that part of the presentation if you do more work in advance. There may be ways for each of you to make use of your strengths in order to produce a successful end result.

A compromising approach is one in which both parties make concessions in order to reduce conflict and increase trust. Using the example above, a solution through compromise might mean that you would agree to be less rigid about when to begin preparing for the presentation, while your colleague would agree to a set schedule and an equal division of labor. Each of you might not get exactly what you want, but the end result would be a successful presentation with input from both participants.

Accommodating and competing approaches go hand in hand. A competing approach involves advocating for your own terms to be accepted, while the accommodating approach involves accepting the terms of the other party. Each method results in one person's needs being met while the other party makes sacrifices. This technique can bring an end to a conflict, but it does not always provide true resolution, since the outcome generally does not reflect an agreement that satisfies both parties.

Another conflict management style is avoidance, in which resolution of the conflict is postponed. This is not always a desirable approach for resolving conflicts among family, friends, or coworkers who have continued contact, since it does not deal with the underlying reason for the disagreement. However, it can be a good way to deal with single events that happen between strangers, such as road rage incidents or the use of personal insults. In these cases, postponing an immediate resolution can be beneficial to the personal safety and peace of mind of the participants.

What Constitutes Successful Conflict Management?

Conflict management succeeds when opposing parties are able to resolve their differences and continue to live or work together peacefully and cooperatively. Ideally, a good resolution not only ends the conflict but also creates better understanding and empathy between the parties. The process depends very much on the personalities of the people involved, so a satisfactory outcome is not always possible. However, good conflict management strives to strengthen relationships in the process of overcoming antagonism.

Properly managed conflict requires the active participation of those involved, and learning to control emotions and reactions is one of the best ways to ensure that a conflict comes to a successful end. When tempers flare during disagreements, people may say hurtful or inflammatory things that may increase the anger and tension. Taking time to think before responding helps to break this cycle. It is always a good practice to keep calm and remain focused on the bigger picture.

A willingness to listen and compromise also facilitates the management of conflict. Since disagreements often arise over differing needs and opinions, efforts toward understanding and kindness can create goodwill between adversaries. An act of good faith on the part of one person, either by making an apology or being the first to offer a compromise, can put the other person more at ease. A mediator can also help people end a dispute on their own terms by creating a safe environment for them to come to an understanding.

What Are Some Barriers to Resolving Conflict?

The process of conflict management is usually initiated by someone outside the sphere of the conflict itself, but it relies upon the willing participation of both parties in order to succeed. If the people involved do not want to resolve their differences, it can be difficult to bring the conflict to a reasonable or mutually beneficial end. While collaboration and compromise can be forced, a resolution of that kind often ends up leading to resentment.

Lack of trust is also an impediment to resolving conflict. This may be a factor when an initial conflict is seemingly resolved but the same problem recurs later. If, for example, a coworker tries to take credit for your work, resolving one instance of this will not adequately settle the conflict if that person returns to the same behavior in the future. Additional efforts toward achieving resolution may be harmed by the possibility that the resolution is impermanent or unreliable. Once trust is broken in a relationship between two people, whether at work or in personal life, it can take a long time to rebuild.

What Are the Benefits of Successful Conflict Resolution?

Successful conflict resolution achieves two things. The first is the reduction or elimination of conflict. No one likes to suffer through an unpleasant disagreement or dispute, so the mere fact that a conflict has been settled can bring relief to the people involved and sometimes to a wider circle of friends and coworkers as well. While it may help you to talk about a conflict with trusted confidantes, this may sometimes have the unintended effect of increasing tension or stress in those around you. Successful conflict management can restore peace and harmony not only for you but also for others in your circle.

Secondly, when conflict is resolved in a positive and constructive way, it can improve relationships by leading to better understanding, increased trust between individuals or groups, and improved self-knowledge. Conflict can bring problems to light that were previously unknown, and the resolution of these problems can present opportunities for people to get to know themselves and others better.

For example, suppose that you are about to leave on a two-week vacation, but a coworker hands you a large assignment that needs to be completed right away. This might make you angry, or you may think that your colleague is being insensitive. If you say nothing, resentment can build and become a distraction, affecting your work and your relationship with your colleague. However, if you approach your coworker respectfully and point out that you are leaving soon, it may turn out that he or she was unaware of your vacation or had forgotten about it. If each of you listens to the other, you may find a compromise and might even agree to communicate more clearly in the future.

What If a Conflict Cannot Be Resolved?

There will always be times when conflict cannot be constructively managed or resolved. This may be due to the unwillingness of one or both parties to work toward a solution, or they may simply have irreconcilable differences or fundamentally incompatible points of view. Sometimes, a disagreement may even lead to the threat of physical violence.

One way to sidestep conflict is to distance yourself from the person or situation that is causing it. If you have a particularly difficult relationship with a neighbor, you might consider looking for a new place to live. If a coworker refuses to change the way he or she treats you, you may consider looking for a new job. These are disruptive and difficult choices to make, but they may be less disruptive than continuing to deal with a constant source of conflict.

In some situations, you may need to call on authorities for help. In cases where a conflict involves abuse or harassment, the police or social services may have to be brought in to put an end to the conflict by force. In the workplace, human resources can help deal with inappropriate or threatening behavior from another employee.

Another strategy is to use a proxy, someone who takes over the responsibility for managing the conflict in your place. This typically happens in lawsuits during which lawyers for each side negotiate with each other in place of their clients.

Mediating Conflict

What Is Mediation?

Mediation is a process of resolving a dispute through the use of a neutral third party. When two people or groups are in conflict and cannot resolve their differences on their own, mediation provides a pathway to resolution. The goal of mediation is to bring both sides of a dispute together to resolve their differences in a way that is mutually beneficial, although not every situation can be resolved in this way.

Mediation seeks to help participants reach a voluntary agreement in a fair and just manner. A mediator does not have the authority to force people to come to an agreement. In fact, mediators do not take sides or even make decisions about the outcome of the process. Instead, they offer advice on how each side can better understand and accommodate the other to reach a mutually satisfactory end to the conflict.

Although a professional mediator is usually trained in how to ease tense situations and promote understanding, anyone can act as an informal mediator by stepping in to help two people reconcile their differences. A coach, a teacher, a supervisor, and even a parent can help students, coworkers, or children get past their disagreements. Most importantly, a mediator should be someone who is not directly involved in the conflict. A mediator must remain impartial, because mediation does not work unless both parties trust that the process will be handled fairly and that equal attention will be paid to the needs of both sides.

Mediation is far less costly and time consuming than going to court over a dispute. In some cases a judge may order parties to engage in some form of alternative dispute resolution, of which mediation is one, to resolve their differences without the direct involvement of the legal system.

In What Kinds of Situations Can Mediation Be Helpful?

Whenever two people or groups cannot resolve their differences on their own, mediation is an option worth considering. Mediation has the potential to resolve disagreements as long as both parties are willing to sit down and talk through their differences. In large-scale conflicts, such as international disputes over resources or territory, mediation is handled by a team of people working together. In most cases, however, the work of a single mediator is usually sufficient to manage the process successfully.

Sometimes, an impartial third party (mediator) can be brought in to help with disputes in the workplace. © STOCKLITE/ SHUTTERSTOCK.COM.

Mediation is commonly used in labor union disputes, divorce proceedings, custody battles, business or property conflicts, breaches of contract, clashes between neighbors, employer/employee disagreements, or any other civil dispute. Criminal cases are handled by the legal system and are not candidates for mediation.

Even small disputes are candidates for mediation. Imagine a case where one of your neighbors leaves a bright light on in her driveway at all hours and it keeps you awake at night. If talking to her about it has gotten you nowhere, you might see if she is willing to agree to mediation as a way to resolve the problem. During the mediation process you might learn that her car has been broken into repeatedly and she leaves the light on to protect her vehicle. You might come to understand each other better and work out a compromise, maybe one in which she agrees to point the light away from your windows while you agree to add thicker curtains to help you sleep.

How Does Mediation Work?

Unlike a legal dispute with both sides using lawyers to make their cases, mediation requires people to talk directly with one another in the presence of a mediator. The mediator's role is to keep the negotiations on track and ensure things don't get ugly or out of hand. While a less formal process than a court proceeding or an arbitration, mediation generally follows a standard pattern. Each mediator will have his or her own approach, but in broad terms mediation includes the following steps.

Usually people meet at a neutral location and sit across from each other at a table. The mediator then makes opening remarks in order to define the goals of the session and establish ground rules about acceptable conduct. The mediator also tries to encourage and reinforce the idea of cooperation and goodwill among the participants.

Next, both sides make opening statements that lay out their understanding of the disagreement, how they feel they have been affected by it, and what they see as a possible solution. This allows both parties to fully talk about their feelings and expectations, something that may have been difficult to do previously. If necessary, the mediator may intervene to clarify or summarize what has been said, but each opening statement is meant to be made without interruption from the other side.

The mediator will then encourage discussion between the parties and attempt to find areas of common ground. At this stage of the mediation, both sides discuss their needs and concerns so that everyone involved knows what is at stake and what issues the other side considers important. It is common during this stage for the mediator to have short meetings in private with each side to assess how well they think the mediation is proceeding and to get a sense of how each side feels about the progress.

As the session draws to a close, the mediator will summarize the state of the negotiations and, if the parties have agreed to a settlement, put the agreement in writing in the presence of both parties. At this point it is up to the parties involved if they want to seal the agreement through legal channels or simply promise to abide by the decision. If agreement was not reached, the mediator may make suggestions for a future mediation attempt or suggest alternate methods for the participants to work out their differences. In the end, a mediator has no legal authority to compel people to agree or to find a solution to their problems. Rather, the mediator's role is that of guide or adviser to both sides in equal measure.

What Are Some Different Types of Mediation?

Mediation is one way for people to resolve their differences outside of the courts, but there are other approaches that use similar methods to achieve this end. Conciliation is a process similar to mediation but one that does not require the parties to meet face to face. Instead, a conciliator acts as a go-between, offering advice to each side separately while conveying messages back and forth. This process works best when there is a great deal of tension or discord between the participants or when being in each other's presence distracts from the goals of cooperation and compromise.

Just as it sounds, party-directed mediation is a means of conflict resolution that requires both sides of a dispute to come together to resolve their issues without the intervention of a mediator. This type of mediation works best when the level of contention is low and trust is high and when the stakeholders have a vested interest in building better relations. Party-directed mediation can produce ***win-win solutions*** where both sides leave the negotiation with their needs met, but it requires the greatest amount of work on the part of those involved to reach resolution.

Win-win solution:
A solution providing a good result for everyone involved.

Arbitration is a legal process used as an alternative to litigation. Whereas mediation places the people involved at the center of the discussion, arbitration does not. Instead, an arbitrator gathers evidence from both sides and, after considering the facts of the case, makes a ruling that both parties are legally bound to accept. An arbitrator acts much like a judge and is empowered with similar legal authority.

What Are Advantages of Mediation?

Mediation is one of the least adversarial forms of conflict resolution. This means that it not only helps end a dispute but it does so in a mutually beneficial way for those involved. Rather than building resentment, as can happen with decisions imposed from the outside, successful mediation brings opposing sides together to come up with a solution of their own making. Since there is no clear winner and loser in a mediated conflict, there are fewer negative feelings as a result.

Mediation tends to be far less costly than litigation since hiring lawyers can be very expensive. The results of mediation are also more predictable than trial judgments because mediated solutions evolve over time with input from all sides instead of being delivered as a single pronouncement from the court. As mediation progresses, each side helps to shape the outcome. In a court case, however, the judge or jury hears both sides and makes a single, final decision.

By ending conflict through promoting cooperation and collaboration, mediation also has the benefit of helping to preserve relationships.

This is especially important in corporate dealings where two parties hope to continue to do business together. Mediation's use of direct face-to-face dialogue increases the chances of understanding and empathy in a way not possible with more detached, proxy-based negotiation, during which an outside party makes the decision for others.

What Are Some Barriers to Mediation?

Mediation is a voluntary endeavor, not a required one. Therefore, willing participation on both sides is necessary. In other words, if both sides will not literally "come to the table," mediation is not possible.

Also, when there is a high degree of contentiousness between parties, or when trust has completely broken down between them, it may not be possible for a mediator to bring everyone together successfully. Protracted disagreements often provoke strong negative emotions. Anxiety, anger, fear, and resentment are common by-products of conflict. While mediators are trained to handle negotiations sensitively, if two people can't be in the same room without getting into a fight, there is little a mediator can do to encourage meaningful dialogue.

Mediation is not an option in criminal cases since a mediator is not a legal authority and has no power to enforce laws. Criminal offenses are handled by the police and the criminal justice system, not a mediator.

What Are Alternatives to Mediation?

When mediation is not possible for whatever reason, or if mediation itself fails, taking legal action is the most common alternative. Filing a lawsuit is a way of legally recording a dispute and seeking a solution to a problem through the court system. While both parties may need to be present in the same courtroom, they need not have direct contact, and should violence erupt there are law enforcement officers on hand to contain it.

Arbitration is another legally binding alternative to mediation. Like litigation, it does not require contact between disputants in order to reach a settlement, which may be for the best depending on the situation. If there is no hope for a peaceful, cooperative resolution to a disagreement, then mediation has little chance of success and must be abandoned in favor of more authoritative solutions.

Regulating Stress and Emotions

What Is Stress?

Stress is an extreme physical, emotional, or psychological response to an external situation or event. It is your body's way of dealing with external pressures or demands, either real or perceived. When you are frightened or feel endangered, your breathing and your pulse quicken in order to give you a better chance of either running away from the threat or defending yourself against it. When the threat is eliminated, your body returns to its prestress state.

Psychological stress can also be triggered in response to an external stimulus, as with a fear of heights or public speaking. However, since it originates inside our own minds and is strongly tied to our perception and experience, psychological stress can also be triggered simply by our thoughts about certain events. Anticipating an unpleasant event is enough for some people to feel anxious, worried, or restless even though the event itself is hours or days away. For example, have you ever felt nervous about going to the dentist well in advance of your appointment? In this way, psychological stress can last for longer periods than physical stress and has the potential to cause both mental and physical health problems.

Being stressed is more than being annoyed or angry at something or someone. Stress is a physiological (of or relating to the way your body functions) state that involves multiple involuntary bodily functions. However, the same reactions that are helpful in the short term can, over time, overwhelm your ability to function and interfere with normal coping mechanisms. While bodily stress reactions have evolved as self-protection mechanisms, excessive *anxiety* can result in extreme reactions such as panic attacks, which can leave you powerless.

Anxiety: *An abnormal and overwhelming sense of worry and fear that is often accompanied by physical reaction.*

Experience plays a large role in determining what you perceive as stressful. For instance, if you were once bitten by a dog, you may

feel stressed when in the presence of dogs. In contrast, if you have had only positive experiences with dogs, you may feel happy and calm when surrounded by them. Many reactions to stress are subconscious or instinctive and, therefore, are difficult to control. However, while the body's initial reaction is hard to regulate, the choices you make can play a large role in helping keep psychological stress from spiraling out of control.

To manage workplace stress so you don't get to this point, you need to identify its underlying causes and determine what level of control you have over them. © INESBAZDAR/ SHUTTERSTOCK.COM.

What Are Some Major Types of Stress?

Events in your life that trigger stress are called stressors. A short-term stressor is a fleeting situation or event resulting in stress that only lasts as long as the event itself. For example, you might feel a great deal of stress leading up to an important test, but once it is over you most likely feel a sense of relief. A long-term stressor is something that causes stress either constantly or occasionally over a long period of time. If you are living in poverty, for example, you might have ongoing worries about buying enough food or paying bills. Money problems are often a source of constant worry that add a high level of stress to people's daily lives.

What makes something a stressor varies from person to person; broadly speaking there are three common types of stress. The first is survival stress. When in fear for your safety, your body instinctively prepares to address the threat either by confronting it or fleeing from it. This is commonly known as the fight-or-flight response. Your body reacts to this type of stress by heightening your sensory awareness and increasing your breathing and heart rates.

Another type is environmental stress. This is caused by things you encounter in daily life that are less acute than survival stress. For instance, loud noises, bright lights, crowds, and automobile traffic can all cause or increase tension and anxiety. Workplace stress, which is often caused by conflicting tasks and personalities, is another common environmental stressor. Phobias, such as fear of heights or insects, also fall into this category.

The third type of stress is internal or anticipatory stress. This type of stress is caused by thinking about or dwelling on stressful situations that occurred in the past or will take place in the future. For example, many

Exercise and Stress Relief

Numerous studies have shown that one way to reduce stress is with daily physical exercise. According to the Mayo Clinic, "Being active can boost your feel-good endorphins and distract you from daily worries." Exercise increases the production of endorphins in the brain, the neurotransmitters that make you feel good. This can help improve your mood and reduce anxiety. In addition, exercise requires you to focus on your physical movements, drawing your attention away from the problems of the day.

The Department of Health and Human Services recommends that adults get 150 minutes of moderate exercise (such as walking) or 75 minutes of vigorous exercise (like running) on a weekly basis. Before starting a new routine, check with your doctor in case you have any existing injuries or health issues. You should choose a physical activity that you enjoy so you'll be more likely to do it even when you're stressed. Since it can be easy to forget or neglect your exercise program, prioritize physical activity by writing it into your schedule. You can also enlist the help of a friend or family member to keep you motivated.

people find preparing for a job interview to be a stressful activity, and the anxiety it causes usually goes far beyond the interview itself. These stressful feelings can become overwhelming and interfere with daily life if they last for days or weeks.

Major long-term stressors include personal finances, family and romantic relationships, health problems, and workplace conflicts. These all have both environmental and internal components. When confronting these issues, it is important to differentiate between environmental stressors that you cannot easily control, such as workplace problems or family conflict, and internal aspects that you can, such as your own thoughts, feelings, and reactions. Identifying the sources of stress in our lives is the first step in understanding and learning how to deal with them.

What Are Some Problems Associated with Chronic Stress?

The human body has evolved to deal with short-term stressors of all kinds and releases compounds, such as adrenaline and cortisol, into the blood stream during stressful situations to give you a temporary boost of strength or speed. These compounds are hard on your body, but in short-lived situations, the trade-off is usually worth it. With long-term stress, however, these same physiological reactions are sustained over time and can result in dire health consequences, including increased incidents of heart disease, depression, obesity, insomnia, digestive problems, and premature aging. Long-term stress tends to weaken your immune system, making you more likely to catch colds, the flu, and other illnesses. Furthermore, it has the effect of lengthening recovery times from these ailments.

Sometimes a short-lived traumatic event, such as a car accident or sexual assault, can lead to chronic stress. This is sometimes referred to as post-traumatic stress disorder (PTSD). A person suffering from PTSD may feel anxiety when thinking about a past stressful event but will also be reminded of it when in similar circumstances. If you were attacked in a parking garage, for example, just being in a parking lot of any kind in the future could trigger flashbacks of the original attack.

Regardless of the source, stress can be particularly damaging to your work life. In addition to health issues, prolonged stress can make you more distracted, unable to focus, irritable, short-tempered, tired, and generally less productive. These problems can lead to a downward spiral in which stress at work increases as your job performance worsens.

What Are Some Causes of Stress in the Workplace?

Studies have shown that workplace stress is the number one source of stress in people's lives, and the greatest cause of workplace stress is excessive workload. Being overworked creates anxiety about work performance, and the pressure to get things done quickly leads to frustration and low job satisfaction.

If you are not provided with enough time to get your work done satisfactorily, you will need to choose between either cutting corners and producing lower-quality work or putting in longer hours to accommodate the workload. Regardless of the cause, the pressure of being overworked produces a great deal of stress that tends to increase over time.

Trying to balance the needs of work and home is another source of job-related stress. Staying late to get the job done might alleviate the stress of being overworked, but it will likely increase the stress you experience in personal and family relationships. Attempting to reconcile the competing needs of work and personal life is often a struggle, especially when succeeding at work takes away from personal time or when your personal life has a distracting effect at work. Work is a vital and necessary part of most people's lives, but when your boss requires one thing and your spouse, child, or parent wants another, you are likely to suffer a great deal of stress as you try to deal with the competing demands.

Personality conflicts with coworkers can also lead to stress. Since workplaces bring different kinds of people together into extended daily contact, conflict between coworkers is common. Conflict can be caused by something as simple as loud and outgoing people interacting with others who are shy and quiet or as complicated as coworkers actively sabotaging each other's efforts in an attempt to get ahead. Unless you have the option of working completely alone, you will likely be faced with a coworker conflict at some point in your working life.

What Are Some Strategies for Managing Stress?

In order to manage stress effectively it is important to identify its underlying causes and determine what level of control you have over them. In the case of external factors, sometimes the easiest option is to change your whole environment in order to eliminate the problem. For example, if your work is too stressful, you can look for another job, or if a neighbor is overly bothersome, you can move to a new place. These solutions are easier said than done, however, and they will not succeed if the underlying causes of stress are more internal than external.

Perhaps the best way to deal with psychological stress is to learn to manage your internal reactions to stressful situations. With practice, you can teach yourself how to remain calm and avoid making bad situations worse. Slow, deep breathing is one way to keep stress from overwhelming you. As soon as you feel yourself getting stressed, pause what you are doing and focus on your breathing as you slow it down. This will help your body relax and keep your emotions from intensifying. If someone or something is adding to your stress, do what you can to isolate yourself while you gather your thoughts.

Clear communication can be an important tool in alleviating stress. If you are overworked, you can make an attempt to explain the situation and the effect it is having on you to your supervisor. If this is not possible, or if the amount of work is expected of you no matter what, it can help to talk about your feelings of frustration or anger with someone. Seek out a trusted coworker, friend, or family member who will listen to your concerns and help you gain perspective on the situation. Stress increases when you keep your negative feelings about it bottled up inside. Even when you cannot change the situation itself, you can change the way you respond to it. For example, you might focus on the things you like about your job, whether it is the people, the work itself, or the simply the paycheck.

This same principle can be applied in situations outside of work as well. For example, you may find that you get angry or frustrated while driving, especially if you are stuck in traffic and eager to get home. Because there is nothing anyone can do to make the journey faster, try to spend your time doing something positive rather than worrying about what you cannot change. That may mean playing your favorite music or just enjoying the time alone in the car.

Lastly, if you are unable to resolve issues of stress and anxiety on your own, seeking the help of a professional therapist or counselor is a valuable alternative. A therapist offers complete confidentiality, which may put your mind at ease if you are worried about your words getting back to the people you need to vent about. A therapist is also trained to be an active listener and to help you sort out the root causes of your stress, while at the same time providing sound, clinical advice about how to cope with what is bothering you.

For More Information

BOOKS

Billikopf, Gregorio. *Party-Directed Mediation: Facilitating Dialogue between Individuals*. 3rd ed. Davis: University of California, 2014.

Friedman, Gary J., and Jack Himmelstein. *Challenging Conflict: Mediation through Understanding*. Chicago: American Bar Association, 2008.

HBR Guide to Managing Stress at Work. Boston: Harvard Business Review Press, 2014.

Jeong, Ho-Won. *Conflict Management and Resolution: An Introduction*. New York: Routledge, 2010.

Levine, Stewart. *Getting to Resolution: Turning Conflict into Collaboration*. San Francisco: Berrett-Koehler Publishers, 2009.

Pryor, Will. *A Short and Happy Guide to Mediation*. St. Paul: West Academic Publishing, 2014.

Raines, Susan S. *Conflict Management for Managers: Resolving Workplace, Client and Policy Disputes*. San Francisco: Jossey-Bass, 2013.

Scott, Elizabeth Anne. *8 Keys to Stress Management: Simple and Effective Strategies to Transform Your Experience of Stress*. New York: Norton, 2013.

PERIODICALS

Davey, Liane. "Conflict Strategies for Nice People." *Harvard Business Review*, December 25, 2013. This article can also be found online at https://hbr .org/2013/12/conflict-strategies-for-nice-people/.

Goode, Erica. "The Heavy Cost of Chronic Stress." *New York Times*, December 17, 2002. This article can also be found online at http://www.nytimes .com/2002/12/17/science/the-heavy-cost-of-chronic-stress.html.

Parthasarathy, Swami. "Self-management Key to Stress Management." *Economic Times*, April 8, 2014. This article can also be found online at http://articles.economictimes.indiatimes.com/2006-04-08/news /27434662_1_stress-management-intellect-discriminates-and-judges.

WEBSITES

"Conflict Resolution." *University of Wisconsin-Madison*. http://www.ohrd.wisc. edu/onlinetraining/resolution/index.asp (accessed November, 6, 2014).

"Q&A on Stress for Adults: How It Affects Your Health and What You Can Do About It." *National Institute of Mental Health*. http://www.nimh.nih.gov/ health/publications/stress/index.shtml (accessed November 30, 2014).

"Stress Management." *Mayo Clinic*. http://www.mayoclinic.org/healthy-living/ stress-management/in-depth/exercise-and-stress/art-20044469 (accessed November 30, 2014).

"Stress Management Tips." *American Institute of Stress*. http://www.stress.org/ management-tips/ (accessed November 30, 2014).

"To Stress or Not to Stress?" *American Heart Association*. http://heart.org/ HEARTORG/GettingHealthy/StressManagement/Stress-Management_ UCM_001082_SubHomePage.jsp# (accessed November 30, 2014).

Entering the Workplace: Professional Ethics, Etiquette, and Conduct

Overview: Entering the Workplace: Professional Ethics, Etiquette, and Conduct

How Will My Behavior and Image at Work Impact My Professional Success?

Experts agree that professional success depends not only on the quality of your work but also on your relationships with others. These relationships begin the minute you make contact with an employer, a colleague, or a prospective client. Taking care with your appearance and *body language* can help you project a professional image and make a great first impression. Once you have landed a job, you can begin building and maintaining the relationships that will help you grow your career. At the foundation of these relationships is the ability to understand and follow rules that dictate how you should behave in relation to others.

Part of knowing how to get along in the workplace is having a basic grasp of the rules of business etiquette. Many of these rules will come naturally, such as shaking a person's hand upon first meeting. However, before starting your first job, it is a good idea to review a book or website devoted to the subject of professional etiquette. This research may be especially useful if your new job requires international travel. Your colleagues in other countries may often have different expectations for interpersonal interactions than do those in the United States.

Understanding your employer's ethics policy is also important. It can teach you about your organization's values and how to make good ethical decisions on the job. An ethics policy can also come in handy when confronted with choices about how to treat others and may advise you on making good use of company resources.

How Can I Make a Great First Impression?

Research shows that the first opinions we form about someone's intelligence, competence, and other traits are long lasting. Further, first impressions

Body language: *The gestures, movements, and mannerisms by which a person communicates with others, including facial expressions, tone of voice, and posture.*

Many workplaces have a written code of conduct on how employees should behave with customers and among themselves. © RAWPIXEL/ SHUTTERSTOCK.COM.

tend to linger even in the face of new, contradictory information. For this reason, before interviewing or entering the workplace as a new employee, you should put some thought into the image you want to project.

Making a good first impression can start even before you are interviewed. In addition to looking at your résumé, many employers will check out your online presence. When job searching, make an effort to update your LinkedIn (http://www.linkedin.com) page and any other business-related blogs or websites with which you are affiliated. You should also look at personal websites and social media profiles, such as on Facebook (http://www.facebook.com) and Twitter (https://twitter .com), taking care that material viewable by the public is appropriate.

At a job interview, first impressions start with your physical appearance, including attire and grooming. Standards for each will vary depending on the industry and your position, but there are a few rules to follow. One good tip is to know your prospective employer's corporate culture and make sure what you wear to your interview is a match. Furthermore, you should dress for the specific job you want. Hiring managers tend to assume that you can do the job you are dressed for, so if you are unsure, it is better to be slightly overdressed than slightly underdressed. As a new hire, you should make sure you understand your company's formal dress code, as well as how other people in the company interpret it. "Casual Fridays" might not mean the same thing in a Manhattan brokerage house as it does in a tech start-up in Seattle, for instance.

Body language also plays an important role in first impressions, and you should keep a few basics in mind both when interviewing and after you are hired. Smiling and making direct eye contact with someone signals friendliness and that you are open to social interaction. Good posture is also important, as it can indicate things about your personality and mood. For example, if you exhibit good posture, you are likely to be seen as confident, but if you slump, others may believe that you are bored. Keeping these tips in mind can set the tone for a positive interview or introduction.

How Can Good Etiquette Help Me in the Workplace Both inside and outside the United States?

After you are hired, you will want to turn your attention to what you can do to get along with your new colleagues and supervisors. As with any social situation, interactions are more pleasant when good manners and courtesy are used by all. The rules governing business etiquette are not substantially different than what you have been taught in other situations, and, for the most part, they are easy to learn. A good business etiquette book or online guide can be a valuable source to refer to when specific questions arise.

One of the most important things you can do to demonstrate that you appreciate new opportunities is to send thank-you notes after a meeting or job interview. If you have met or interviewed with multiple people, each should receive a thank you. If you are hired, it is important to learn and remember the names of colleagues, managers, and clients that you encounter regularly. Doing so will make you seem engaged and will make others feel good.

As more U.S. companies operate in a global marketplace, it is likely that you will need to interact with workers from other cultures, either in person or virtually. When visiting job sites, clients, or business partners in other countries, it is important to behave professionally in a sometimes radically different cultural context. Even in your home office you may find yourself in a videoconference with clients in Japan or colleagues in India. While you may not need to have as much knowledge about international business etiquette in the latter situation, it is still important to have a good grasp of the basics, such as proper greetings and titles, in order to smooth conversation and avoid making a potentially offensive mistake.

What Are Some Good General Things to Know about Business Etiquette when Visiting Other Countries?

Once you understand how to behave in the workplace, it is relatively easy to apply your knowledge to new situations. You may not be able to completely comprehend all of the nuances of social situations in a culture different from your own, but there are some general rules that can help you navigate them. These guidelines include educating yourself about the country and its customs, following your host's lead, and, when in doubt, erring on the conservative side in terms of dress and behavior.

If you anticipate traveling to another country for business, you should make it a habit to do a little research before departure. You should find facts about the country itself, such as the geography, as well as about the people and their culture. Being able to make small talk with your hosts about their homeland communicates respect. You might also want to familiarize yourself with current local news, if you are able, but be sure to steer clear of controversial news stories in conversation.

It may be somewhat difficult to research the basic rules of etiquette followed in another country, especially as practices may vary between regions. This is particularly true in large countries such as China. Still, it is worth familiarizing yourself with basic local customs such as how to greet people and whether or not it is customary to bring gifts to your hosts when visiting on business. You should also read up on table manners, as business is often conducted over meals and expectations may be different than what you are used to in the United States.

Furthermore, even if you have done research, it can be hard to navigate social interaction in a foreign culture, especially if you do not understand the language. While most hosts will either speak English or provide an interpreter, you still may face confusion in restaurants and other, less formal periods of your trip. When in doubt, it is a good idea to observe your hosts and follow their lead. In some countries, for example, a business lunch will be an extended affair with a long period of socializing before the actual business at hand is mentioned. In such cultures, immediately launching into a sales presentation or deal negotiation will appear rude and may create tension that will work against your team. Waiting for your host to transition into business, while it requires patience, may have a big payoff.

On a final note, when visiting another country for business, it is always best to be conservative in both dress and behavior. For instance, if you are not sure whether it is appropriate to use first names with your Japanese counterpart, you should avoid doing so. In most cases, it is better to be too formal than to be too casual, which can be interpreted as being disrespectful. In conversation, you should introduce open-ended topics that require elaboration, while avoiding expressing strong opinions yourself. Doing so will keep the conversation flowing and will give you an opportunity to learn from your host's speech and behavior.

What Are Workplace Ethics and Why Are They Important?

Workplace ethics has become a hot topic. Typically, the term is used to mean the values an organization seeks to demonstrate with its operating policies and how it expects its employees to behave. Ethical values include things such as honesty, fairness, responsibility, and transparency. The particular values emphasized will depend on both the employer and the common practices in the industry to which it belongs. Compliance with federal and state laws regulating businesses is also part of what defines good conduct, as is following with the norms of the broader community.

Research suggests that companies that work to create an ethical culture are more successful than those in which unethical behavior occurs unchecked. This is in part because consumers value companies that have a reputation for ethical policies and fair treatment of employees. In addition, such a company is more likely to attract and keep talented people as employees. Workers who feel as though they are respected and treated fairly not only are less likely to leave but also are more productive, which helps the business economically.

In less ethical organizations, dissatisfaction and turnover tend to be higher. Furthermore, when misconduct becomes widespread, it can lead to public scandal and can even have repercussions for the economy. For instance, analysts have pointed to unethical lending practices in the banking industry as a major contributor to the global financial crisis of 2007–09.

What Are Ethics Policies and Codes of Conduct?

Employers use ethics policies and codes of conduct to lay out values and specific expectations for their employees. Ethics policies often begin by introducing traits or practices a company values, usually both moral and practical. For instance, an ethics policy may emphasize fairness, transparency, and respect for others, as well as a commitment to profitability for shareholders.

Codes of conduct, which may be part of a broader ethics policy, will usually provide examples of behavior prohibited during working hours and, sometimes, after hours. Employers also typically include information about the consequences of breaking the rules, along with a description of the procedures employees can follow to report misconduct by others.

What Is Employee Misconduct?

In broad terms, *misconduct* refers to a violation by an employee of an employer's stated values and rules. Some types of misconduct may be obvious and standard across companies, such as behavior that violates state and federal laws. Other violations may be specific to an industry or organization. For this reason, it is important to understand your employer's specific expectations. Furthermore, because employers may update policies, especially with regard to changing technology and the laws that govern it, you should stay abreast of your employer's rules.

Misconduct can occur in many situations and can be a minor infraction by a single employee or a major systemic transgression affecting the company's finances. Some behaviors, such as stealing large amounts of money from company accounts, are clearly misconduct. In other cases, it may not be easy for you decide whether a behavior violates company ethics, especially if it is something many employees do. Using your employer's computers and Wi-Fi for personal business is an example of this type of gray area. When in doubt, it is always best to consult your employee handbook or ask a trusted peer or supervisor for a definitive answer. In addition, it is usually best to err on the side of caution rather than risk discipline for running afoul of your employer's ethics policy.

Should I Report Misconduct If I See It?

Many employees will eventually be forced to decide whether or not to report wrongdoing they observe. While this is a personal decision, there is evidence to suggest that, when you report misconduct, everyone benefits. Studies have shown that misconduct tends to beget more misconduct. In companies where misconduct is widespread, employees faced with an ethical dilemma may be more likely to do the wrong thing. In contrast, when the corporate culture supports ethical behavior and deals appropriately with misconduct, employees are more likely to do the right thing, even when misconduct might be tempting.

Because of the economic power of corporations, notions of social responsibility can also play a part when you are weighing whether or not to turn in a wrongdoer. For example, energy and communications giant Enron filed for bankruptcy in 2001 after it became known that the company had been using fraudulent accounting practices to hide years of corporate losses. Thousands of employees and former employees lost their retirement savings, and other stockholders and the U.S. economy took hits as well. Experts have speculated that the damage caused by the collapse of Enron might have been lessened had one person aware of the fraud alerted authorities earlier on.

How Do I Report Misconduct?

When you see someone at work doing something wrong, you may be tempted to talk over the situation with coworkers, especially if you are feeling unsure about what to do. While such discussions might help temporarily relieve emotional stress, they are generally a bad idea. Revealing sensitive information can make you appear untrustworthy and unprofessional even if what you are saying is true. Moreover, if your accusations end up being unfounded, you may have damaged a coworker's reputation, not to mention your own. Spreading misinformation about a peer or supervisor can get your fired and potentially even lead to criminal prosecution.

Rather than discuss misconduct by a coworker with others, you should find out how to officially report misconduct in your organization. Companies will often have a hotline or designated e-mail address you can use to report misconduct anonymously. However, in some cases, especially in smaller companies, you may not have this option. Still, most companies work to keep misconduct reports confidential, and many also have policies in place to prevent retaliation by the reported employee. Letting the appropriate personnel investigate misconduct helps ensure that the matter will be resolved in a fair way. In cases where you see misconduct that endangers lives or seriously violates the law, you may need to make a report to the government or to law enforcement.

For More Information

BOOKS

Collins, Denis. *Business Ethics: How to Design and Manage Ethical Organizations.* Hoboken, NJ: Wiley and Sons, 2012.

Ferrell, O. C., John Fraedrich, and Linda Ferrell. *Business Ethics: Ethical Decision Making and Cases.* Stamford, CT: Cengage Learning, 2014.

Johnson, Dorothea, and Liv Tyler. *Modern Manners: Tools to Take You to the Top.* New York: Potter Style, 2013.

Lehman, Carol M., Deborah Daniel DuFrene, and Robyn Walker. *BCOM: Business Communication.* Stamford, CT: Cengage Learning, 2015.

Maxwell, John C. *Ethics 101: What Every Leader Needs to Know.* New York: Center Street, 2005.

Pachter, Barbara. *The Essentials of Business Etiquette: How to Greet, Eat, and Tweet Your Way to Success.* New York: McGraw Hill Education, 2013.

Post, Peggy, and Peter Post. *Emily Post's The Etiquette Advantage in Business: Personal Skills for Professional Success.* 2nd ed. New York: William Morrow, 2014.

PERIODICALS

Sharkey, Joe. "The Hot Potato of Business Etiquette." *New York Times*, May 16, 2006. This article can also be found online at http://www.nytimes.com/2006/05/16/business/16road.html?_r=0.

Tugend, Alina. "In Life and Business, Learning to Be Ethical." *New York Times*, January 11 2014: B5. This article can also be found online at http://www.nytimes.com/2014/01/11/your-money/in-life-and-business-learning-to-be-ethical.html.

WEBSITES

Adams, Susan. "The New Rules of Business Etiquette." *Forbes.* October 5, 2011. http://www.forbes.com/sites/susanadams/2011/10/05/the-new-rules-of-business-etiquette/ (accessed January 8, 2015).

"Business Ethics." *Chicago Tribune.* http://articles.chicagotribune.com/keyword/business-ethics (accessed January 8, 2015).

"Business Ethics." Markula Center for Applied Ethics. *Santa Clara University.* http://www.scu.edu/ethics/practicing/focusareas/business/ (accessed January 8, 2015).

Gebler, David. "Business Ethics and Social Responsibility." *Free Management Library.* http://managementhelp.org/businessethics/ (accessed January 8, 2015).

Haidt, Jonathan. "Can You Teach Businessmen to Be Ethical?" *Washington Post.* January 13, 2014. http://www.washingtonpost.com/blogs/on-leadership/wp/2014/01/13/can-you-teach-businessmen-to-be-ethical/ (accessed January 8, 2015).

Napier-Fitzpatrick, Patricia. "Top 10 Business Etiquette Tips for New College Graduates." *The Etiquette School of New York.* http://etiquette-ny.com/top-10-business-etiquette-tips-for-new-college-graduates/ (accessed January 8, 2015).

Professional Ethics

What Are Workplace Ethics?

Workplace ethics are standards of conduct that define the way a business should operate and the way the people employed by that business should behave. Good conduct is in part defined by compliance with federal and state laws regulating businesses. In addition, common practices in your industry, as well as the values and culture of your workplace, will determine the standards that serve as a model for your behavior at any job. Finally, the ethical standards of the broader community may also help shape expectations about best ethical practices at work.

Generally speaking, values emphasized in the workplace may include integrity, fairness, responsibility, transparency, and self-control, among others. Workplace ethics come into play in both large and small ways in all work environments, from corporate offices to mom-and-pop restaurants. An ethical dilemma may concern something as small as deciding if it's okay to take extra pens home from the office. Or it can involve something as large as figuring out what to do about a once-trusted boss you suspect is cheating investment clients out of their retirement savings.

At the basic level, employees should do what they were hired to do with care and diligence; without ethics, there is no trust, no respect in the workplace.
© RAWPIXEL/
SHUTTERSTOCK.COM.

Why Are Workplace Ethics Important?

Workplace ethics are important for a number of reasons. First, research suggests that companies with solid ethical practices are more successful than those in which unethical behavior is tolerated or encouraged. Their success may be partly attributed to the fact that an ethical company committed to fair practices will build a good reputation among consumers. Also, such a company is more likely to attract and retain top talent. Workers who feel as though they are treated fairly and respected are not only less likely to leave, but they are also typically more productive, which contributes to the business's bottom line.

On the other hand, employees who work for a company in which misconduct is not punished or, even worse, rewarded, are more likely to engage in misconduct themselves. Employees whose personal ethics do not allow such behavior may choose to leave, which can lead to a further decline in the ethical quality in those organizations. When misconduct becomes widespread, chances are good it will come to public attention, and it can become a nightmare for a business forced to spend a large amount of money to restore its image. In some cases, misconduct can have huge consequences that reach far outside a single company or industry. For example, analysts have pointed to unethical lending practices in the banking industry as a major factor in the U.S. financial crisis of 2008–09.

As an employee, clearly defined standards of conduct can provide you with important guidance about how to behave in various situations and help you navigate difficult situations and make sound choices. If you are aware of the rules, you can make sure your behavior conforms to them. Furthermore, a work environment where all employees are held accountable for their conduct will generally be a more fair and pleasant place to work.

How Are Workplace Ethics Defined by Individual Employers?

In most cases, employers begin to communicate expectations about character and behavior during the hiring process. Job listings may specify that candidates possess particular personal characteristics, such as "honest" or "responsible." Upon hire, most new employees receive a copy of the company's employee handbook, which may formally lay out more rules, possibly including a code of ethical conduct. Companies that do not publish a code of ethics still typically provide a description of rules and regulations. Some of these will address practical aspects of your job, such as the dress code, while others detail how you should behave. In either case, guidelines vary depending on the industry and employer but may define things such as appropriate interactions with other employees and customers and proper use of company resources. When you accept a job, you are often required to sign a contract agreeing to the offer's terms of employment, including company rules and codes of ethical conduct.

Besides providing employees with information about how to comply with the company's ethics standards, many businesses provide training for employees regarding conduct. Training may cover specific topics, such as sexual harassment, which is both an ethical and a legal concern. Or training may be more general and can include ethics work-shops or company discussions that explore types of ethical dilemmas that may come up and how to deal with them. Also, some employers offer resources such as websites or reading material that provide guid-ance on ethics issues.

Why Is Workplace Culture Important in Matters of Ethics?

Workplace culture, while a somewhat murky concept, can be one of the key factors influencing employee behavior. Workplace culture may include things like the way employees communicate with each other and with supervisors, the dress code and the extent to which it is respected, the overall appearance and atmosphere in the office, and the manner in which disciplinary procedures are enacted.

While there are many variables regarding what makes a particular workplace culture "ethical," in general companies whose policies are clearly defined and reflected in day-to-day operations are more likely to have employees who are guided by these values. When employees observe their employers following the law and consistently applying the rules they have in place, employees will likely be more motivated to do the same. When cutting corners is the standard, or when blatant miscon-duct goes unremarked or undisciplined, unethical behavior may be seen as normal. For employees in this kind of company, doing the right thing may be like swimming against the current.

How Do Managers Impact Workplace Ethics?

Managers serve an important role in modeling a company's values to their employees. When your manager follows the rules that you are expected to follow and makes sure that others do too, you are more likely to form a positive relationship with a foundation of trust. It is especially important to have this trust because of the power that managers may have over their direct reports' job security, pay, and advancement potential.

Some recent research has suggested that, when ethical misconduct is uncovered in the workplace, managers themselves are involved more than half of the time. In many ways this makes sense, as there may be less oversight of managers, especially high-level managers, than of rank-and-file employees. Still, when managers routinely disobey the rules they are charged with enforcing, it is probable that employees will begin to catch on, which puts them in a tough spot. Some employees may be influenced to relax their own standards and could potentially end up in trouble as a result. Others may want to report misconduct, but they may be too fearful of retaliation to do so. When managers are caught in misconduct and disciplined, it often has a positive effect on employee morale. Knowing that the same rules apply to everyone can be reassuring, and that communicates a high level of respect for employees at every level of the organization.

What Are Some Examples of Common Ethical Dilemmas in the Workplace?

One of the most common ethical dilemmas confronted by employees is using company time and resources for personal business. For instance, is it acceptable to make personal phone calls or send nonbusiness related e-mails during the workday? Or if you are sitting in on a conference call but not participating, can you surf the web or send text messages at the same time?

While many companies have policies regarding the use of company time and resources for personal matters, there are usually exceptions. Taking a call about a family emergency might be considered acceptable, for instance, while making a call to confirm dinner plans with a friend may not. If you are in doubt about what constitutes acceptable behavior, it is always best to check with your employer. Some companies, especially young companies in new media fields, may allow or even encourage small breaks to promote employee productivity and morale.

Another common ethical dilemma many employees confront at some point involves decisions about what to do when you see a coworker behaving unethically. You might, for example, be confronted with a coworker who is stealing from the company or one who is harassing another coworker. You might even be asked to participate in someone else's misconduct, as when an employee leaves work without permission and asks you to cover so your supervisor won't find out. In more serious cases, you could be aware of cases of law-breaking and fraud, which can be especially tricky if supervisory personnel are involved.

Issues related to other people's conduct are especially hard to resolve. Getting along with coworkers is essential, and few people want to be branded a troublemaker or backstabber. In these cases, it is a good idea to investigate what sorts of safeguards are in place for whistle-blowers. While many cases of employee misconduct are matters to be dealt with internally, cases that involve serious breaches of the law may need to be reported to an outside agency. If this happens, it may be a good idea to consult an attorney before proceeding.

How Do Companies Evaluate the Ethical Conduct of Employees?

Employers may use a variety of measures to gauge employee attitudes and behavior regarding workplace ethics. Some employers routinely administer anonymous surveys to measure how employees view the conduct of their managers and how comfortable they feel reporting misconduct of managers or other employees. Companies may also test employees to see how well they understand the conduct that is expected from them and others. Collecting data in this manner can help an employer spot potential problems and can also help shape employee education and training programs.

Many companies now take into account an employee's conduct when preparing performance reviews. During a review, you might get feedback about how well you comply with company values, in addition to an evaluation of how well you perform job duties. Such evaluations can give you a clear picture of how well you've understood your employer's expectations and where there might be room for improvement.

What Are Some Ways Employers Enforce Rules about Ethics?

Most employers have some system in place to deal with employee misconduct. At the foundation of such a system is a clearly defined procedure that employees can use to report ethical violations committed by others without fear of retaliation. This process is typically set up to ensure confidentiality and may even allow for anonymous reporting, especially in cases where employees are turning in higher-ups in the company.

In addition to a system for reporting unethical conduct, most companies have devised a standard method of disciplining employees who have violated company rules. The types of penalties applied to misconduct are often detailed in employee handbooks and can include temporary suspension or dismissal, depending on the seriousness of the violation. Misconduct that violates the law and leaves your employer open to criminal or civil penalties will often be treated more harshly than violations of internal rules alone. Disciplinary procedures applied fairly to all employees is known to contribute to employee morale in the workplace.

Ethics Policies and Codes of Conduct

What Is an Ethics Policy?

An employer's ethics policy is a statement of the company's basic values, which employees are expected to embody in their work and conduct in the workplace. Such policies typically begin by focusing on general traits or practices a company seeks to promote, be they moral values or more practical ones. For example, an ethics policy may mention the importance of honesty, fairness, and respect for others in the workplace, as well as a commitment to profitability for people who own stock in the business.

An ethics policy may also include a more specific code of conduct, which usually provides examples of what types of behavior are encouraged or prohibited during working hours as well as those that are expected after work. Ethics policies generally describe the consequence for violating the code of conduct and detail the process for reporting violations.

Usually, you will be provided with a copy of your company's ethics policy when you are hired. You will typically also be expected to sign a document stating that you have read and understood the policy. Some large companies may have specific ethics policies tailored to different corporate divisions such as sales, accounting, or management. Employees who work internationally may also be given separate guidelines for dealing with companies and governments that follow different cultural practices and rules of law.

How Do Companies Benefit from Having an Ethics Policy?

Experts have suggested that a robust ethics policy can set the tone for establishing ethical conduct among employees at all levels of an organization. Some research has also suggested that the presence of an ethics code alone will make employees more likely to behave ethically, while

specific codes of conduct can help employees understand expectations and how to conform to them.

A reputation for ethical practices, in turn, benefits a company in a number of ways. Organizations perceived as ethical are likely to be deemed more trustworthy by consumers and, hence, more likely to receive business. In contrast, consumers sometimes avoid corporations whose employees have been caught engaged in unethical behavior, particularly when it is known to be widespread. In addition, ethical companies may be more likely to attract and retain top talent, in part because workplaces where honesty, fairness, and other such values are promoted may provide a more attractive work environment to employees.

How Common Are Employee Ethics Policies and Codes of Conduct?

Research suggests that, in the early twenty-first century, more than 85 percent of Fortune 500 companies have some form of ethics code in place, up from around 14 percent in 1990. In the United States, the prevalence of such policies is closer to 100 percent. The rise in codes of conduct can be explained in part by pressure from consumer protection groups concerned with corporate ethics, especially in light of scandals such as the financial misconduct of officials at the energy firm Enron. The company's bankruptcy in 2001 resulted in the loss of billions of

Preventing Sexual Harassment in the Workplace

Most companies have ethics policies that prohibit sexual harassment, but many employees have differing opinions about what constitutes sexual harassment. It is important for all employees to familiarize themselves with the different types of behavior that can be defined as harassment and what to do if it occurs.

- Avoid communication that could be perceived as sexual harassment. This could include dirty jokes, posters, or e-mails.
- Don't assume that your coworkers want to hear sexually charge comments or jokes. In addition, many people do not appreciate comments about their appearance or what they wear.
- Flirting or asking for dates can also be considered sexual harassment.

- Pay attention to nonverbal and body language clues. If someone shrinks away when you try to talk to him or her, this is an indication that you are crossing a line.

If your company doesn't provide sexual harassment education sessions, suggest that one be arranged. You can also request that pamphlets and posters about the topic be distributed around the workplace. If an incident does occur, document the incident, including as much detail as possible. Then report it to your supervisor so a formal complaint can be filed. If your company fails to investigate, you should report the harassment to the local authorities. Educating yourself about sexual harassment is the first step to preventing it.

dollars, including the retirement savings of many employees, and prompted a public outcry against corporate greed and the lack of ethical oversight for upper-level management.

While Enron had a code of conduct in place prior to its collapse, company officials deliberately sidestepped the code. In response to Enron's collapse, as well as several other corporate scandals, the federal government enacted the Sarbanes-Oxley Act in 2002, which outlines standards that U.S. public company boards and senior management must follow. Section 406 of the act outlines that public companies must disclose whether they operate under a code of ethics and, if so, whether there are any circumstances under which company officials may choose to waive its provisions.

How Did Ethics Policies Develop?

While ethics policies had existed in some form previously, the codification of ethics in corporations began to occur in the 1960s and 1970s, prompted by several pieces of legislation defining the rights of workers. In 1964 the U.S. Civil Rights Act was signed into law, prohibiting

Human resources:
The department in a company that is responsible for hiring and managing employees.

employers from discriminating on the basis of race, religion, or national origin. In response, many companies added employees to their *human resources* departments to ensure compliance with the law. Employers were also affected by passage of the U.S. Occupational Safety and Health Act (1970), which forced corporations to police the conditions of the work environments they provided. These two pieces of legislation made corporate officials aware of the need to take employee rights seriously and to have policies in place to make sure government regulations were enforced.

In many corporations, ethics training began in earnest in the 1980s, and a number of these companies also began appointing ethics officers. Some industries were rocked by repeated scandals and, in response, voluntarily set up bodies to oversee ethical practices. For example, in 1986, the Defense Industry Initiative on Business Ethics and Conduct was formed to help regulate defense contracts. Participating companies agreed to publish a code of ethics, train employees on these codes, and set up regulatory systems to make sure that policies were being followed.

The motivation for businesses to establish and enforce ethics policies increased even more in 1991 when the U.S. Sentencing Commission put into place the Federal Sentencing Guidelines for Organizations, which governs federal judges' imposition of sentences on U.S. companies implicated in wrongdoing. These guidelines lay out tough penalties to be charged against organizations whose employees commit federal crimes. However, companies that have implemented a program to detect and prevent law breaking are generally afforded some amount of leniency.

In addition to the Sarbanes-Oxley Act, the early twenty-first century brought other legislation influencing corporate ethics practices. The Dodd-Frank Wall Street Reform and Consumer Protection Act was passed in 2010 in response to corporate misconduct that caused the financial crisis of 2007–09 and the recession that followed. This act again brought federal regulations to bear on corporate financial practices and on the ways in which corporations enforce compliance with these regulations among their employees.

How Are Employee Ethics Policies Created and What Is Included?

When company officials deem it necessary to produce an ethics policy, they often look to existing documents in the organization, such as the company's *mission statement*, along with information taken from employee handbooks. Ethics policies and codes of conduct are generally internal documents created by a team of staff members, which may include management, human resources, and corporate attorneys. Team members may consider recent federal and state laws, practices in their industry, and the organization's existing corporate culture. Team members also typically keep in mind the standards of the broader community around the company, especially when many employees are drawn from it.

Many ethics policies begin with a statement from the company's chief executive officer or other leader. These statements endorse the contents of the policy and are used to establish the importance of the code at all levels of the organization. The introduction may also specify to whom the policy is addressed. Most policies also include a summary of corporate values, which typically overlap with the company's overall mission statement. Such a statement is usually general, and the values mentioned are often explained with more concrete behavioral examples in the section that follows.

The essence of an ethics policy is typically composed of the code of conduct, which spells out the manner in which you should behave in your work environment with regards to, among other things, interpersonal interactions, handling of financial transactions, and use of company funds and property. The code of conduct may also deal with ethical dilemmas that may arise, such as conflicts of interest, and how to approach them. A code of conduct could also touch on compliance with all applicable laws, particularly those regarding sexual harassment and workplace discrimination.

In addition, most ethics policies describe the way a company administers the policy and how you, as an employee, can use that system. This section may indicate where you can go for an explanation of the code of conduct, especially as new situations arise that may be difficult to follow without additional information. It also describes how to report employee misconduct, as well as what consequences violators will face, the most serious of which is usually dismissal. Some policies also specify the protections that are in place for whistle-blowers (people who report the misconduct of a coworker), underlining the company's commitment to non-retaliation against those who report ethics violations. A guarantee of protection against retaliation is important, as many employees may be hesitant to report supervisors or to report misconduct that is widespread.

Mission statement:
A formal summary of the aims and values of a company, organization, or individual.

Do Small Businesses Have Ethics Policies?

Some small to midsize businesses have ethics policies and codes of conduct similar to those found in large corporations. These codes often focus on the same types of concerns addressed by corporate policies. Small businesses may have much shorter ethics policies than do larger organizations, particularly those who do business globally.

Very small companies often skip formal codes of conduct. Companies with fewer than 20 employees in particular may assume the character of a family, even when not officially a "family business." In such cases, introducing a formal ethics policy may be awkward, and expectations may be communicated verbally rather than in written documents.

Is an Ethics Policy Legally Binding?

As an employee, signing an ethics policy shows that you agree to follow its terms and accept the consequences for violating them. While an ethics policy is not legally enforceable, it does provide some protection for employers when faced with wrongful termination suits after dismissing an employee over an ethics violation. An ethics policy that explains a company's system of protections for whistle-blowers can also help protect an employee reporting an ethics violation, especially one by a senior staff member who has influence on the employee's career.

Corporations as a whole are not legally bound by their own codes of conduct and cannot be prosecuted for activities that violate them except when these activities are also illegal. This issue sometimes arises with regard to companies that outsource aspects of their business to countries where labor laws and local practices allow unacceptable conditions for workers. For example, bad publicity about the use of sweatshop labor has forced some U.S. companies to change their practices in this area, but such changes are entirely voluntary and, some critics have charged, also superficial.

What Does the Future Look Like for Ethics Policies in U.S. Companies?

Ethics policies and codes of conduct are likely to continue to grow in the twenty-first century. The increased presence of digital communication and social networking technologies makes the behavior of employees both in and outside work more visible. Cell phones and other mobile devices also make it easier for employees to use company time for personal business. Employers have responded by addressing these issues in ethics policies and will likely continue to do so as technology evolves. Some privacy advocates have expressed concerns about the possibility of companies making employment decisions based on the monitoring of behavior (for example, via social media such as Facebook or Twitter) that occurs outside the workplace.

Changes in the workforce are also likely to play a part in ethics policy creation as more employees work from home or other remote locations rather than in traditional, centralized offices. Corporations with many remote workers will have to worry less about issues such as workplace violence. However, other concerns, such as misuse of intellectual property or sexual harassment via e-mail communications, could become more pressing.

In recent years, concerns have grown about the impact of human activities on the environment. Environmental activism has put pressure on companies to reduce waste and develop sustainable practices. Many companies have responded by including a commitment to protecting the environment as a core value, mentioning it in the corporate ethics policy and encouraging employees to conserve resources and recycle. This trend is likely to grow in the coming years as business practices respond to changes in the availability of natural resources, government regulation, and social attitudes about being environmentally conscience.

Examples of Employee Misconduct and Unethical Behavior

What Is Employee Misconduct?

The term *misconduct* can apply to a variety of behaviors by employees in the workplace. It generally refers to an employee's violation of his or her employer's core values, which may or may not be formally stated in an ethics policy. Some violations may be clearly defined, such as those that break state or federal laws. Other instances of misconduct may be specific to an industry or a particular company.

 Misconduct can occur in many contexts. It can be a minor infraction with little impact, or it can be a major breach that affects other employees or the company's bottom line. Misconduct most often occurs in interpersonal interactions, communication, the handling of company funds, or the use of company resources. When misconduct happens on a large scale, it can have devastating effects that ripple outside the company into the broader community.

In some cases, it may not be easy for you to determine whether your behavior violates company ethics. Large corporations typically have ethics policies in place that spell rules out clearly. In the case of smaller companies, it is best to consult a trusted supervisor when in doubt.

What Are Some Examples of Financial Misconduct?

One of the most famous examples of financial misconduct involved high-level employees of the energy and communications company Enron, as well as members of its accounting firm, Arthur Andersen. When Enron went bankrupt in 2001, thousands of employees lost their retirement savings along with their jobs, and stockholders also suffered devastating losses. Sixteen Enron executives were convicted and sent to prison for their roles in fraudulent accounting practices, which involved creating various subsidiary (secondary) businesses to help hide financial losses and keep stock prices high.

Numerous corporations were involved in the financial crisis of 2007–09, which led to the Great Recession, one of the worst economic periods in U.S. history. Lehman Brothers, a financial firm that declared bankruptcy in 2008, routinely used unorthodox accounting practices to hide the company's quarterly losses. Many banks were engaged in questionable lending practices at that time, knowingly offering mortgages to people who were not prepared to repay them and then selling the risky loans. These mortgages, called subprime mortgages, also contributed to the Great Recession, resulting in record *foreclosures* that devastated families and communities.

While these examples involved large companies, individual employees can also be guilty of financial misconduct. One such example might be using your corporate expense account to purchase items for personal use. While spending small amounts of money might seem to have little impact on a company's profits, such misuse of funds is in clear violation of most codes of conduct.

Lying on a timesheet, stealing company supplies, or taking credit for others' work are all examples of unethical behavior in the workplace.
© ALEXANDRA PETRUK/ SHUTTERSTOCK.COM.

Foreclosure: *A legal process by which a bank takes possession of a property because the buyer of the property is no longer able to make payments on the loan he or she took out to purchase it.*

What Are Some Examples of Misconduct in Interpersonal Interactions?

Like most employees, you probably spend a considerable amount of time communicating with coworkers. You must be able to get along well with your fellow employees and function as part of a larger team. Employers often have rules governing interactions among employees, as well as with customers, vendors, and members of the general public. Misconduct in the area of interpersonal interactions can include things such as sexual harassment, discrimination against people based on race or religion, or inappropriate relationships between managers and subordinates.

Sexual harassment is an area governed by law as well as by employer ethics policies. Many companies require you to undergo training to help you understand the types of behaviors that constitute harassment and

Recovering from a Career Mistake

Even the most careful employees can sometimes find themselves in breach of their company's code of conduct. Although errors cannot be undone, there are some things you can do to avoid being terminated from your job and correct your error.

- Apologize. The best thing you can do is admit your mistake. If you take responsibility for your actions and provide a solution to fix the problem, it will help you and your coworkers to move forward.

- Communicate. Provide your manager with regular progress updates that detail what steps you're taking to rectify the situation. Detail how you plan to move forward and what has already been done. Avoid personalizing the situation or how it has affected you.

- Reassess. Think about why you messed up. A regular pattern of misconduct could be a sign that you're unhappy with your job and are trying to sabotage yourself. It may be time to reevaluate your skills and your level of satisfaction. It may be time to move on, particularly if your boss and colleagues no longer trust you.

- Stay positive. If you remain optimistic that you can correct your mistake, your superiors and coworkers are more likely to offer you a second chance and help you with your plan to move forward.

to avoid engaging in them. Certain behaviors are prohibited, such as unwanted physical contact or the use of sexual language in the workplace. With the increasing convenience and popularity of e-mail and text messages, employers have begun to extend rules to include these forms of communication as well. Circulating dirty jokes to coworkers, or even sending them to friends via a work e-mail, can be considered misconduct.

Many companies prohibit romantic relationships between supervisory personnel and those who report to them, even when the relationships are consensual. Relationships between employees and clients may also be prohibited, especially between doctors and patients or therapists and clients. Such liaisons involve a power imbalance and can present the appearance of indecency.

Discrimination against employees on the basis of race, religion, gender, or other personal factors is a violation of the law as well as of most ethics policies. Employers also generally prohibit language that could be considered hateful, even when presented as humor.

What Are Some Examples of Misconduct in Communications?

Misconduct related to company communications can be similar to misconduct in interpersonal interactions. Communication that is overtly sexual, racist, or offensive in other ways is usually prohibited at the workplace or when transmitted via work communication systems such as e-mail. In such cases, employers are concerned with *liability* issues in addition to such a climate being fostered in the workplace.

Sharing confidential information is another type of misconduct. Confidential information may include details such as individual salaries or compensation packages, as well as inside information about company finances, product development, or business strategies. Insider trading, in which people use confidential information to buy or sell stock ahead of the public release of company news, is an example of this type of misconduct.

What Are Some Examples of Misuse of Company Resources?

Companies make use of many different kinds of resources in order to conduct business. These resources include physical items, such as equipment and production supplies, as well as intangibles, such as intellectual property or the hours of service for which they pay their employees. Misuse of company resources is a broad category that encompasses a wide variety of misconduct, ranging from theft of office supplies to trading a company's proprietary information or trade secrets.

Stealing is one of the most obvious examples of misuse of resources. Theft can be relatively small scale, such as taking home a supply of pens or printer paper, or it may include theft of more valuable property, such as laptops or other electronics. While you are probably aware that the latter is theft, you might think your company would not notice the absence of a few office supplies. However, your employer may not share this view, especially if supplies routinely disappear, since the cost of small items can add up over time.

A less obvious type of theft involves the misuse of a company's nonmaterial resources. One of the most frequently cited examples of this kind of misconduct is the use of company time to conduct personal business. For instance, you might leave work for a doctor's appointment

Liability: *The responsibility that a company takes for damage or harm caused by its product.*

or meet a friend socially without reporting the time off or without arranging to make the time up later. The use of work time to make personal phone calls, send e-mails, or socialize with coworkers can also be considered misconduct. Your employer might allow you a limited amount of time for such activities or may make exceptions to certain rules in the event of an emergency. However, the line between acceptable behavior and misconduct may not always be clear, so you should make an effort to clarify your employer's expectations.

Employees sometimes make use of a company's equipment and technology for activities that are not work-related. For example, you may shop online on a workplace computer or use a printer or copy machine for personal documents. Many employers tolerate a modest amount of this type of behavior, but overusing company resources or engaging in forbidden activities, such as the use of a work computer to view pornography, could result in disciplinary action.

What Are the Consequences of Workplace Misconduct?

Most employers have a process in place to detect and deal with employee misconduct. Ethics policies usually offer some guidelines for behavior in the workplace, and they may also outline the procedures that you can follow to report misconduct by others without fear of reprisals. Systems of this kind can help an employer uncover ethics violations, especially those of supervisory employees, whose misconduct may have more significant consequences for the company than that committed by workers at lower levels.

Once misconduct is detected, most large companies have a standard method of disciplining employees who are found to have violated company rules. Ethics policies and employee handbooks often outline the application of penalties for various types of misconduct. Violations that break the law or leave an employer open to criminal or civil penalties are usually answered with the most severe discipline, which may include dismissal. Depending on the nature of the violation, an employer may also be required to report the misconduct to the authorities. Less serious cases of misconduct can sometimes be addressed with ethics training, a temporary suspension, or a demotion. The misconduct may also be noted in your personnel file, which can have an impact on your future career development.

Misconduct can have consequences for you as an individual as well as for the company as a whole. Other employees are unlikely to want to work in an environment where misconduct is allowed to occur unchecked and may decide to seek employment elsewhere. When misconduct is made public, it can affect a company's reputation and cause customers to turn to other competitors.

How Can My Behavior Outside the Workplace Affect My Employment?

With the advent of the Internet and the popularity of social media sites, your activities outside the workplace are more visible to your employer than ever before. While many job seekers are aware that unseemly photos or blog posts can cost them a job opportunity, some who are already employed may not be concerned about this. However, it is also possible that your online presence, if it conflicts with your employer's values, can cost you the job you have.

If you work in a field such as education, you may be held to especially high standards of conduct. A number of cases have been reported in the media where teachers have been suspended or fired as a result of inappropriate photos that surfaced on social media sites. While the legality of such actions is still being contested, you should be aware of your employer's stance on these issues. Some organizations include a morality clause in employee contracts that can allow an employer to take action against you, even when the alleged misconduct happened outside the workplace.

Reporting Misconduct

What Is Employee Misconduct?

Employee misconduct is any behavior that involves an employee violating a company's stated ethical values or official code of conduct. Ethics policies and codes of conduct define misconduct in a particular company. When you are initially hired, your new employer will usually provide an employee handbook, which often includes the company's ethics policy. You may be asked to sign a document agreeing to abide by the company's policies as a condition of employment.

The behavior that constitutes misconduct varies from company to company. Examples of misconduct may range from an individual employee who comes to work under the influence of drugs or alcohol to multiple members of an executive staff involved in fraudulent accounting practices. Some organizations have relatively few problems with misconduct, while in others misconduct becomes so widespread that it causes economic damages far beyond the company itself.

Who Engages in Misconduct?

Employees at all levels of a company can and sometimes do engage in misconduct. It is not always obvious whether or not a person is capable of doing something unethical. While there may not be a single type of employee who is likely to engage in misconduct, research does suggest that more than half of the misconduct that gets reported is committed by someone in a managerial position. There could be several reasons why this is the case. Managers often have less oversight than do rank-and-file workers and, therefore, may have more opportunity to misbehave. On the other hand, misconduct by managers might be more visible to the employees they supervise, particularly if those employees are asked to participate in acts that they know are against company policy. An employee concerned with doing the right thing might report managerial misconduct to protect his or her job.

In some cases, misconduct can be a result of misinformation. Employees who do not have a clear understanding of the organization's policies may be in greater danger of unintentionally making a bad decision. For this reason, many companies provide training on topics such as sexual harassment. The more knowledge employees have, the better equipped they may be to steer clear of misconduct.

Employers have a legal obligation to remedy sexual harassment in the workplace.
© PHOTOGRAPHEE.EU/ SHUTTERSTOCK.COM.

How Common Is Misconduct and How Frequently Is It Reported?

Because misconduct is often secret in nature, it is hard to get an accurate measure of how common it really is. In 2013, 41 percent of those who responded to an annual survey by the Ethics Resource Center reported witnessing misconduct on the job. According to this same report, 63 percent of employees who witnessed misconduct reported it.

Whether or not misconduct gets reported may depend in part on factors that are external to the company. The Ethics Resource Center survey traced a correlation between the state of the economy and the frequency of whistle-blowing, a term sometimes used to refer to the act of reporting misconduct. Data collected by the organization shows that, during difficult economic times such as a recession, the incidence of whistle-blowing increases. Whistle-blowing also increases following public scandals, such as the one associated with subprime mortgage lending schemes that contributed to the housing market collapse of 2008.

Why Is It Important to Report Misconduct?

A number of problems can occur in companies in which management allows misconduct to occur unchecked. Studies have shown that misconduct tends to be self-perpetuating. If the corporate culture is such that misconduct is widespread, employees confronted with an ethical dilemma may be more likely to make a poor choice. Conversely, when unethical behavior is recognized and dealt with appropriately, employees are more likely to make good choices. Studies also suggest that companies that support ethical behavior tend to have happier, more productive employees.

Misconduct Less Likely in Family-Owned Companies

Misconduct takes place across all U.S. industries, affecting large and small organizations. According to business scholars Shujun Ding and Zhenyu Wu, misconduct tends to occur less often in companies owned by families. In their 2014 article "Family Ownership and Corporate Misconduct in U.S. Small Firms," published in the *Journal of Business Ethics*, Ding and Wu explain why. They write that some family-owned or operated firms may care more about company reputation and what the authors call "moral capital" than companies without family interests. They suggest that caring about their reputation makes these companies less likely to create or condone a corporate culture in which misconduct take place.

Ding and Wu also suggest that, in companies where leadership roles are given to family members based on succession, less misconduct happens. Notably, the authors emphasize that their findings only apply to family companies that have been in business for a significant amount of time and who have older leaders-owners.

Bankruptcy: *The condition in which a business cannot meet its debt obligations and petitions a court either for reorganization of its debts or for liquidation of its assets.*

Employee misconduct can have effects that reach outside the company into the broader community and beyond. For example, in 2001 the energy and communications firm Enron was found to be using fraudulent accounting practices to hide corporate losses. When the company filed for ***bankruptcy***, thousands of workers lost their retirement savings, and stockholders took major losses. The damage caused by the collapse of Enron could perhaps have been avoided if one person aware of the fraud had reported early on to outside authorities that it was occurring.

What Should I Do If I See Misconduct?

When you witness a coworker engaged in misconduct, it can be tempting to discuss your observations with others in your workplace. While gossiping may feel good in the moment, it is generally a bad idea. Gossiping can make you appear unprofessional, even if the statements you make are true. Moreover, if they prove to be untrue, you may have damaged someone else's reputation as well as your own. Spreading misinformation about a coworker can lead to termination and potentially even to criminal prosecution.

Rather than discuss your suspicions with peers, you should find out who handles reports of misconduct in your organization. Turning matters over to the appropriate personnel will help ensure an impartial investigation for the accused. It will also allow you to protect yourself, regardless of the outcome of the investigation. If you feel that you need guidance from a more experienced coworker or supervisor, be sure to speak in general terms rather than naming names or providing specific details.

To Whom Should I Report Misconduct?

Most companies have an official system in place for dealing with wrong-doing by an employee. This information is usually published as part of the company's ethics policy. If this information is not readily available, you should ask someone who is knowledgeable about company policies but not directly involved in the situation. Be sure to keep the inquiry general.

In many organizations, especially large corporations, *human resources* (HR) personnel deal with complaints of misconduct. In smaller companies, your supervisor or even the company's owner may be the person you will need to contact. You should always make sure you have reached the right person before you begin to provide specific details.

Human resources:
The department in a company that is responsible for hiring and managing employees.

Will My Report Be Kept Confidential?

To encourage employees to speak up if they see wrongdoing, many companies have a system in place that allows workers to report what they have seen anonymously. Anonymity helps ensure that they will feel comfortable coming forward when they need to do so. It is common for large corporations to have a hotline established for this purpose. In many cases, such hotlines are available for use around the clock. Some firms may also have an internal website or a designated e-mail address where anonymous complaints can be made.

If you are reporting misconduct, you may want or need to address the matter in person with a supervisor or HR professional. In most cases what you say will be kept confidential. However, this may be difficult if it is well known within the company that you were in a unique position to have observed the misconduct. Many organizations have policies in place that can protect you from demotion or mistreatment following a report. These policies can be especially important if you have made a report against someone who has a higher position in the company hier-archy. If you fear for your safety for any reason, you should address these concerns with supervisory personnel and possibly with law enforcement.

Are There Times When I Should Report Misconduct Outside the Company?

Sometimes a company's internal resources may be insufficient to address employee misconduct. If you are witnessing misconduct that violates the law, especially if it endangers people or could cause serious economic harm beyond the company, you may need to report what you have witnessed to resources outside the organization. Reporting misconduct to an attorney, a government agency, or law enforcement officials may also be necessary if you feel unsafe making a report internally. This situation can arise in companies in which people in managerial positions are acting unethically. Some whistle-blowers have also reported misconduct to the news media as a means of exposing wrongdoing.

One of the most famous cases of public whistle-blowing involves misconduct by executives at the Brown & Williamson tobacco company. In 1996 Jeffrey Wigand, the company's former vice president of research and development, went public with allegations that officials at the company had deliberately misled the public about the addictive qualities of cigarettes and the fact that smoking causes lung cancer. Wigand was interviewed for the TV news magazine *60 Minutes* and acted as a witness in a civil suit against tobacco companies. Other famous whistle-blowers include Cynthia Cooper, who exposed misconduct at telecommunications giant WorldCom, and Sherron Watkins, who did the same at Enron.

What Happens after I Report Misconduct?

In many organizations, claims of misconduct are taken seriously and investigated immediately. Typically, once you make a report, HR or supervisory personnel will interview the person you have reported. If that person confesses to the misconduct, disciplinary action may be undertaken promptly. While you might be tempted to ask around to find out what has happened, it is best to avoid doing so. You should also avoid discussing the matter with the person you have accused unless you are officially asked to do so as part of a training or mediation process.

If the employee suspected does not immediately admit misconduct, your claim will be investigated. Investigations are usually conducted by a neutral party and might include interviews with other employees, a review of surveillance footage, or an examination of electronic and other communications. If you are asked to provide information, you should do so, but again, you should avoid gossiping to third parties about your participation in the investigation. You may be asked to sign an agreement that you will not discuss the matter with anyone else, and you may also be asked to sign a statement of the facts as you reported them. It is important to read such documents carefully before signing to make sure that they are accurate.

When the investigation concludes, the company may take action against the person you reported. Punishments may range from counseling and training to suspension or termination. Usually, you will not be given details of the nature of the punishment, but you may be informed that action was taken. Follow-up interviews may be conducted at regular intervals to make sure that the misconduct has ceased.

For More Information

BOOKS

De George, Richard T. *Business Ethics*. Upper Saddle River, NJ: Prentice Hall, 2010.

Martin, Jeanette S., and Lillian H. Chaney. *Global Business Etiquette: A Guide to International Communication and Customs*. Westport, CT: Praeger, 2006.

PERIODICALS

Ding, Shujun, and Zhenyu Wu. "Family Ownership and Corporate Misconduct in U.S. Small Firms." *Journal of Business Ethics* 123, no. 2 (2014).

Kerns, Charles D. "Creating and Sustaining an Ethical Workplace Culture." *Graziadio Business Review* 6, no. 3 (2003). This article can also be found online at http://gbr.pepperdine.edu/2010/08/creating-and-sustaining-an-ethical-workplace-culture/.

WEBSITES

"Blowing the Whistle on Workplace Misconduct." *Ethics Resource Center*. December 2010. http://www.ethics.org/files/u5/WhistleblowerWP.pdf (accessed January 5, 2015).

"Defense Industry Initiative on Business Ethics and Conduct." *Berkley Center for Religion, Peace and World Affairs*. http://berkleycenter.georgetown.edu/organizations/defense-industry-initiative-on-business-ethics-and-conduct (accessed December 4, 2014).

Graves, Jada A. "Your Guide to Surviving a Career Mistake." *U.S. News & World Report*. July 3, 2014. http://money.usnews.com/money/careers/articles/2014/07/03/your-guide-to-surviving-a-career-mistake (accessed December 4, 2014).

"The History of Business Ethics Training." *The Network*. https://www.tnwinc.com/tag/business-ethics-training/ (accessed December 4, 2014).

"How Do I Deal with an Employee's Misconduct?" *United States Department of Agriculture: Farm Service Agency*. April 28, 2011. http://www.fsa.usda.gov/FSA/hrdapp?area=home&subject=mgrs&topic=dem (accessed December 16, 2014).

Imani, Faizah. "What Is Misconduct in the Workplace?" *Houston Chronicle*. http://smallbusiness.chron.com/misconduct-workplace-16111.html (accessed December 16, 2014).

Keller, Helen. "Corporate Codes of Conduct and Their Implementation: The Question of Legitimacy." *Yale University*. http://www.yale.edu/macmillan/Heken_Keller_Paper.pdf (accessed December 4, 2014).

Lunday, Jason. "The Need for More Effective Standards of Conduct." *Corporate Compliance Insights*. http://www.corporatecomplianceinsights.com/the-need-for-more-effective-standards-of-conduct/ (accessed December 4, 2014).

Lype, Bob E. "Employee Misconduct and Workplace Torts."*Bob E. Lype and Associates, Attorneys at Law*. May 8, 2003. http://www.lypelaw.com/employee-misconduct-and-workplace-torts.html (accessed December 16, 2014).

McGregor, Jena. "Ethical Misconduct, by the Numbers." *Washington Post*. February 4, 2014. http://www.washingtonpost.com/blogs/on-leadership/wp/2014/02/04/ethical-misconduct-by-the-numbers/ (accessed January 5, 2015).

"National Business Ethics Survey." 2013. *Ethics Resource Center*. http://www.ethics.org/nbes/ (accessed December 4, 2014).

Silverstein, Ken. "Enron, Ethics, and Today's Corporate Values." *Forbes*. May 14, 2013. http://www.forbes.com/sites/kensilverstein/2013/05/14/enron-ethics-and-todays-corporate-values/ (accessed December 4, 2014).

"Stop Violence against Women: Sexual Harassment." *University of Minnesota*. http://www1.umn.edu/humanrts/svaw/harassment/explore/5prevention.htm (accessed December 4, 2014).

Warner, Russ. "How Do You Deal with an Unethical, Productive Employee?" *Huffington Post*. September 2, 2014. http://www.huffingtonpost.com/russ-warner/how-do-you-deal-with-an-u_b_5741770.html (accessed December 4, 2014).

"Where to Report Misconduct in…" *United States Office of Government Ethics*. http://www.oge.gov/About/Mission-and-Responsibilities/Where-to-Report-Misconduct-in---/ (accessed January 5, 2015).

Workplace Etiquette and Conduct

In This Section

- ■ Making First Impressions
- ■ Proper Meeting Etiquette
- ■ Professional Attire and Workspace Appearance
- ■ Basics of International Business Etiquette
- ■ For More Information

Why Are First Impressions Important?

Whether you are in a job interview, being introduced to your new boss, or meeting a potential client, first impressions are important. Studies suggest that the first ideas we get about someone's trustworthiness, intelligence, competence, and status are lasting, even if we later learn conflicting information about that person. Moreover, first impressions are made within the first 10 seconds of meeting, so it is important to be aware of the way you present yourself to others.

When making a first impression, what you say is important, but nonverbal cues tend to have even more of an impact. Knowing what others will notice about you and use to form an opinion of you can help you maximize the positive when conducting business or *networking*. Knowing something about the importance of first impressions can also help you be more conscious of the way you assess others. This awareness is important because powerful, first impressions may not always be accurate.

It is also important to note that, in the digital age, first impressions may be made online, before any actual face-to-face meeting. To ensure that

Networking:
The cultivation of productive relationships for employment or business.

These young professionals are waiting to interview for a job; they each understand that first impressions can be heavily influenced by what they wear. © SEAN DE BURCA/ SHUTTERSTOCK.COM.

your online presence enhances rather than detracts from your in-person first impression, be sure to manage your online presence by keeping work-related sites or social media profiles professional and up-to-date and personal information and photos private.

How Can I Use Body Language to Make a Positive Impression?

Body language and physical appearance both play a significant role in first impressions. Learning about how people read your expressions, gestures, and posture, as well as your attire and grooming, can help you make a good impression. Understanding these basics can help you avoid mistakes that put people off and damage your chances of getting new business or establishing important professional relationships.

The term *body language* refers to the nonverbal cues that you send others about your personality and your interest in engaging in conversation. Body language may include your facial expressions, gestures, posture, and the amount of eye contact you make with others. According to some experts, body language typically accounts for approximately 50 to 70 percent of all communication. People observe and assess others' body language quickly and usually instinctively.

When you smile and make direct eye contact with someone, you signal that you are friendly and open to social interaction. To remind

Malcolm Gladwell on First Impressions

Malcolm Gladwell, a popular writer on topics of social psychology and current events, tackled the psychology of first impressions in *Blink: The Power of Thinking without Thinking* (2005). In the book, Gladwell debunks the idea that first impressions are just emotional or intuitive responses. Rather, he proves that first impressions are actually a product of quick and often unconscious thinking. In a question-and-answer forum on his website, Gladwell writes that first impressions are "perfectly rational." He continues, "It's thinking—it's just thinking that moves a little faster and operates a little more mysteriously than the kind of deliberate, conscious decision-making that we usually associate with 'thinking.'"

Gladwell argues that first impressions, or what he calls "rapid cognition," can often be more accurate and informative than deliberate thinking over a long period of time. He also points out, however, that not all first impressions will be useful, as some rapid cognition is based on stereotypes about race, gender, body types, and other physical traits.

yourself to make eye contact during introductions, some experts suggest that you make a habit of noting the eye color of everyone you meet. It is important to avoid too much eye contact, however. Excessive eye contact can appear aggressive, especially when the eye contact occurs outside of a conversation. Likewise, excessive smiling can appear forced or insincere and might be especially out of place in a business setting.

Your posture conveys information about your self-confidence and mood. It's another thing that people notice and take into account when they form a first impression. When you stand and sit with an erect spine and squared shoulders, you appear focused and capable. These are traits, of course, you want to project when interviewing for a job or trying to make a sale. Slumping or slouching, on the other hand, may suggest boredom or a lack of confidence. You should avoid crossing your arms or legs while engaged in a conversation, as that can indicate defensiveness. Facing the person you are speaking with and keeping your body open conveys that you feel good about yourself and the interaction. It's acceptable to lean forward a little to indicate attentiveness, but don't get too close. In general, people in professional settings stay at least two feet apart.

Some people naturally gesticulate (make gestures when speaking) more than others. Career experts have noted that while gesturing is fine, in professional settings you should curb any tendencies to be too dramatic. A good habit is to keep your hands close to your midsection and especially avoid putting them at or above your shoulders. Meetings and job interviews can be nerve-racking, but try to keep your body calm and avoid using nervous gestures.

In the United States, a handshake is usually customary when you meet someone for the first time. You should aim for a firm grip but avoid clasping hands too tightly or squeezing. Hugging or cheek kissing, which may be a common way to greet people in social situations, is not appropriate in a professional environment. Failing to make this distinction can make you seem unprofessional.

What Are Some Tips for Dressing to Make a Good First Impression?

Your clothing and accessories, as well as your grooming, will affect the judgments people make when meeting you for the first time. The rules for how to dress professionally vary depending on the job and the industry. However, there are a few basic guidelines you can follow to make sure your appearance is sending the right message about you.

First, you should make sure that your clothes are clean and free of wrinkles. Replace missing buttons, trim any stray threads, and be sure to eliminate items from your professional wardrobe as they become noticeably worn. Shoes should be clean and free of scuffs, as should handbags and laptop cases. While most of these guidelines are easy to follow, good taste, which is also important, is much more difficult to define. If you are unsure about the appropriateness or style of your professional wardrobe, experts suggest that you borrow the eye of a trusted friend. You can benefit from letting someone else take a look at your clothing, jewelry, and other accessories to make sure they are appropriate.

Good grooming will help you make a good first impression. As with attire, standards may vary from industry to industry, but there are a few basic rules you should always keep in mind. Clean hair, teeth, and fingernails are all important. In addition, in most professional situations, you should keep hair neatly trimmed and conservatively styled. Very long hair and split ends may give you a disheveled appearance, which can undermine your professional image, even if your work and qualifications are otherwise stellar.

How Can I Use Social Media to Help Create a Great First Impression?

Before meeting you in person, many employers and others you do business with will evaluate your online presence, including social media sites, both professional and personal. For this reason, it is vital to be aware of what type of information is available online and to manage your online presence so that it doesn't work against you.

When posting on social media sites such as Facebook (http://www.facebook.com), it is important to be aware of privacy settings and to make sure that any images or information you want to keep private, stay private. Always check to see who can view what you post, and make use of privacy controls to prevent members of the general public (including potential business contacts) from viewing private posts. Many people choose to keep information about personal politics and religious views private. These topics, among others, can alter the way others perceive you. Some experts recommend registering your personal accounts in a way that they are not easily viewed by people searching for your name. For example, you can use a first and middle initial with your last name rather than using the more traditional first and last name.

For profiles or websites that you create to represent yourself professionally, visual appearance is key. If you include a picture of yourself, be sure you are well dressed and well groomed in the photo. You should avoid selfies or group shots, which can look unprofessional and, in the latter case, confusing. If you have a cover photo or professional logo, be sure that it is visually appealing and well placed on your page. For full websites, consider hiring someone with knowledge of web design to make sure your site looks professional and is easy to use.

While the visual appearance of your site is important, the content will also influence the first impression you create. When deciding what to include, some strategists suggest that you think about your professional goals, as well as the particular skills and experience you want to promote. Work to create content that reflects these goals, skills, and experiences. Keep the site simple and clear, and avoid information that is out of step with your overall vision. If you do include personal information, such as a biography, make sure you highlight experiences that match your professional goals and avoid those that are unrelated. For instance, describing extensive international travel might be important for someone seeking to do global marketing. It may be less helpful if you want to emphasize deep knowledge of one particular city's market. On a final note, make sure that the spelling and grammar are correct and that the copy on your profile or site is error free.

What Else Will Help Me Make a Good First Impression?

If you are meeting with a prospective employer or client at his or her place of business, you should be aware that staff in the reception area may be asked about their first impressions of you. You should err on the side of caution and assume you are being observed from the moment you arrive. If you are seated in a reception area, experts suggest that you keep your profile to the desk so that you will not need to worry about making too much or too little eye contact with the person working the reception desk. Keep anything you have brought with you at hand to avoid scrambling to gather everything when it is time for your meeting.

Résumé: *A document providing a detailed description of a person's previous work experience, educational background, and relevant job skills.*

Preparation before your meeting or interview is key to making a good first impression. Before a job interview, for instance, you should take time to research your prospective employer's company history. You should also be knowledgeable about the company's current projects and about the specifics of the job for which you are interviewing. It is important to be prepared to discuss the specifics of your *résumé*. Similarly, if you are meeting with a potential new client and plan to make a sales presentation, you should make sure you have thorough knowledge of the product or service you are offering and be able to address any questions that may arise. In most cases, solid preparation will increase your confidence, which is essential for those looking to acquire new accounts.

Another good strategy to make sure your first meeting is successful is to know beforehand who will be attending. Once you have the names of participants, you can do a little background research. LinkedIn (http://www.linkedin.com), a professional networking site, is a good resource to use for this information.

Proper Meeting Etiquette

Why Is Proper Meeting Etiquette Important?

Participation in workplace and business meetings is generally an important part of a person's work life. These meetings often happen face-to-face, but they may also be conducted via phone or video conferencing. Work-related meetings can involve just one other person or many people. You may meet with coworkers, your supervisor, or people you supervise. Other meetings might include people from outside your workplace, such as customers, potential customers, or people from another company or agency. Since your behavior and contribution to a meeting can make a long-lasting impression, your participation in workplace meetings could potentially be a key element in advancing your career.

Meetings are more pleasant and productive when all participants show common courtesy and respect. If you are attending a meeting, you are generally expected to arrive on time and stay until the meeting is over. During the meeting, you should pay attention to the proceedings and avoid interrupting others, and you should always take care to mute your cell phone. However, there is more to workplace and business meeting etiquette than these common courtesies. The rules of meeting etiquette are designed to facilitate clear, respectful communication, which is key to all meetings. These rules help meetings run in a smooth and organized manner, which allows the participants to have a sense of accomplishment and feel that their time was put to good use.

Why Do I Have to Participate in Meetings at Work?

If you have been invited to attend a meeting at work, it is likely that your participation in the meeting is expected and needed. Supervisors or coworkers may share important information at the meeting, or you

Following proper meeting etiquette shows respect for meeting participants and can encourage cooperation.
© RAWPIXEL/SHUTTERSTOCK.COM.

may have information and ideas that your coworkers would like you to share. Workplace meetings can have a variety of purposes, including information gathering, training, decision making, evaluation, planning, and brainstorming. It is important to know the purpose of a meeting in order to determine the proper rules of etiquette to follow.

What Are Some Expectations of Good Meeting Etiquette?

You should always come to a meeting prepared with an understanding of the meeting's purpose, which you can learn from its agenda. The agenda is a list of items that will be discussed at the meeting, and you may receive it a few days in advance. If you do, you should read it carefully. If you have questions about the agenda, you should contact the person or group in charge of the meeting as soon as possible. The agenda may also be handed out or posted at the beginning of the meeting, or participants may be asked to help develop one. If you have suggestions for topics to discuss, you should make them at this time.

You should come to a workplace meeting prepared to take notes with paper and pen. If you would prefer to take notes with an electronic device such as a laptop, tablet, or phone, you should inquire beforehand whether the use of such devices will be considered appropriate.

Case Study: Charlie Recovers from Behaving Poorly at a Meeting

Charlie is the general manager of a chain of grocery stores. Each Monday morning he has a standing meeting with the managers of each store. Charlie is in charge of leading the meetings and determining the agenda. Usually the meetings are productive, and Charlie has a chance to check in with each manager, discuss current issues or obstacles, and talk about how to achieve goals. But, at the last meeting, Charlie messed up. He had slept fitfully the night before and felt like he was coming down with a cold. To make matters worse, right before the meeting, he received a call from his wife letting him know that the family car had broken down. Due to all of this, he forgot to send out an agenda to his team beforehand and arrived to the meeting 10 minutes late. Once there, the managers noticed that he wasn't paying much attention. He seemed far more absorbed in drinking coffee and eating a bagel than listening. During the meeting he answered his phone twice and even sent out text messages while people were talking.

Back at his office after the meeting, Charlie reflected on his actions. He realized that he had acted poorly at the meeting and that his behavior strongly suggested that he was uninterested in the perspectives of the other managers. Instead of berating himself for his behavior, Charlie admitted that he was tired, under the weather, and stressed out. He acknowledged that, although these were not excuses for his behavior, they did explain why he acted the way he did.

In response, Charlie sent a brief e-mail to his team in which he apologized frankly for his behavior and reiterated how much he appreciated their presence and hard work. He vowed to himself that in future meetings he would act in a more professional way and not let his personal problems affect his work performance.

It is important that you bring all materials that you will need for participating in the meeting, particularly if you will be making a presentation.

You should do your part to make sure that the meeting begins and ends on schedule by arriving on time. If you have been invited to a meeting but cannot attend, you should let the appropriate contact know as soon as possible so that the other participants know that they will not need to wait for you. If the meeting will be held in a place that is unfamiliar to you, plan ahead to allow yourself time to locate the building and find parking. However, you should not arrive at the meeting site more than five minutes before the meeting is scheduled to start. If you arrive too early, you may interrupt others who are using the space for an earlier meeting, or you might hinder those who are preparing for the meeting in advance. You should also do your best to avoid being late so that you will have time to settle into your seat and get out paper or a device to take notes. You will generally be expected to stay until the meeting is over. If leaving early is unavoidable, you should make sure that you leave with as little disruption as possible.

Everyone in the room should know the name and title or position of everyone else at the meeting, and this sometimes requires introductions. When introducing yourself, brevity is always best. Exchanging business cards is often appropriate in meetings where the participants are meeting for the first time. If you receive a business card at a meeting, it might be a good idea to put it on the table in front of you so that you can remember the giver's name.

While a person's job position may dictate his or her role at a meeting, the participants may also have assigned roles. The chair or facilitator will be expected to keep the meeting focused on the agenda. One person will usually be designated to take notes, and this person will keep track of all decisions that are made and report them after the meeting. Other participants will be expected to listen actively, ask questions, and contribute their own ideas.

A good workplace meeting will have clear rules established from the beginning. You should use these rules to conduct yourself properly during the meeting. Rules generally dictate that one person should speak at a time and that there should be no conversations that take place aside from the main discussion. Everyone should have a chance to speak, and those who are speaking should respect time limits so that the meeting can finish on time. It is also important to assume positive intent on the part of the other participants. If rules are not stated or developed early in the meeting, you should try to determine the unwritten speaking rules. Is this a meeting where you need to raise your hand to speak? Is it okay to interrupt to ask questions, or should all the questions be held until a specific point in the meeting?

There are several details of workplace etiquette that you should observe during a meeting. You should sit up straight and be careful not to fidget, rustle papers, or tap your feet. Try to turn your face toward whoever is speaking and listen attentively. If you can't hear the speaker, you should find a respectful way to let him or her know, and when you are speaking, make sure that everyone can hear you. It is often acceptable to have coffee or another beverage at a meeting, but avoid eating unless food had been provided for everyone. You should keep your phone in your pocket, bag, or purse with the sound off. Answering your phone or texting during a meeting is not polite or professional. If you need to use the phone, you should excuse yourself.

At the end of the meeting, you should thank the facilitator. When you leave, be sure to clean up after yourself. Remove all food and beverage containers, and remember to check the table, your seat, and under the table to make sure that you pick up any items that need to be discarded. You should also take away everything that you brought with you, including papers and pens. If you have met someone with whom you would like to follow up later, it is good etiquette to send that person a note as soon as possible after the meeting.

What Is the Proper Etiquette for Planning or Facilitating a Meeting?

When you have called a meeting, you are responsible for making sure that there is a clear agenda and that the meeting's goals can be accomplished within the allotted time frame. You should send out the agenda at least a few days before the meeting and be willing to answer questions about it. You may also distribute or post an agenda as the meeting starts. If you need the meeting participants to develop the agenda, you should lead the development process at the beginning of the meeting.

As the facilitator, you should make sure that all participants at the meeting know what is expected of them. Everyone should know who the official note or minute taker is, who will be presenting, and when other participants will have the opportunity to comment and ask questions. If you are not sure whether the participants have met before, you should organize brief introductions. Establishing the rules for the meeting at the beginning will enable everyone to participate in respectful and useful ways.

Are There Different Etiquette Rules for Video or Phone Meetings?

Whether you are in the same room as other meeting participants or meeting via phone or video, you should always make an effort to communicate in a considerate manner. All of the rules for face-to-face meetings apply to video and phone meetings. In addition, you should introduce yourself each time you talk, and it may be helpful for you to keep notes so that you can address the other participants by name.

Sound is another important consideration when you are participating from a remote location. You should turn off any devices that might make sounds that could interfere with communication, and you should also avoid loud keyboard typing. Be very careful to speak with a natural tone and voice level, and try to keep from interrupting others.

What Are Examples of Meeting Behaviors That Should Be Avoided?

People sometimes have low expectations of business meetings, and low expectations can lead to inappropriate behavior. You should do your best to avoid becoming distracted, since this may offend or distract other participants. Doing other work at a meeting is disrespectful to the others who are present since it will convey to them that you consider the meeting to be unimportant. Unless you are using an electronic device for note taking or other meeting-related purposes, it should be put away. Other people will know if you are checking Facebook or playing a game. You should also avoid texting or taking phone calls during a meeting.

While it is important that you participate in a meeting, you should be careful to not talk too much or respond too frequently to the speaker. Sometimes you may need to voice an opinion or a point of view that is different from those of others, but you should avoid doing so in a confrontational or argumentative manner so that you do not embarrass or anger other people.

Body language: *The gestures, movements, and mannerisms by which a person communicates with others including facial expressions, tone of voice, and posture.*

Be attentive to what your *body language* is saying and do not slump or stare at the clock if you are bored. You should also avoid engaging in side conversations, since that conveys that you are not interested in what the speaker is saying. If there is a break in the meeting, you should not stay away longer than the designated time, and if you must leave before a meeting is over, let the facilitator know before the meeting starts.

Professional Attire and Workspace Appearance

How Can My Image Affect My Success in the Workplace?

Most career experts agree that the image you project in the workplace can be very important to achieving career success. Prospective employers as well as current supervisors, coworkers, and customers will all make note of external appearances when judging you and your work. Working on your professional image can help you land and keep a job, as well as help you move up in the company hierarchy.

While many things affect your image, two of the most important are your attire and the appearance of your workspace. Specific expectations in these areas can vary considerably from company to company and even within a company from job to job. However, there are several things that will tend to make a good impression across the board. In terms of attire, matching your clothing and accessories to workplace culture, as well as to the specific demands of your job, is key. In addition, a clean and neat appearance is part of the foundation of a professional image, which is true for both your personal appearance and your workspace.

How Can I Project a Professional Image at Work?

Career experts note that your appearance is an important part of first impressions, so prior to a first interview you should research the company and position so that you can dress appropriately. Hiring managers often assume that people who look the part can do the job. Coupled with the right skills and qualifications, the right image can help you get hired. In addition, dressing appropriately for a job interview demonstrates that you have researched the position and correctly interpreted employer expectations, abilities that are important for job seekers to possess.

In an office environment, how you dress and keep your workspace can influence how others perceive you. © AVAVA/ SHUTTERSTOCK.COM.

As a new hire, you should take some time to familiarize yourself with the organization's rules and corporate culture. Many companies have a formal dress code that is detailed in an employee handbook. It is important to note that guidelines may vary depending on where you work in the organization. A person in sales who routinely meets with clients will have a different wardrobe than someone who makes service calls to repair technical equipment, for example.

Formal rules do not tell the whole story, however, and it is equally important to determine how the dress code is put into practice by employees throughout the organization. Both a large corporate bank and a midsize tech start-up may have a business casual Friday, for instance, but the former's version might still be conservative, with clothing and accessories, while quirkiness may be tolerated, and even encouraged, at the latter. Getting to know your own workplace will help you navigate these differences and dress accordingly.

What Are Some General Tips for Dressing Professionally?

Whatever style of dress is the rule at your workplace, making sure your clothes are clean, wrinkle-free, and well maintained is fundamental to looking professional. All of your clothing should be free of visible stains, and suits, dress shirts, pants, and skirts should be ironed or professionally dry cleaned. Also, if you are a pet owner, you should make sure to eliminate any pet hair clinging to your clothing before entering the office. You should also be sure to check for loose threads or missing buttons and make repairs as needed.

In terms of specific clothing, the first step is to find out what is appropriate in your particular situation. There are some good rules to consider, however. For executive and managerial positions, a classic suit is often appropriate, especially in conservative industries such as banking. For many other professionals, a slightly less formal approach will be fine on most days. Experts often advise investing in a few classic, well-made pieces that will form the basis of your work wardrobe and can

Five Questions to Ask Yourself When Choosing a Business Casual Outfit

1. Would I wear this to meet my boy/girl friend's mother for the first time?
   - If you answer YES, it's most likely business casual.
2. Would I wear this clubbing?
   - If you answer YES, go change; if you answer NO, you're safe.
3. Would I wear this to sleep?
   - If you answer YES, pick something else; if you answer NO, you're OK.
4. Would I wear this to do yard work?
   - If you answer YES, find a new outfit; if you answer NO, you're acceptable.
5. Would I wear this to a costume party?
   - If you answer YES, back to the closet; if you answer NO, you're fine.

When in doubt, it is a good idea to err on the side of caution and overdress.

SOURCE: Layton, Julia. "What Does Business Casual Mean for Women?" http://lifestyle .howstuffworks.com/style/fashion/office-wardrobe/business-casual-for-women2.htm.

ILLUSTRATION BY LUMINA DATAMATICS LTD. © 2015 CENGAGE LEARNING.

be mixed and matched with more trendy separates for the sake of variety. For example, women may want to buy a good suit with both pants and a skirt. When you have an important meeting with a client, you may choose to wear the full suit, while on other days you may elect to wear the pants with a nice sweater or wear the skirt with a tailored blouse.

Business casual outfits may be the norm in more informal work environments and sometimes for positions that are lower in the company hierarchy. In most companies, business casual for men means wearing a collared shirt with nice pants. Women usually have more options, including sweaters, blouses, skirts, and pants. T-shirts and jeans should generally be avoided in business casual environments, although there may be exceptions to this rule.

In jobs that require manual labor, such as construction, durable jeans, work pants, t-shirts, and sweatshirts will make the most sense. In fact, overdressing for your job can be as much of a mistake as under-dressing, as it indicates that you do not understand the job's require-ments. While getting clothing dirty may be unavoidable in some trades, you should still strive to appear neat and clean wherever possible, espe-cially if you have contact with customers.

In many service professions workers are required to wear a uniform. All or part of the uniform may be provided by the company, or you may be expected to provide part or all of the uniform in a color or style specified by the company. For example, some restaurants provide aprons to members of their wait staff and ask employees to wear the apron with a white shirt and dark pants. As with any job, you should make sure that your uniform is clean and well maintained and that the pieces you provide conform to the specifications you have been given.

It is important to make sure that your clothing fits well. Clothing that is too tight or too loose detracts from a professional appearance and should be avoided. Women should also stay away from very low necklines and high hemlines. Men should generally avoid leaving more than a couple buttons open on a shirt collar.

How Can I Accessorize to Look Professional?

Accessories can put the finishing touches on any outfit. They can also detract from your look if not well chosen and maintained. As with clothing, it is always a good idea to consult your employee handbook regarding accessories, as well as taking cues from your coworkers and especially your supervisor.

Both men and women should keep shoes clean and free of scuff marks. Also, you should make sure that your shoes match in style with your clothing. Casual styles work best in a more laid-back office, while more formal business attire requires dressier shoes for both men and women. Many women like to wear heels, which can complement both formal and informal business attire. You should generally avoid very high heels, however, as well as open-toed shoes. Experts suggest that you avoid high heels over 3 inches tall in most professions. Furthermore, if you are dressing for a job interview, you should avoid wearing shoes that are not properly broken in, as they can make you appear uncomfortable and may make walking difficult.

Bags and briefcases can also help you project a professional appearance. Leather bags and briefcases in neutral colors can work well for more formal business attire. As with shoes, it is important to keep bags clean and scuff-free. In more casual work environments, cloth and canvas bags can be an attractive, washable alternative to leather. However, you should avoid bags with overly loud designs or inappropriate pictures and slogans. Bags and shoes do not need to match in color but should be similar in style.

Both men and women should keep jewelry simple. Men are often advised to stick to a watch, cuff links when required, and a wedding ring if they wear one. Women are typically given a bit more latitude and can wear necklaces, earrings, bracelets, and rings. There are numerous styles you can choose from, but they should match your clothing style and workplace vibe. Less is often more when it comes to accessories. Also, wearing jewelry can be a safety hazard in some positions, especially in manufacturing. Common sense should rule in such situations.

How Can I Look Professional on a Budget?

Dressing for work can be expensive. Particularly when you are just starting out in your career, it may be hard to afford to buy enough quality items to look good five days a week. One solution to this problem is to find some quality consignment shops or second-hand stores. With persistence, you can find well-made, stylish items that are gently used, at a fraction of their original cost. Outlet stores can also be a good option, although it is important to check clothing carefully before purchasing. Some factory outlets sell clothes that are of lower quality than their full-price counterparts.

To maximize your options, you can also mix in some less expensive, trendy items with a few classic pieces. For example, an inexpensive, patterned shirt paired with a nice suit can look polished and appropriate. It is a good idea to keep the colors and style of your current wardrobe in mind when making new purchases.

What Should I Do to Keep My Workspace Looking Professional?

Most people realize they will be judged based on personal appearance, but you may not have thought about how the appearance of your workspace may affect your professional image. As with attire, expectations regarding workspace appearance vary from company to company and position to position and may depend partly on whether you have an office or a small cubicle to yourself or if you share common space with other employees. Regardless of these differences, there are a number of things you can do to make sure that your workspace reflects your professionalism.

First, it is always a good idea to make sure your area is neat and clean. You may not be responsible for cleaning the floor or emptying the trash, but you should refrain from leaving food wrappers, old mail, or other items in your space that add clutter. Keeping things well ordered not only makes it easier to find what you need but also communicates that you are organized, which is a trait prized by most employers. Keeping your space neat and clean is especially important if it is shared with others.

Most people spend many waking hours at work and enjoy personalizing their workspace with photos, knick-knacks, and other items. While it is generally acceptable to add a few personal touches in this manner, you should always decorate your workspace with restraint. When choosing items for your workspace, some experts suggest neutral items such as plants and calendars. Both add color to your area without adding controversy.

Some companies may have specific rules about what is and is not acceptable. For instance, many employers prohibit religious items in the workplace, particularly if they are visible to clients. You can find this type of information in an employee handbook or check with a supervisor. Generally speaking, you should avoid displaying items that may be offensive to others, including material that is sexual in nature. You should also avoid things that are overly cute, as they can detract from your image as a mature, competent professional.

Basics of International Business Etiquette

Why Is It Important to Learn Proper Business Etiquette for Companies Outside the United States?

Knowledge of international business etiquette is key to good communication with coworkers, clients, and other associates. Those who know the rules governing social interactions in the workplace are in a better position to build the relationships that make business operations run smoothly. They also project a more professional image, which is helpful in daily interactions with others and in building a career.

As U.S. companies expand their global reach, more employees will need to interact with workers from other *cultures*. When visiting job sites, clients, or business partners in other countries, you will need to know how to behave professionally in a sometimes radically different cultural context. Stateside, you might find yourself in videoconferences or on phone calls with people from other cultures. Although much knowledge about international business etiquette may not be needed in the latter situations, it is still important to have a good concept of the basics in order to facilitate communication and to avoid making an embarrassing, or potentially offensive, social blunder.

Culture: *The set of shared attitudes, values, goals, and practices that characterizes an institution, organization, or group.*

What Are the Basics of Business Etiquette When Visiting Other Countries?

Standards for business etiquette vary from country to country. Although it may be difficult to grasp all of the nuances of social situations in a culture different from your own, there are some good rules that can help you navigate them. These guidelines include educating yourself about the country and its customs, following your host's lead, and, when in doubt, erring on the conservative side in terms of dress and behavior.

Customary greetings in Japanese business are either a bow (as shown in this photo) or a handshake. © RAWPIXEL/ SHUTTERSTOCK.COM.

If you are traveling to a different country for business, it is important to educate yourself about your destination before you arrive. Knowing the basics of a country's geography, as well as some information about the country's culture, will help you avoid appearing unprepared or rude. You should have a general sense of where the country is located, which countries border it, and where the city you are visiting is in relation to other cities. It's also a good idea to research the basic rules of etiquette followed in the country, including how to greet people and whether or not it is customary to bring gifts to your hosts when visiting on business. Familiarize yourself with what constitutes good table manners in your host country, as business often is conducted over meals, and expectations may be different than those you are used to in the United States.

Even with some amount of background, it may be hard to anticipate the nuances of all social interaction in a foreign culture, which is why it is a good idea to observe your hosts and follow their lead. For instance, in some cultures, a business lunch will be an extended affair with a long period of socializing before any actual business is discussed. In such cultures, launching into negotiations or other "shop talk" too early can appear rude and may create tension that will be counterproductive when you do get down to business. Exercising patience and waiting for your host to turn the conversation to business will help keep things on course.

Although it is good to follow the cues of your hosts, there may be times when you are still unsure exactly how best to present yourself. In such cases, it is always best to err on the conservative side in your attire and grooming, as well as in your social interactions. For instance, if you are not sure whether to address your counterpart in an overseas office by his or her first name, you should avoid doing so. Being too formal is less likely to be frowned upon than is being too casual, which can be interpreted as disrespectful. In conversation, introduce topics that require elaboration by asking open-ended questions. Doing so will keep the conversation flowing and will give you an opportunity to learn from your host's speech and behavior.

What Are Some Specific Etiquette Tips for Japan?

According to experts, Japanese business culture, like the broader culture itself, tends to be conservative and group oriented. Therefore, it is best to approach meetings in Japan with patience and reserve. Observe *hierarchies* and be especially respectful to older team members, who also tend to be the most senior. Respect the cultural emphasis on privacy by avoiding small talk of an overly personal nature.

Hierarchy: *The levels of management within a business organization, from the lowest to the highest.*

In Japan, business cards are very important, and the exchange of cards should reflect this emphasis. When receiving or offering a card, always use both hands, and never slide the card across a table. When possible, offer your card to the most senior person present. If the card is printed in both English and Japanese, the Japanese side should be facing up. You should always refrain from writing on any cards you are given and from shoving cards into your wallet, as both are considered rude. Cards should be put into a card case at the end of your meeting.

What Are Some Tips for Doing Business in China?

As China has joined the global marketplace in the last decades, business travel to the country has become increasingly common. Chinese professionals may be less Americanized than their counterparts in other countries, such as Japan which has a lengthier history of business dealings with the United States. Still, the rules of patience and regard for senior team members apply. In addition, experts note that forming a strong relationship with one key contact in the company may be very important when doing business in China.

If you are conducting business over dinner, there are several things you should know. For instance, in many restaurants service is almost continuous, and you do not need to pause to wait for it to finish if you are in the middle of discussions. Also, barring allergy or dietary restriction, it is generally considered good manners to try a small amount of everything served, even if it is unfamiliar. Avoid eating everything on your plate, however, as doing so may be taken as a signal that your host did not provide enough to eat.

What Are Some Tips for Doing Business in India?

Many Indians speak English, and business meetings in large cities will typically be conducted in English. However, there are a few important cultural differences to be aware of when Americans travel to India. Although Indian men will often shake hands with both men and women, Indian women typically do not shake hands with Western men. Observe your hosts for cues as to how to navigate introductions.

One thing that often confuses American business travelers is that, in India, it is common to eat with your hands rather than using flatware. You should eat with your right hand and should not touch serving spoons or other community items with that hand. You should also not use your left hand to eat, as this is considered rude, even if you are left-handed. If you are uncomfortable eating with your hand, many upscale restaurants will provide a spoon if requested, but following local custom signifies your respect for Indian culture.

What Should I Know about Hosting Travelers from Other Countries?

Before you host international business travelers, you should learn about the travelers' country and culture of origin. Although many international business travelers speak English, it is best to ask ahead of time if anyone in the traveling group would prefer to have a translator available. Also, if you will be reviewing written material during meetings, it is courteous to have them available in both English and in the native language of your guests. Some countries, such as China, may have multiple dialects, so make sure to identify the dialects of those present beforehand.

If you will be taking your guests out to eat, be aware of any dietary prohibitions that might apply. Choosing a restaurant with a wide selection of options is always a good bet. Even if you are unaware of any specific cultural issues regarding food, a broad menu can accommodate a variety of tastes and diets.

What Are Some Etiquette Tips for Videoconferences and Phone Calls?

Although you will not need quite as much cultural background when communicating via videoconferencing or phone, there are still a few things to know. As in any videoconference, you may want to consider basics such as positioning of team members to reflect seniority and role in the meeting. If you know ahead of time how your international business partners will be positioned, you might consider this as well. More specific to conferencing with foreign partners will be how you handle such details as greetings, eye contact, and the amount of small talk that occurs before the business portion of the conference begins. Brush up on the basic etiquette in these areas before your meeting, and make corrections as needed once the conference is under way.

Phone calls may be somewhat less complicated to navigate, but you should still have a sense of cultural expectations beforehand. Know in advance how to address the other person and whether it is appropriate to begin with small talk. You should also know how to transition into the business portion of the meeting smoothly.

How Can I Make Sure My Written Communications Are Appropriate?

Communicating via e-mail or mail with international partners or clients requires the same basic knowledge you would need to write any business correspondence. You should make sure you know the proper way to open and close the correspondence, as well as the proper tone to take. Some people may have a tendency to be less formal when composing an e-mail, so avoid this pitfall, especially when writing to people in conservative cultures. Never use emoticons or Internet slang in business correspondence.

If possible, it's a good idea to have your initial correspondence checked over by someone familiar with the norms of the country in question. This helps to ensure the appropriate tone. In a country such as Senegal, for instance, business communications are often written in a more respectful style than in the United States. Failing to adjust your style for your audience can make the communication less effective and even potentially offensive.

For More Information

BOOKS

Crowley, Katherine. *Working with You Is Killing Me: Freeing Yourself from Emotional Traps at Work*. New York: Warner Business Books, 2006.

Kaner, Sam. *Facilitator's Guide to Participatory Decision-Making*. San Francisco: Jossey-Bass, 2014.

Pachter, Barbara. *The Essentials of Business Etiquette: How to Greet, Eat, and Tweet Your Way to Success*. New York: McGraw-Hill, 2013.

Post, Peter, and Peggy Post. *Emily Post's The Etiquette Advantage in Business: Personal Skills for Professional Success*. New York: William Morrow, 2005.

Sutton, Robert I. *The No Asshole Rule: Building a Civilized Workplace and Surviving One That Isn't*. New York: Warner Business Books, 2007.

Tropman, John E. *Making Meetings Work: Achieving High Quality Group Decisions*. Thousand Oaks, CA: Sage, 2003.

Whitmore, Jacqueline. *Business Class: Etiquette Essentials for Success at Work*. New York: St. Martin's, 2005.

PERIODICALS

Brennan, Emily. "Chinese for Faux Pas? Ask Eden Collinsworth." *New York Times*, October 5, 2014, TR3. This article can also be found online at http://www.nytimes.com/2014/10/05/travel/decoding-etiquette-in-china-handshakes-to-meals.html http://www.nytimes.com.

Maltby, Emily. "Expanding Abroad? Avoid Cultural Gaffes." *Wall Street Journal*, January 19, 2012. This article can also be found online at http://www.wsj.com/news/articles/SB10001424052748703657604575005511903147960?mg=reno64-wsj&url=http%3A%2F%2Fonline.wsj.com%2Farticle%2FSB10001424052748703657604575005511903147960.html.

Zimmerman, Eilene. "Smartphones Should Know Their Place." *New York Times*, March 11, 2012, BU9. This article can also be found online at http://www.nytimes.com/2012/03/11/jobs/etiquette-for-using-personal-technology-at-work-career-couch.html?_r=0.

WEBSITES

Adams, Susan. "Business Etiquette Tips for Foreign Travel." *Forbes*. June 15, 2012. http://www.forbes.com/sites/susanadams/2012/06/15/business-etiquette-tips-for-international-travel/ (accessed February 4, 2015).

Giang, Vivian. "10 Etiquette Rules for Meetings That Every Professional Should Know." *Business Insider*. November 24, 2013. http://www.businessinsider.com/10-etiquette-rules-for-meetings-that-every-professional-needs-to-know-2013-11 (accessed November 3, 2014).

Goman, Carol Kinsey. "10 Simple and Powerful Body Language Tips for 2012." *Forbes*. http://www.forbes.com/sites/carolkinseygoman/2012/01/03/10-simple-and-powerful-body-language-tips-for-2012/ (accessed February 4, 2015).

———. "Seven Seconds to Make a First Impression." *Forbes*. http://www.forbes.com/sites/carolkinseygoman/2011/02/13/seven-seconds-to-make-a-first-impression/ (accessed February 4, 2015).

Hecht, Alan, Stephanie Janson, and Carol McQuiggan. "Videoconferencing Etiquette and Meeting Tips." *The John A. Dutton e-Education Institute, Penn State University*. https://courseware.e-education.psu.edu/resources/Videoconf_etiquette4.pdf (accessed November 4, 2014).

Hering, Beth Braccio. "10 Commandments of Dressing for Work." *CNN*. http://www.cnn.com/2011/09/16/living/workplace-professional-dress-cb/ (accessed December 12, 2014).

"Meeting Participants Roles and Responsibilities." *Exforsys*. October 18, 2009. http://www.exforsys.com/career-center/meeting-management/meeting-roles-responsibilities.html (accessed November 4, 2014).

Parrish, Rogue. "Business Etiquette for Women Traveling Abroad." *USA Today*. http://traveltips.usatoday.com/business-etiquette-women-traveling-abroad-52425.html (accessed December 28, 2014).

Root, George N., III. "10 Rules for Proper Business Meeting Etiquette." *Houston Chronicle*. http://smallbusiness.chron.com/10-rules-proper-business-meeting-etiquette-2857.html (accessed February 4, 2015).

Sherman, Lauren. "Wardrobe Essentials for the Young Professional." *Forbes*. http://www.forbes.com/2008/07/09/cities-professionals-young-forbeslife-cx_ls_0709style.html (accessed December 12, 2014).

"10 Etiquette Tips for Business Meetings." *Emily Post*. http://www.emilypost.com/emily-post-business-etiquette-training-meeting-tips (accessed November 3, 2014).

"Workplace Housekeeping—Basic Guide." *Canadian Centre for Occupational Health and Safety*. http://www.ccohs.ca/oshanswers/hsprograms/house.html (accessed December 12, 2014).

Teamwork, Collaboration, and Leadership Skills

Overview: Teamwork, Collaboration, and Leadership Skill

When Did the Concept of Teamwork Originate?

Throughout history people have worked in teams, joining together in clans or tribes to protect themselves from predators and to seek food and shelter. Many definitions of the word *team* exist. Most commonly a team is a group of individuals with various and often complementary abilities, skills, and strengths working together toward a common purpose, whether in a family or a work environment. A team has some degree of shared accountability and ownership and is formed according to particular needs. Team members are generally chosen based on their ability to accomplish predetermined goals or tasks.

Work teams became more common in businesses and organizations beginning in the late twentieth and early twenty-first centuries. This was due, in part, to the popularity of quality circles among U.S. manufacturers in the 1980s. A management technique that first originated in post–World War II Japan, a quality circle brings employees from different areas of an organization and with different skills and knowledge together to solve organizational problems rather than relying on managers to make all the decisions. By the 1990s many companies were using work teams to tackle particular problems, projects, or tasks, and by the early twenty-first century teamwork was an integral part of day-to-day life in most organizations and businesses.

How Do Teams Form?

Teams can form informally or formally. An informal team might, for example, form among a group of workers who decide that the employee lounge isn't a very comfortable place. They might meet casually during

Building a successful team takes some analysis. Each team member has unique strengths and differences which can be pieced together effectively by a good leader who recognizes the fit. © TOTALLYPIC.COM/ SHUTTERSTOCK.COM.

their breaks to figure out ways to get new furniture and books in the lounge. On the other hand, a department manager working on an important project might assemble a formal team, selecting people from different departments and with varying abilities to work on the project collaboratively. In this case the manager might establish formal meeting times and specific goals for the group.

Whether formal or informal, teams work best when goals and objectives are clear. With a formal team a manager might establish goals at the team's first meeting. With an informal team, the general reason for coming together may be clear, but a first step might be to collectively define goals and objectives.

In addition to agreeing upon goals and objectives, teams need to establish ground rules for working together. These should include commonsense guidelines such as being responsible to the group, as well as more complex issues such as how conflict will be resolved. Other common first steps include designating roles, assigning specific tasks, and creating a time line.

Who Makes Up a Team?

Individuals on teams will have their own unique work, social, and communication styles. They are also likely to have strengths in some areas and weaknesses in others. For example, you might be great at creative brainstorming but have a hard time organizing tasks. Team members will likely also have a range of experience. Often people with different abilities are brought together in a team to ensure that a variety of tasks can be accomplished, to spur creativity, or to learn new skills from each other.

Team members typically come from diverse cultures and traditions and may be of different races, ethnicities, genders, religions, or sexual orientations. When each team member contributes from his or her own unique background, there are more possibilities for creative work and solutions. When working with diverse groups, do not make assumptions about process or communication style. Behavior that may be considered positive in one culture might be considered rude in a different culture. Make sure to take logistics into account when working with a diverse group that might require particular accommodations. For example, are meeting places wheelchair accessible? Are meetings scheduled during a Jewish or Muslim holiday? Remember that the needs of all team members should be considered.

What Is Team Culture?

The word *culture* describes the beliefs, values, customs, habits, and attitudes a group of people share. When people form teams, they develop a team culture. Every team will have a particular culture reflective of each individual and their interactions with the group, a certain leadership style, and a larger organization the team represents.

If the organization your team is working for is very strict about time, team meetings will likely start and end promptly. If people on your team have personal relationships with each other, the team culture might be that people chat a lot before or after meetings. If your team is dealing with a sensitive issue, such as domestic violence, people may use pseudonyms. Each of these is an example of team culture.

How Can Team Culture Positively Affect Problems and Conflicts?

When a strong team culture is established, problems and conflicts can often be dealt with effectively. If challenges arise, team members will understand how to proceed and will have confidence that the issue can be resolved. Group dynamics, which describes how well team members work together, can be influenced by strong team culture. Similarly, team culture may be influenced by a change in group dynamics. For example, if a new person joins the team, both the group dynamics and the team culture may be affected.

Often the problems and conflicts a team encounters are due to negative interactions between individuals or poor group dynamics. With a strong team culture, stong emotions and stress can be lessened. Problems and conflicts will be viewed not as individual issues but as team issues. Team members will consider how a problem or conflict impedes goals and discuss what they can do to resolve the problem in order to reach their goals rather than seeing a problem or conflict as a personal attack.

How Is Negotiation Used on Teams?

Negotiation takes place when two or more people try to come to an agreement. A team is made up of individuals, and each individual offers unique and differing skills, ideas, values, and behaviors. Informal and sometimes formal negotiating will be necessary in order for everyone on the team to come to an agreement about how to accomplish all the tasks, as well as to determine how group processes will happen.

When negotiating, the needs and opinions of all parties should be taken into account. Cultural and identity issues should also be considered. In some cultures, for example, a back-and-forth manner of speaking and "interrupting" is considered the norm, whereas other cultures value not interrupting until the speaker is completely finished.

Teams might opt for a formal negotiation process for a range of issues. Formal negotiation is often used when there is a major problem or conflict that needs to be resolved quickly. Generally, in a formal negotiation the team members decide when and where to meet, designate a time frame for making a decision, and make sure everyone understands the issues involved. Ground rules are adhered to or created. The group tries to come to a "win-win" solution, where all sides feel they have been heard and everyone feels they made positive gains. At the end of the negotiation, group members should determine a course of action for implementing any agreements.

Being on a team also typically involves many informal negotiations, whether among the whole group, among small task-oriented subgroups, or between specific individuals. Even something as minor as where people sit at the conference table or who will be the week's note taker can require informal negotiation with give and take from those involved.

Why Are Compromise and Collaboration Important on Teams?

By definition, teams collaborate. They work together, collaboratively, toward a common goal. Having clear goals, trust, effective communication, and positive relationships will help foster a collaborative environment. Collaboration can sometimes be challenging. Individuals might not work well together, for instance, or might have trouble integrating their ideas with others.

When team members do collaborate, they work together to find a formula that uses their differing skills and resources to come up with creative and needed solutions. Collaboration helps people come to a win-win situation because, unlike compromise, individuals are not giving up their particular ideas or beliefs. Instead, all ideas are being considered equally and respectfully and are integrated to accomplish goals.

Sometimes team members need to compromise. When attempting a compromise, work toward achieving give and take from all sides. For example, one individual might decide that it's okay to compromise about the size and color of a brochure but not about its written content. Often, a back-and-forth discussion of various ideas and compromises is necessary. Each side makes concessions before a compromise can be reached.

Compromise is not always the first choice in approaching a matter because usually people have to "give up" something to come to an agreement. This can create harsh feelings and other issues. However, sometimes compromise is the only way to move forward, especially when group members face a challenging conflict. In addition, being willing to compromise on minor issues, such as meeting times, can help to establish trust among team members, which will be helpful when engaging in future collaborative work.

What Is the Role of a Team Leader?

If you are chosen as a team leader, you must be able to inspire your team and establish a course of action for meeting team goals. A leader who is authentic and engaged in the work will be able to influence team members to be effective and responsible. You will need to encourage innovation and creative thinking, while understanding when it is important to "stay the course." It is important to provide support, encouragement, boundaries, and inspiration.

Leaders build relationships between members of the group, taking into account group dynamics. You should be proactive and make decisions about whether or not to intervene if you see something is not working or notice that a problem is brewing. Leaders are, to an extent, neutral, so they can be trusted to be fair and judicious when problems or conflicts arise. Because a leader is often looked at as a role model, you should be respectful to all, affirm and value people's work, give constructive criticism when needed, and demonstrate responsibility to your tasks and the group.

It is also important for you to have an overall view of the team and its goals and to act strategically when necessary. You need to be aware of internal factors, such as group dynamics, and external factors, such as the team's responsibility to the organization or how different stakeholders will to react various situations. It is a good idea to look at the big picture and consider how the team as a whole needs to move forward as well as how all the parts need to work separate and together.

What Skills Do I Need to Be an Effective Leader?

All leaders have their strengths and weaknesses, but there are some skills and traits that are particularly important. Being self-confident and assertive, even if it is a quiet assertiveness, will help motivate your team and give members confidence in your leadership. It's important to be flexible and to adapt to changing circumstances. As a leader you need to instill confidence in your team members so they are comfortable changing direction when needed. Part of being flexible is admitting to and learning from mistakes and then moving on. Leaders need to receive both positive and negative feedback gracefully and must be able to offer evaluation of others in productive ways.

Time management: *Skills and scheduling techniques used to maximize productivity.*

Delegating tasks fairly and respectfully with an understanding of relationships and group dynamics is essential. Know how to motivate yourself and others to get tasks done and to accomplish goals and objectives. Consider how to foster positive relationships. Think strategically about how goals will be met. To be an effective team leader, you also should have strong organizational, planning, and *time management* skills.

In addition, leaders need to possess good written and oral communication skills. In our increasingly technological world, your communication skills will need to be versatile so that you are effective whether you are e-mailing, blogging, texting, or instant messaging. Team members need to feel you are clearly communicating expectations and that you are always open to hearing from them. Your communication skill set should include the ability to negotiate and resolve conflicts. Additionally, you need to be respectful of cultural diversity when communicating as well as in all other aspects of leadership.

In the early twenty-first century many business experts talk about the importance of emotional intelligence, or EI, in leadership roles. Emotional intelligence means you are sensitive to both your own emotions and to the emotions of those around you. This awareness and sensitivity enables you to form positive relationships. When you have EI, you have strong social skills, empathy, integrity, and cultural sensitivity. People see you as someone who is trustworthy.

Are There Different Ways to Approach Leadership?

Not all leaders are the same, and not all projects require the same type of leaders. Some leaders are loud and like to make quick decisions, whereas others are more understated or analytical. Different situations call for different types of leadership. A team working in an emergency situation may need a leader who is commanding and comes to quick decisions. A team organizing a fund-raiser might need a leader who enables a slow, creative process.

There are many different styles of leadership. Some of the more common leadership styles include managerial, procedural, transformational, authoritarian, adaptive, charismatic, strategic, participative, and laissez-faire. Leadership styles are characterized by how the leader interacts with the group and how decisions are made. Each approach has pros and cons. For example, an authoritarian leader is very direct and tells team members very specifically what to do. A laissez-faire leader acts more as an adviser and lets the group make decisions. In a team with an authoritarian leader, results may happen quickly because there is a single decider. However, creativity may be stifled. With a laissez-faire leader, people may feel very involved, and the creative juices may flow freely, but tasks may take a long time as decision making can be slow and conflicts may arise.

Leaders don't typically rely on only one management style. Most use a combination of styles that are best suited not only to the work and the team but also to their personal strengths and skills. Being able to match the task, the team, and your own personal preferences to the right combination of leadership styles and attributes is in itself a sign of good leadership.

For More Information

BOOKS

DuBrin, Andrew J. *Leadership: Research Findings, Practice, and Skills*. Independence, KY: Cengage Learning, 2015.

Levi, Daniel Jay. *Group Dynamics for Teams*. Thousand Oaks, CA: Sage Publications, 2013. Print.

Mackin, Deborah. *The Team-Building Tool Kit: Tips and Tactics for Effective Workplace Teams*. New York: AMACOM, 2007. Print.

Nelson, Bob, and Lundin, Stephen. *Ubuntu! An Inspiring Story about an African Tradition of Teamwork and Collaboration*. New York: Crown Business, 2010. Print.

PERIODICALS

Kasanoff, Bruce. "10 Ways to Build a Winning Team." *Business Insider*, November 13, 2014. This article can also be found online at http://www.businessinsider.com/ways-to-build-a-winning-team-2014-11.

Mickan, Sharon, and Sylvia Rodger. "The Organisational Context for Teamwork: Comparing Health Care and Business Literature." *Australian Health Review* 23 (2000): 179–92.

Vicens, Quentin, and Philip E. Bourne. "10 Simple Rules for a Successful Collaboration." *PLoS Computational Biology* 3, no. 3 (2007): e44. This article can also be found online at http://www.ncbi.nlm.nih.gov/pmc/articles/PMC1847992/.

Whitfield, John. "Collaboration: Group Theory." *Nature* 455 (2008): 720–23. This article can also be found online at http://www.nature.com/news/2008/081008/full/455720a.html.

WEBSITES

"Building a Collaborative Team Environment." *Office of Personnel Management*. http://www.opm.gov/policy-data-oversight/performance-management/teams/building-a-collaborative-team-environment/ (accessed January 30, 2015).

"Building a Great Team Culture." *Global Leadership Foundation*. https://global-leadershipfoundation.com/wp-content/uploads/2013/04/Building-A-Great-Team-Culture1.pdf (accessed January 30, 2015).

Cardinal, Rosalind. "How to Make Team Goals That Work." *Huffington Business*. December 11, 2014. http://www.huffingtonpost.com/rosalind-cardinal/how-to-make-team-goals-th_b_6308308.html (accessed January 30, 2015).

Haselmayr, Melanie. "Five Types of Office Collaboration Tools: Which Is Right for Your Team?" *Forbes*. July 11, 2013. http://www.forbes.com/sites/allbusiness/2013/07/11/5-types-of-office-collaboration-tools-which-is-right-for-your-team/ (accessed January 30, 2015).

Rowe, E. "Team Leadership." *University of Vermont*. http://www.uvm.edu/extension/community/buildingcapacity/?Page=teamleadership.html (accessed January 31, 2015).

Warrell, Margie. "Great Leaders Build a Culture of Courage in a Climate of Fear." *Forbes*, March 25, 2014. http://www.forbes.com/sites/margiewarrell/2014/03/25/culture-of-courage/ (accessed January 30, 2015).

Teamwork Skills and Developing Healthy Team Dynamics

What Is Team Culture?

A company's culture comprises all the ways in which things get done, from developing new ideas to decision making and production. Organizational culture can even include how people dress, talk to customers or clients, and market their services or products. Each workplace has a culture that reflects its values, habits, and history, and that culture influences everything from its productivity and performance to its employees' attendance and punctuality.

A collaborative environment is the hallmark of team culture. A business with a strong team culture generally will organize groups, or teams, as a strategy for accomplishing goals. Team culture places high value on shared commitment to a process of working together, and members share collective responsibility for the work they do. This culture puts into practice the beliefs that everyone has important contributions to make and that cooperation among team members produces better results than an individual could accomplish if working alone. It also recognizes that members

Every team culture has unique character traits influenced by the mix of experience and the environment. © RAWPIXEL/ SHUTTERSTOCK.COM.

Hierarchy: *The levels of management within a business organization, from the lowest to the highest.*

Stakeholder: *Any group or individual who can affect or is affected by the achievement of the organization's objectives. A firm's stakeholders include employees, consumers, the community, and government.*

of a team are dependent on one another to get the job done. A company with a well-established team culture usually values individual expertise while helping employees understand and appreciate the roles and expertise of others. It likely also is committed to employee training, development, and advancement, because each employee is a valued member of the team.

Participatory decision making is also typically a feature of team culture. This kind of decision making both limits and extends personal freedom of expression. Team members are limited in their ability to take initiative on their own, but they are encouraged to contribute their own ideas and innovations to the group, which benefits from the variety of individual perspectives. Information should flow to the whole group, rather than following a *hierarchy*, in order to allow the team to make informed decisions. Ideally, the team should share information and resources with all members, allowing for flexible leadership and adaptability to changing situations.

What Are the Benefits of Team Culture?

Team culture encourages individuals with diverse backgrounds and experience to contribute to a company's goals. Because of the diversity of the U.S. workforce and the complexity of many business operations, most twenty-first-century businesses employ people with a variety of backgrounds, perspectives, and experiences. A diverse workforce generally has a better chance of coming up with creative solutions to problems. The majority of businesses recognize ethnic, religious, and geographic diversity as assets that will make their company stronger.

Team responsibility for all aspects of a job means that there may be many people involved in carrying out a task. You may notice a detail that another person might miss, and when each individual is empowered to bring ideas or insights forward to the group, the project benefits from this added level of observation. When teams are made up of representatives from multiple company departments, many different *stakeholders* may be represented in decisions. The involvement of multiple people in a project also makes it possible for the work to continue if one or more team members leave the group.

Personality and Team Culture

Personality plays an important role in workplace interactions, including team work. Teams function best when the atmosphere is truly collaborative, with all members contributing and communicating well with each other. Sometimes, however, personality differences can lead to misperceptions that hinder team performance. For example, team members who are extroverts are likely to speak up sooner, and more often, than those who are introverts. Even when acting in the interests of the team, extroverts run the risk of being perceived as bullies who force their ideas on other team members. Introverts, who often like to have time to think through an issue before joining a conversation, are also frequently misunderstood when they work on teams. While quietly thinking through possible strategies, they run the risk of being perceived by their more extroverted peers as complainers with nothing to contribute.

Regardless of your role on a team, it is important to understand the personalities of your fellow team members. If you are an extrovert, remember that your more introverted peers have valuable contributions to make but often need time to get their minds around their ideas before voicing them. Conversely, if you are an introvert, remember that more vocal members of your team are doing what comes naturally to them. They may think out loud and might need the feedback from others to flesh out their ideas. Don't assume they are trying to silence you or push their own ideas.

As a team leader, get to know the personality types on your team. If your team includes both introverts and extroverts, create a team environment that benefits all members and promotes productivity. Providing an agenda or talking points ahead of key team meetings will give introverts a chance to think through their ideas before the discussion starts. During meetings, make sure that everyone has a chance to speak, but avoid putting introverts on the spot. Don't silence the most vocal members of the team, but try not to let them to set the tone and the agenda. Your team will benefit most when everyone is comfortable offering and discussing ideas.

How Is Team Culture Used in Business?

Team culture is practiced in a variety of ways in the business world. For instance, a food service business may organize shifts into teams. Team culture can enhance the mutual sense of responsibility toward the work that needs to be done. On a successful team, each member understands who is responsible for each area of work and knows where he or she can pitch in to help the team complete a successful shift.

Health care is another field in which team culture plays an important role. The proper functioning of a health-care team requires professionals with varied backgrounds and responsibilities to share information.

Members of health-care teams need to know which colleagues are responsible for making decisions, and they need to be confident that each member's contribution is being considered. To be successful, the team should have a firm commitment to follow through on decisions once they are made and should have a mutually agreed-upon method for resolving conflict.

Team culture is also increasingly important in manufacturing, where complex concerns with financing, raw materials, production, and marketing take place on a global scale. Industries with a wide range of stakeholders have found that, by engaging employees at a variety of levels and locations and collaborating across the industry, they can address complicated environmental and economic problems. For instance, the jeans manufacturer Levi Strauss assembled a team that was tasked with reducing water consumption in the making of jeans. By forming a multidisciplinary team, it was able to design jeans that require much less water to make.

Software engineering and other creative high-tech industries often have intensively collaborative team cultures. Innovation in technology requires continual feedback, ongoing learning, and accountability, all of which are important aspects of working with a team. Complex software projects, in particular, can be personally draining without the boost of team morale.

Why Do I Need to Understand Team Culture?

Most modern businesses recognize the benefits of collaboration, and most make use of teams to some degree. No matter what industry or career you are in, you are likely to spend part of your workday as a member of a team. Companies use teams to accomplish special projects, to develop innovations, and as a way for departments to work together. New developments in technology make it increasingly possible for teams to collaborate over distances. It is important, therefore, to understand and embrace team culture in order to advance in twenty-first-century business.

How Can I Be a Valuable Member of a Team?

Every team works in its own unique fashion, but there are guidelines that can help make teamwork successful. You can be a more valuable member of a team if your expectations for the group are in line with how good teams work. A team should know or establish its purpose at the beginning, and members should be aware of the team's goals and understand the limits of its scope and responsibilities. They should also know what success will entail and how it will be measured.

For you to become a valued member of a team, you should be aware of the reasons why you were chosen to participate. What skills, experience, relationships, qualities, or expertise do you bring to the group? It is important that you know what is expected of you, but you don't have to limit your participation because of these expectations. Your team will benefit from your creativity and from the synergy (increased effectiveness that results when two or more people or businesses work together) created by your collaboration with others.

In addition to understanding your own role, you should understand the roles of other team members. Is someone expected to be the team leader or facilitator? You should know the backgrounds and expertise of other members and align your expectations accordingly. This includes being aware of the level of commitment that each person is expected to make. You should know how long you will be asked to work on the team and how much time you should devote to the team's work. You should also be aware of the timetable for completing the project, including the final deadline and any intermediate milestones. It is every team member's job to try to keep the team on schedule.

How Do Teams Make Decisions?

There are many models for team decision making. It is important for you to know how your team will make decisions. In the least participatory model, a team leader makes some or all of the decisions for the team. However, for this model to work in a team culture, the whole group must understand and accept the leader's responsibility for making decisions. The team members must feel empowered to give input on the decisions, and the leader must inform all team members about decisions that have been made.

If team members are experts in various fields, decisions may be made by a team leader after a discussion among all of the members. Each participant should have the opportunity to offer relevant information to the whole group on his or her topic of expertise. The group can then discuss the issues with the understanding that one person will be making the final decision. The team may also decide to delegate decision making to a smaller group within the team. However, a team does not usually rely on majority-rule decisions, because majority rule may result in weak commitment from the minority voters.

The consensus model is another effective decision-making method for teams. Consensus does not necessarily mean that everyone in a group is in complete agreement. Rather, it means that everyone has had the opportunity to contribute and that everyone accepts responsibility for the decision. During the discussion, it is important for you to listen to other team members and for each person to feel that he or she has been heard. You should also be willing to modify your ideas based on new information from other team members. Consensus decision making requires a high level of team member involvement and commitment in order for the group to come to an agreement.

What Are Some of the Pitfalls of Team Culture?

Teams cannot be successfully implemented in a work environment without planning, training, and commitment from both management and employees. Teamwork requires company resources as well as full support from management. For teams to be successful, they should have goals that will be better attained through teamwork than by individuals working separately. Before implementing a team, an organization should consider whether a team approach is the best way to accomplish the goal. Planners should also consider which workers have skills that will make them a good fit for the team and what training they will need in order to do the necessary work.

Not every work-related project or goal is best addressed by a team. When a task is very interdependent, assigning it to a team may be a good idea. However, if a work project can be accomplished more efficiently by an individual, trying to turn it into a team effort could waste time and energy. Although teams involve more people, this does not always make it possible for them to accomplish more. Assigning a project to a team may also make the project more costly, since teams may have increased communication and management expenses. To evaluate efficiency, a team should have periodic evaluations that answer questions about whether it is on track to complete its tasks, whether the right people are on the team, and whether the team's original goals are being met.

How Can I Improve My Teamwork Skills?

Teamwork skills are very similar to leadership skills because each person must assume responsibility, communicate effectively, and facilitate the work of others. These are skills that can be learned and practiced. Many high schools, colleges, and universities know the value of teaching teamwork and have incorporated learning how to work in small groups into their curriculum. Community colleges offer specific courses in teamwork, and they teach such skills as making and keeping contracts with small groups, group decision making, conducting meetings, and giving and receiving constructive feedback.

There are several professional-development speakers and writers who emphasize teamwork. Some address the health of the whole organization and how teams should work together, while others focus on specific aspects of team members, such as gender or job position. Some professions necessarily emphasize teamwork in their routine schooling and training, including teaching, coaching, and nursing.

Recognizing and Appreciating Diversity among Your Team

What Is a Diverse Team?

A team consists of two or more people who come together to work toward a shared mission. Each member has a specific role or function that helps the team reach its goals. Teams are used in a wide variety of workplace, organizational, government, and educational settings. They help build relationships and a sense of community, which can have long-term positive effects on the success of an organization or a business. The members of a team share responsibilities, and they are accountable for one another's actions and accomplishments. Often, teams are formed when a project is too big or complicated for an individual to tackle alone.

Homogeneous: *Made up of the same or a similar kind or nature.*

Since all people are unique individuals, teams will naturally be diverse in some ways. Some differences among team members may be obvious, while others may be subtle or even imperceptible. In a thriving team, the members view diversity as an advantage that gives the group a competitive edge. A team made up of people who have different backgrounds, characteristics, and personalities may be more effective at developing innovative ideas than a relatively *homogeneous* group. Members of a diverse team may spark one another's creativity and come up with original insights that they may not have been able to discover by working independently.

Why Should I Recognize and Appreciate the Diversity of My Team?

The concept of diversity encompasses all unique aspects of an individual. It includes many different qualities, such as a person's race, gender, sexual orientation, disability, class, cultural background, experience, and personality. Honoring the diversity within a team can help teammates forge good working relationships with one another, and this can make the team far more likely to succeed in accomplishing its goals.

Team values can vary greatly and reflect a wide range of backgrounds, opinions, and priorities. © MONKEY BUSINESS IMAGES/ SHUTTERSTOCK.COM.

Since some groups of people have experienced discrimination over time, it is important that conscious or unconscious prejudices, such as racism or sexism, do not cloud your ability to work well with people who might be different from you.

There is a difference between recognizing diversity and appreciating it. If you recognize diversity, you acknowledge that your teammates are different from you and that this difference matters. Appreciating diversity means that you respect and value all the things about a person that makes him or her different from you and that you welcome that person's identity. People who are in positions of power are not always aware that some groups of people are sometimes treated unfairly and subjected to discrimination because of certain differences. To improve your own awareness, you should make an attempt to see the world from the perspective of others.

How Do the Diverse Backgrounds of Team Members Affect a Team?

Background knowledge refers to the skill sets and educational backgrounds that individuals bring to a team. A team member may have acquired certain kinds of expertise through previous professional positions or an internship. College, graduate school, training programs, and certification courses also provide skills that can be used in a team

Discrimination against Women in the Workplace

Although women have made significant strides in the workplace, those who work full time are still paid 78 cents for every dollar a man makes in the United States. Even "millennials," the youngest generation of workers, experience the pay gap. Many people think that this gap relates to the fact that some women leave the workforce to take care of children, but research done by the American Association of University Women (AAUW) shows that the pay gap begins early, long before women decide to have children.

While some women choose to pursue careers that pay less, AAUW research has shown that men and women who do the same job, with the same experience and credentials, are paid unequally.

If a man has the same qualifications as a woman, why is he making more? Researchers attribute the pay gap to discrimination on the part of management, although it is not usually overt. In fact, those in charge of setting salaries often discriminate unconsciously.

setting. Some team members might also have gathered useful experience in unconventional ways. A single mother may have strong organizational skills, while a person living on limited income may have learned a lot how to manage money.

There are many benefits to assembling a team that is made up of members with diverse backgrounds. For example, in a university, a team might include administrators, professors, staff, students, and community members. When there are many different perspectives within a team, the members may discover numerous original and inventive ways to accomplish their tasks through the process of working together.

How Do the Diverse Characteristics of Team Members Affect a Team?

Teams may be made up of members who come from different cultures, ethnic or racial groups, or socioeconomic classes. They may be different genders, sexual orientations, or religions, and they may have varying disabilities or political beliefs. They may also come from different geographic locations, or their first language may not be the one most common to the group. Most people have more than one facet to their identity, and these elements combine to shape their perspectives. For example, a team member could be a Muslim woman who uses a wheelchair. Her gender, religion, and disability all contribute to her sense

Language Spoken at Home, 2009–2013

2009–2013 American Community Survey 5-Year Estimates

	United States					
			Percent of specified language speakers who ...			
	Total Surveyed		Speak English "very well"		Speak English less than "very well"	
Subject	Estimate	Margin of Error	Estimate	Margin of Error	Estimate	Margin of Error
Population 5 years and over	291,484,482	+/−3,346	91.4%	+/−0.1	8.6%	+/−0.1
Speak only English	79.3%	+/−0.1				
Speak a language other than English	20.7%	+/−0.1	58.3%	+/−0.1	41.7%	+/−0.1
Spanish or Spanish Creole	12.9%	+/−0.1	56.4%	+/−0.1	43.6%	+/−0.1
Other Indo-European languages	3.7%	+/−0.1	68.1%	+/−0.1	31.9%	+/−0.1
Asian and Pacific Island languages	3.3%	+/−0.1	52.1%	+/−0.1	47.9%	+/−0.1
Other languages	0.9%	+/−0.1	69.2%	+/−0.3	30.8%	+/−0.3

SOURCE: U.S. Census Bureau, 2009–2013 5-Year American Community Survey, Table S1601. http://factfinder.census.gov/faces/tableservices/jsf/pages/productview.xhtml?pid=ACS_13_5YR_S1601&prodType=table.

ILLUSTRATION BY LUMINA DATAMATICS LTD. © 2015 CENGAGE LEARNING.

of who she is, and this in turn influences how she might work within a group.

Clear ground rules about a respectful work environment and the value of individual experiences are essential in diverse groups. As part of maintaining a respectful environment, you should avoid making assumptions. Suggesting that your team meet at a restaurant for dinner might seem like a good idea, since you might expect it to be an experience that everyone would enjoy, but there might be considerations that have not occurred to you. Is everyone able to afford the cost? Does the team include single parents who may need to stay home with young children? Is everyone able to eat the food, or do some members have dietary concerns? Is the restaurant wheelchair-accessible? It is important for members of a team to address potential assumptions that may have a negative impact on some members of the group. By discussing concerns as they arise, team members can improve trust and understanding within the group and foster a better work environment.

Communication is another important aspect of teamwork. Some team members may express themselves differently than others, and verbal and *nonverbal communication* styles may vary among different cultures. Depending on an individual's cultural background, interrupting a person who is speaking may be viewed as an indication of either excited

Nonverbal communication: *Communication without words. It includes facial expressions, eyes, touching, and tone of voice, as well as less obvious messages such as dress, posture, and distance between people.*

engagement or disrespect. Becoming aware of these differences can help team members communicate more effectively.

 When people from different backgrounds work closely together, they should be careful to avoid stereotyping, or assuming that people who have one thing in common are alike in other ways. One example of a stereotype would be an assumption that all young people are irresponsible. Even an assumption that you believe has positive intent, such as the belief that young people are technological experts, is still a stereotype and should be avoided. The members of your team are individuals who have unique combinations of interests and traits, and while you may know a few details about a person, such as age, gender, or cultural background, these details do not provide a full picture of that person's identity. It is essential for all members of a team to be open-minded and willing to respect one another's differences.

How Do the Personalities of Team Members Affect a Team?

Teams are most successful when they include diverse personality types. A group of introverts may not function as well as a group that includes both introverts and extroverts. Likewise, a group of intuitive thinkers could be improved by the addition of analytical thinkers.

Teamwork requires people to work closely over extended periods of time, and this can sometimes result in personality clashes. When a team member annoys you or acts in a way that you don't understand, you should try to keep in mind that different personalities make the group work better as a whole. There are a variety of personality tests, such as the Myers-Briggs test and the Enneagram, that team members can use to learn about their personality traits. Consider having each team member take a personality test and then have the group discuss the results with one another. This could help them gain a better understanding of their similarities and differences. The process could also help them identify and plan for potential areas of conflict.

Another simple and useful personality system for the workplace was developed by psychologist John Holland. He theorized that each person fits one of six different personality types: realistic, investigative, artistic, social, enterprising, or conventional. Each personality type is associated with specific traits. If each type is present within a team, the members' collective strengths and weaknesses can be balanced out.

What Happens to a Team When Diversity Is Not Valued?

When diversity is not recognized or appreciated, it can adversely affect the success of the team. Some team members may feel left out or disrespected, and this may lead them to disengage from the project or decide to quit working with the team entirely. Those who leave will inevitably take expertise, special talents, and company knowledge with them. If a problem within a team is severe enough, a member may even decide to initiate legal action against the company.

If a team fails to honor diversity, poor leadership may be a contributing factor. Sometimes a team leader may not take enough authority in directing the group toward acting and speaking in an inclusive and respectful manner. Team members who are not committed to diversity may dominate conversations and thus create an unpleasant or unsafe atmosphere for other members. Conversely, a leader can also take too much authority, *micromanaging* the group in a way that excludes some of the participants. Some members of the group may become resentful or frustrated if they feel that their points of view are not valued.

Micromanage: *To control every part, no matter how small, of an activity or enterprise.*

Individual team members can also play a part in creating an environment in which diversity is not respected. If a team member expresses insensitive remarks or assumptions or treats certain team members differently, this could result in a negative atmosphere for everyone in the group. On the other hand, individuals who are committed to diversity may be so concerned about pleasing a group leader or other members that they may hesitate to object when another person says or does something discriminatory. Teams can manage such conflicts by establishing effective problem-solving practices for handling issues related to diversity.

How Can a Team Resolve Conflicts Effectively?

No matter how committed a team may be to respecting diversity, problems may still occur. A Jewish person who celebrates Shabbat on Fridays may feel left out if the rest of the team attends after-hours gatherings on Friday evenings. A woman may become upset when she hears others make sexist remarks. A team can deal with conflict before it happens by engaging in discussions about diversity. This process can be critical in managing hurt or angry feelings that may arise, and it can help to ensure a positive outcome. The team leader should work with the group to establish clear and agreed-upon methods for managing conflict. A good conflict-resolution process can improve the group's working relationship and bring the team members closer together. Addressing problems as soon as possible can prevent them from growing into larger issues.

There are many team-building activities that can help members establish good relationships and learn to work together more effectively. Many such activities can be found on the Internet or in books. For example, each member might tell a story about his or her name, or the leader might ask the group to make a decision together about an imaginary situation, such as what 10 items they would like to have on a deserted island. Activities like these can help establish trust and allow team members to get to know one another better.

Diversity training may also be helpful in creating an inclusive culture. Outside firms that specialize in this type of training can be brought in for a session or series of sessions to help team members learn about common problems that may occur when working with a diverse team. By providing this kind of training to their employees, companies can demonstrate to the workers that they are committed to honoring diversity and that discriminatory actions will not be tolerated.

How Can a Team Leader Help the Team Recognize and Appreciate Diversity?

While teams work as a group, a team leader is important for the group's success. Teams often have one leader, but some teams may decide on a structure that shares leadership positions. There may be different leaders for particular tasks, or leadership roles may be rotated among two or three members.

In general, it is the role of the team leader to make sure that the team recognizes and appreciates diversity. If you are chosen as leader, you should monitor the way the team members interact with one another to ensure that communication is respectful. Try to set an example for the rest of the group by modeling appropriate speech and behavior. You should be an attentive listener who will consider the needs of individuals as well as those of the team as a whole. It is also important to treat each member with respect and dignity, regardless of his or her background, personality, or other qualities that might constitute differences.

As leader, you should constantly consider how you can create an even more inclusive and supportive team. This may involve motivating the team to develop ideas for strengthening diversity and create action plans for implementing their ideas. It may be necessary to change the structure of meetings to ensure that everyone has an equal chance to speak. Sometimes even changing the physical environment of where people are sitting can have a positive effect on team interaction. You can affirm positive group dynamics while working to change those that are negative, and you should regularly assess your own behavior and how it contributes to team culture.

Identifying Your Strengths and Weaknesses

Why Is Understanding Individual Strengths and Weaknesses an Important Part of Teamwork?

Teamwork plays a significant role in the twenty-first-century business world. Many companies often rely on teams of employees to solve problems and get work done. The success of a team depends on the individual contributions of each team member. As such, each team member must be willing to assess his or her own strengths and weaknesses and make adjustments for the benefit of the team as a whole. A strong team regularly assesses the habits, skills, and processes of its members in order to see continued improvement.

Effective communication, the ability to self-manage, and strong social skills are the building blocks of a good team. There are many ways to measure these skills based on the work output of the team and the contributions of each individual team member.

What Are the Qualities of a Good Team Member?

To be an effective team member, you should be an active, responsive participant; have strong listening skills; be tuned into other team members' emotions; and contribute thoughtfully and respectfully to the group. It's important to complete your share of responsibilities on time, lend enthusiasm to motivate the group, and clearly identify the team's goals and purposes. In addition, you should be assertive; open to criticism and feedback; and offer respectful, helpful feedback to others. You need to be willing to learn from your experiences, grow your skills, and be open to compromise when disagreement arises.

In addition to the qualities listed above, good team members tend to have strong communication, social, and self-management skills.

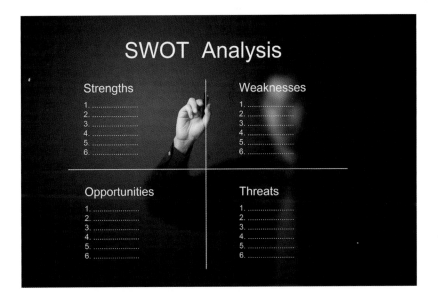

Self-assessment and the ability to identify your own strengths and weaknesses could help you relate better to those around you.
© DUSIT/SHUTTERSTOCK.COM.

Communication encompasses a variety of skills, all of which are necessary for productive interactions among team members. You communicate meaning both verbally and nonverbally, through tone of voice and in the written word. Accurate use of language and the clarity of your communication can build your credibility. Furthermore, *active listening* can show respect and build trust with other team members.

Individuals with high levels of emotional intelligence can observe their own and others' feelings and responses and can make choices about their behaviors based on those observations. Teams whose members have high levels of emotional intelligence generally are able to collaborate, appreciate one another's contributions and perspectives, be sensitive to individual and group emotions, and resolve conflicts.

Self-management skills are also vital to successful teamwork. An individual with these skills, often described with such adjectives as *efficient, diplomatic,* and *organized,* contributes to the team's ability to get work done efficiently and effectively. Self-management includes being able to manage time, set goals, avoid stress, and maintain good emotional and physical health. Procrastination is a common problem in teamwork and can have devastating effects on collaborative projects. Strong self-management skills combat procrastination and help individuals stay in control of their work habits to complete quality work on time.

Active listening: *The act of mindfully hearing and attempting to comprehend the meaning of words spoken by another in a conversation or speech. It can involve nodding one's head, making sounds that indicate attentiveness, and paraphrasing what the other person said.*

Seeking Out Personality Assessment

Many personality tests are available online, often at no cost. Such assessments may provide you with initial oversight into your personality, skills, and growth areas, thus helping you function more effectively as a member of a team. However, the scientific reliability of these tests has not been studied. If you want scientifically rigorous results, you may want to seek out a career counselor who is licensed to administer assessments such as the Myers-Briggs Type Indicator.

The National Career Development Association offers advice for individuals who are considering career counseling.

In addition to administering assessments, licensed career counselors can discuss your assessment results with you and help you see your skills and growth areas within the context of your work environment and the teams on which you work. You can explore the benefits of career counseling and find licensed counselors at http://www.ncda.org. You may want to see if it would be practical for your workplace to hire a career consultant to work with all team members. This will save individuals the costs of counseling, while providing benefits to the company by strengthening individual and team performance.

How Does Self-Evaluation Contribute to Teamwork?

Because the effectiveness of a team is so closely tied to the skills and habits of each individual, it is important to make sure team members are aware of their strengths and weaknesses. Providing opportunities for self-evaluation, which paves the way for awareness and improvement, is key to strengthening any team.

Choosing the best people to serve together on a team is impossible without team members understanding who they are and how they interact with others. Strong teams are often made up of people who complement one another's skills. Team members with diverse abilities can allocate tasks based on individual talents, enrich discussions with varying perspectives, and double-check each other's work. It is helpful, therefore, to have a strong sense of your strengths and weaknesses in order to have frank discussions with others about how you could best serve a team.

For example, imagine that your enthusiasm works well to motivate a group, but your ability to follow through on tasks needs improvement. If you are working with others who have similar habits, your team will have lots of energy but won't get much done. Knowledge of self can allow you to be honest with team members about what you can contribute.

However, that does not mean team members cannot succeed at tasks for which their skills are not a match. Some teams may benefit from having members working outside of their strengths to learn new skills. In such cases, however, it is important that the other team members know that an individual is working outside his or her comfort zone so they can provide any needed support.

What Are Some General Methods of Self-Evaluation?

Your perception of others and of yourself is subjective, which means that everyone sees the world and the people in it differently. Your view of yourself is also influenced by your ego, which often gets in the way of providing an accurate self-assessment. To combat this, psychologists have developed several tools to help. One of the most popular is the Myers-Briggs Type Indicator (MBTI). This questionnaire-based assessment was created in the 1920s and remains a commonly used test to measure individual preferences and perceptions. A certified professional usually administers the test in order to accurately interpret and explain the results.

By assessing your answers to almost 100 questions, the MBTI measures your preferences within four sets of differing traits, such as introversion and extraversion and thinking and feeling. Your answer will provide insight into how you perceive the world around you and how you approach decision making. The MBTI can also offer a glimpse into your communication style and social habits. It is important to note that the test measures preferences for certain habits or behaviors rather than your actual abilities. Still, it can suggest which careers and relationships fit your personality, though the MBTI does not promise to predict job performance.

Another tool that can help you understand your attributes is a four-section matrix called the Johari window. This tool and its accompanying activity ask you and your peers (such as team members) to choose five to six words that describe you from a list of about 60 adjectives. The window's four sections each contain a specific sampling of the results.

The first section, called the open arena, includes the adjectives that both you and your peers chose. This agreement points to the highest level of accuracy and understanding. The second section identifies the adjectives chosen just by you—not your peers. As these tend to be traits you keep hidden from others, the second section is called the hidden section. Although you can choose not to share this information with your teammates, sharing the information helps to build trust and understanding. A third section, called the blind spot, contains adjectives chosen just by your peers. These traits can be surprising, flattering, or offensive, so peers must take care of how or even if they communicate these to you. Adjectives from the list that were not chosen by either you or your peers go into the fourth, or unknown, section. These traits either simply do not apply to you or are unfamiliar to you or your peers.

Large open arena sections indicate that both you and your peers have a high level of understanding about your attributes. Teams can use the Johari window exercise multiple times to continue building trust and understanding and to learn more about how the team is developing.

How Can I Evaluate My Strengths and Weaknesses as a Communicator?

Communication skills are many and varied. As such, when taking an assessment of communication skills, it is important to be clear about which skills the assessment is measuring. There are many surveys available online, including one that evaluates multiple communication skills at skillsyouneed.com. This free survey of about 50 questions rates communication skills as average, above average, or below average and includes a numerical score. The site also provides strategies for improving those skills. Another communication assessment can be found online at mindtools.com. Also free, this survey provides a numerical score and discussions of skills, along with suggestions for improving them.

Keep in mind that assessing your communication skills does not always provide complete or accurate results. To increase accuracy, pair self-assessments with similar evaluations completed by team members or peers. For example, a 2009 study published by BMC Medical Education showed how a medical school attained accurate results from a specific assessment of medical students' communications skills. This tool was successful because it combined a self-assessment survey done by medical students with a similarly worded survey completed by the students' patients.

How Can I Evaluate My Social Skills?

Like communication, social skills are broad and varied. Assessing your own social skills can be complex, as they are difficult to separate from emotions. Some researchers believe that no tool can accurately and completely measure social skills. There are, however, several online tools available, including a free survey on the skillsyouneed.com site that evaluates listening, emotional intelligence, and teamwork.

One way to begin evaluating your strengths in social situations is to listen to your emotions throughout the day. Which social situations feel satisfying and which make you uncomfortable? Your feelings about specific activities might give good hints about your strengths and weaknesses. For example, if you enjoy quietly taking notes on what happens in meetings, you might have strong listening and reporting skills. If you find satisfaction in solving interpersonal conflicts, you might have strong emotional intelligence.

Feedback from others can provide valuable clues about your social strengths and weaknesses. Such feedback may include performance reviews and team assessments at the end of a project. Many people, however, are not comfortable offering feedback on weaknesses and might gloss over bigger issues in the interest of not hurting anyone's feelings.

Indirect feedback from colleagues, friends, and family can provide more reliable information about social skills. For example, when a colleague chooses you to speak for the group in a difficult situation, he or she clearly values your ability to read an audience and tailor your message accordingly. Similarly, when others pass you over for situations that require conflict mediation, they may be telling you that this is a social skill you need to work on.

How Can I Evaluate My Self-Management Skills?

Knowing our self-management strengths and weaknesses is key to understanding how we can effectively contribute to teams. Valued self-management skills include effective time management, setting realistic goals, following through on promised work in a timely manner, and demonstrating flexibility when approaching problems. You can assess your success in these areas on your own and with the help of peers.

As with social and communication skills, self-management skills can be evaluated using surveys and questionnaires. Some of these tools are available online (mindtools.com offers a survey on time management, for example). You can also monitor your habits by tracking your daily activities and comparing your accomplishments to a work plan or daily goals. Team members can help each other reflect on self-management strengths and weaknesses by responding to similar surveys about one another, then comparing results.

How Can I Maximize My Strengths and Compensate for My Weaknesses When I Work as Part of a Team?

Your strengths are assets, so it's best to use them to their fullest as an individual and in a team. For example, if you are good at public speaking, use that skill to benefit your team. Teams with a supportive atmosphere and little at stake are good for testing and practicing weaker skills. On the other hand, situations in which teams are facing high stakes or tight deadlines might require members to contribute their strongest attributes. Clearly communicating your perceived strengths and weaknesses to colleagues can help streamline the team's processes.

Consider thinking about weaknesses as strengths in disguise. Social skills considered weak in some circumstances can be valuable in other situations. For example, perhaps you have hurt a team member's feelings by being too direct with feedback. Although it would be a good idea to focus on using a more positive delivery, you may find yourself valued for your honesty. Teams can and do benefit from members who are not afraid to point out difficulties, and your bluntness might help with this.

Overcoming Obstacles and Conflicts

Why Do Obstacles and Conflicts Occur within Teams?

Obstacles are roadblocks that prevent a team from moving forward on a project in the way that it had initially planned. They occur because of outside factors (a resource being unavailable when needed, for example) or because of internal factors within the team, such as conflict. Conflicts are disagreements that occur between two or more people regarding any number of subjects. In general, conflicts stem from team members' poor communication skills or the poor leadership skills of the team leader. They also occur when team members prioritize their own needs over the team or do not take into account team members' points of view. Sometimes they happen as a result of a team member doing too much work or not doing enough.

When a group of people gather together to work toward a shared goal, they are likely to encounter obstacles that slow them down. Team members may clash over differing personalities, values, communication styles, and skill levels. At times this is useful, stimulating creativity and meaningful discussions. Obstacles and conflict become a problem, however, when they interfere with a healthy team dynamic. If the tension is causing widespread or deep-seated discontent, it will prevent the group from functioning at its best. Indeed, a team's long-term success depends on its ability to successfully handle obstacles and address conflicts. If it cannot deal with such issues, the team may not accomplish its mission. Team members may quit, or the team may disband altogether.

How Do Obstacles and Conflicts Impede Teamwork?

Individuals can often accomplish more if they band together and work as a team. Each person contributes a different set of skills, experience,

Obstacles and conflict in the workplace can be challenging.
© IOFOTO/SHUTTERSTOCK
.COM.

and personal traits that add value to a group. If your team is plagued by obstacles and conflict, however, it may accomplish less than the individuals would have if they had worked alone. Loss of enthusiasm, inferior work quality, missed deadlines, decreased productivity, and unhappy personnel are common symptoms of poor teamwork and may indicate that there are obstacles and conflicts occurring that need to be worked out. Faced with discord, you may form cliques that fracture the group even more. Others may quit or are dismissed and must be replaced, which slows your team's progress toward unity and top performance.

In contrast, a healthy team dynamic creates a more pleasant and successful work experience. You complete projects quickly, and the quality of your work improves. Team members interact frequently and feel comfortable speaking to each other without fear of conflict. This improves communication and generates a spirit of enthusiasm, patience, and goodwill. When your team works well together in an efficient, friendly way, the entire organization functions more effectively.

How Does Poor Communication Contribute to Obstacles and Conflicts within Teams?

Poor communication between teammates is often the root cause of conflict. If you cannot effectively express information, as well as your ideas and feelings, the team is likely to run into problems. A language barrier is one cause of poor communication. In the United States, the labor force includes a large number of immigrants whose first language is not English. Companies also frequently interact with contacts in foreign countries where different languages are spoken. Different cultural behaviors and manners may also contribute to miscommunication.

Another common source of conflict are team members who purposefully refuse to communicate. This may be a way of deliberately withdrawing from the group or attempting to exert authority by withholding

What Should I Do If I Am Uncomfortable with Conflict?

For some people, conflict within a team is not just uncomfortable, it is extremely stressful. People who feel this way will likely try very hard to avoid it at all costs. Often this tactic manifests itself as passive aggression. That is, instead of straightforwardly addressing a conflict, a person who is uncomfortable with conflict may quietly express his or her displeasure and anger. Signs of passive-aggressive behavior include acting cold or standoffish, not performing tasks well or at all, and speaking sarcastically, among other characteristics.

If you are uncomfortable with conflict, the next time a conflict arises within your team, do whatever activity works best for you to calm yourself down. This might mean taking a few deep breaths, meditating, drinking a cup of chamomile tea, or going out for a walk to get some fresh air. Some people feel better if they can vent their feelings to a trusted confidante. Then, simply accept the fact that conflict is a naturally occurring, normal part of team behavior. When different personalities with different life experiences and identities gather together for a period of time, conflict is virtually guaranteed to happen. By accepting the presence of conflict, you'll see that it is a normal occurrence and nothing to be too concerned about.

In addition, becoming comfortable with conflict means accepting that conflict is not only natural but also, at times, healthy. Conflicts alert the team that something isn't working and that they need to work collaboratively toward a solution. They are similar to a "check engine" light blinking on your car. The presence of a conflict is simply a symptom of a larger problem that will need to be solved in order for the team to be successful.

information. Other people are simply reserved and do not enjoy talking. Still others have things to say but hesitate due to lack of confidence or poor communication skills. Some may speak up but have a hard time expressing themselves.

How Does the Presence of Different Personality Types Contribute to Obstacles and Conflicts within a Team?

Conflicts and obstacles often stem from personality traits that irritate other people in the group. For example, feeling enthusiastic, you may try to take control of tasks that are the responsibility of another, leaving that person upset. Or instead of cooperating and helping everyone perform at their best, a team member undermines coworkers through backstabbing and other unfair practices. Bullying is another type of conduct that ruins morale, whether it is done by a team member or the team leader.

In addition, some people have difficulty understanding why other personality types act the way they do. If you are an introvert, you may not know how to interact with extroverts. If you tend to make quick choices, you may not understand those who need a longer time to deliberate and weigh options. As an analytical thinker, you may not comprehend a team member who acts from his or her intuition.

How Does Poor Leadership Contribute to Obstacles and Conflicts within Teams?

Obstacles and conflict within a team may sometimes be the result of poor leadership. If your leader lacks managerial skills and does not provide the team with a strong sense of direction, he or she may be unknowingly generating obstacles and conflicts for the team. It is important to make sure that the team has specific goals and a plan for achieving them. In this scenario, tasks may be left undone, or the same job might wind up being done by two different people, which wastes valuable resources. If your leader provides each team member with a clearly defined role and specific responsibilities, obstacles and conflicts are less likely to occur.

Moreover, if the group is to perform at its best, the leader must function as part of the team. Otherwise, his or her knowledge and abilities might not be available when the team needs them. Some leaders neglect their teams and are not sufficiently involved in the project. In this instance, your group will probably lack direction and an understanding of who has authority over various aspects of the work. At the other end of the spectrum are dictatorial leaders. They refuse to share power and do not respect the opinions, expertise, and individual needs of team members. These types of leaders operate in a detached way instead of involving everyone in the process. For example, your leader might dominate team meetings and spend the time issuing orders instead of encouraging members to participate in a dialog about the project. In this environment, no one but the leader feels comfortable making meaningful comments. On the other hand, free-flowing, open, and spontaneous communication indicates that the team is functioning well.

How Do the Stages of Team Development Explain How Obstacles and Conflicts Happen?

There are several stages of team development, which were first identified by theorist Bruce W. Tuckman in 1965. Instead of proceeding through each level in a linear way, teams sometimes move back and forth between stages. They might also remain at one level indefinitely, often stage one or two, because they fail to achieve more effective teamwork.

In the initial stage, known as "forming," team members usually try to avoid conflict as they become acquainted with each other and the project at hand. Wanting to be accepted, they seldom discuss their feelings, beliefs, or weighty issues. Instead, they focus on tasks such as organizing the group, scheduling meetings, and establishing assignments for each person. This stage of team building tends to feel comfortable and safe but is not particularly productive.

During the second stage, called "storming," conflicts arise as the group encounters major issues that must be resolved. Individuals begin to express their differences of opinion and align with team members who agree with them. Their patience with each other wears thin, and they make less of an effort to be courteous. The team might engage in open bickering, or the conflict might remain partially hidden. Some individuals feel uncomfortable with this new group dynamic, while others welcome the opportunity for an open but risky airing of grievances and other topics that were previously off limits. At this level of team building, some groups become so bogged down that they cannot progress to the next two stages, where performance is highest.

By the third stage, "norming," team members have generally moved beyond their conflicts to reach a deeper understanding and appreciation of each other. The group has established norms, defined the role and responsibilities of each person, and agreed upon a plan for reaching its goals. The team has begun to feel united, mutually supportive, and committed to its purpose.

Not all teams reach the fourth stage, "performing," where the group achieves its greatest efficiency and productivity. Here, team members know each other, identify with the group, and feel loyalty toward it.

They depend on each other a great deal and participate fully in the group process, but the team is so flexible that individuals also have the freedom to work independently. At this high level of teamwork, individuals assume different roles and responsibilities whenever necessary to accomplish the task as competently as possible. In addition, conflicts and obstacles are less likely to happen. But, when they do, the team has the skills to competently address them.

How Can Communication Skills Help Teams Overcome Obstacles and Conflicts?

Straightforward, courteous communication is the most useful tool for resolving differences among team members. If you have a conflict with a coworker, it is usually best to talk to the person in a spirit of honesty, self-discipline, and professionalism. This is the mature way of handling an interpersonal dispute, and it tends to be more effective than complaining to management or to other people on the team.

A system that allows open, honest communication is essential for a group to work effectively. Without it, team members are likely to vent their frustrations by complaining behind each other's backs and looking for ways to get back at those who have offended them. Without launching into attacks or accusations, explain your point of view and how you feel about the situation. Listen carefully to what your teammate says in response, and try to understand that perspective. Think about your own behavior to determine whether you might be causing some of the difficulties. Finally, ask for suggestions that might help the two of you work together more constructively.

In addition, building better relationships with your team may help you improve how you communicate with them. It could also build team cohesion. To build better relationships with all members of your team, look for opportunities to do thoughtful things for them. If something goes wrong, avoid focusing on punishing the person who made the mistake. Instead, try to influence the team to view the incident as a learning experience for everyone. When a conflict arises, do not have a knee-jerk reaction. It is much more effective to carefully consider why the person is behaving in that way.

To become better acquainted with your colleagues and deepen your understanding of their viewpoints, spend time together. For example, you could meet them for lunch or socialize in some way that is not related to your job. This will cultivate a deeper, more comfortable, and more cordial relationship. Establishing common ground and genuine appreciation for each other strengthens the team.

How Can a Leader's Skills Help Teams Overcome Obstacles and Conflicts?

Like all members of the group, leaders must develop teamwork skills. In particular, they should be especially adept at helping their team overcome obstacles and conflict. If you are the leader, your job is to guide, nurture, inspire, and reassure individuals in order to help them flourish. If each individual prospers, so will the team as a whole, and obstacles and conflicts are less likely to happen. This is a case of the group becoming greater than the sum of its parts, accomplishing more than what the individuals could on their own. In addition, as a leader you will ensure that all team members are equally sharing the workload. No one is doing too much work and getting burned out, and no one is simply skating by on the work of others.

The leader should also make sure that the team is challenged to do its best in a spirit of camaraderie, not competition. Good team management involves acknowledging the accomplishments of the individuals, valuing their strengths, and balancing their weaknesses by recruiting other members who are strong in those areas. As the leader, you should become acquainted with the members of your team so that you understand their personalities and can adjust your approach accordingly. This will help you avoid potential conflicts in the future. For example, you will most likely need to be gentle in dealing with a shy or self-doubting person who has great talent. If you create a safe place, that individual may feel confident enough to share fully with the rest of the group. A fearless, adventurous team member might also be enlisted to provide balance in this situation.

What Else Can Team Members Do to Overcome Obstacles and Conflicts?

Teams that are dedicated to overcoming obstacles and conflicts will put the needs of the team ahead of their own as well as create a plan that outlines the type of behavior that is expected within the team. It is helpful if the team leader spearheads these efforts, but all team members can make personal efforts to do the above actions.

To overcome obstacles and conflicts, place the larger needs of the team ahead of your own personal needs. This is not to say that you should sacrifice your health or personal life for the well-being of the team. Rather, you should develop solutions to obstacles and conflicts that benefit the team's overall mission, not your own particular mission. An added benefit of this approach is that you will be considered a good team player and, therefore, a valuable asset.

Obstacles and conflicts often happen because team members do not know how they are supposed to act in a specific team. They might have learned in a previous position that the best way to achieve a leader's appreciation is to speak badly about fellow teammates. Or they may think that they are not allowed to express frustration or any negative emotions and, therefore, keep all of their feelings bottled up. Having a group brainstorming station in which the leader and team members speak openly about team culture and define what types of behaviors are appropriate (and which ones aren't) will likely help the team be on the same page and overcome future problems more successfully.

For More Information

BOOKS

Avery, Christopher M., Meri Aaron Walker, and Erin O'Toole Murphy. *Teamworking Is an Individual Skill: Getting Your Work Done When Sharing Responsibility*. San Francisco: Berrett-Koehler, 2001.

Blanchard, Kenneth H., Sheldon M. Bowles, Donald Carew, and Eunice Parisi-Carew. *High Five! The Magic of Working Together*. New York: William Morrow, 2000.

Jamail, Nathan. *The Leadership Playbook: Creating a Coaching Culture to Build Winning Business Teams*. New York: Gotham, 2014.

Lencioni, Patrick. *The Advantage: Why Organizational Health Trumps Everything Else in Business*. San Francisco: Jossey-Bass, 2012.

PERIODICALS

Bishop, James W., and Ashish Mahajan. "The Use of Teams in Organizations: When a Good Idea Isn't and When a Good Idea Goes Bad." *Lab Medicine* 36 (2005): 281–85. This article can also be found online at http://labmed.ascpjournals.org/content/36/5/281.full.pdf+html.

"The Critical Role of Teams." *The Ken Blanchard Companies*. www.kenblanchard.com/img/pub/pdf_critical_role_teams.pdf (accessed January 26, 2015).

Smith, Jacquelyn. "How to Identify Your Workplace Strengths." *Forbes*, August 30, 2013. This article can also be found online at http://www.forbes.com/sites/jacquelynsmith/2013/08/30/how-to-identify-your-workplace-strengths/.

Symons, Andrew B. "A Tool for Self-Assessment of Communication Skills and Professionalism in Residents." *BMC Medical Education*, January 8, 2009. This article can also be found online at http://www.biomedcentral .com/1472-6920/9/1/#abs.

WEBSITES

"The Basics of Working on Teams." *Massachusetts Institute of Technology*. http:// hrweb.mit.edu/learning-development/learning-topics/teams/articles/basics (accessed November 23, 2014).

"Diversity and Inclusion Training." *Workplace Answers*. http://www .workplaceanswers.com/diversity-and-inclusion/ (accessed January 28, 2015).

Feigenbaum, Eric. "About Barriers to Effective Communication within the Workplace." *Houston Chronicle*. http://smallbusiness.chron.com/barriers-effective-communication-within-workplace-3185.html (accessed January 7, 2015).

Felce, David, and Jonathan Perry. "Assessing Work-Related Social Skills: Existing Approaches and Instruments." *Welsh Center for Learning Disabilities, Cardiff University*. http://www.projectatlas.org/publications/assessingwork .pdf (accessed December 19, 2014).

"How Good Is Your Time Management?" *Mind Tools*. http://www.mindtools .com/pages/article/newHTE_88.htm (accessed February 4, 2015).

"Johari Window." *businessballs.com*. http://www.businessballs.com/ johariwindowmodel.htm (accessed December 15, 2014).

Lau, Edmond. "Why and Where Is Teamwork Important?" *Forbes*. http:// www.forbes.com/sites/quora/2013/01/23/why-and-where-is-teamwork-important/ (accessed January 26, 2015).

"Leadership." *The Happy Manager*. http://www.the-happy-manager.com/ (accessed January 7, 2015).

Linn, Allison. "Wage Gap Starts Right after College, Research Shows." *Today*. October 23, 2012. http://www.today.com/money/wage-gap-starts-right-after-college-research-shows-1C6639835 (accessed January 28, 2015).

Lubber, Mindy S. "How Timberland, Levi's Use Teamwork to Advance Sustainability." *Greenbiz*. May 9, 2011. http://www.greenbiz.com/blog/2011/05/09/ how-companies-court-stakeholders-accelerate-sustainability (accessed January 26, 2015).

"Management: Developing Self Management Skills." *Scottish Qualifications Authority*. http://www.sqa.org.uk/files_ccc/CB3496_self_management.pdf (accessed February 4, 2015).

McFarlin, Kate. "Importance of Different Personalities in a Workplace." *Houston Chronicle*. http://smallbusiness.chron.com/importance-different-personalities-workplace-10733.html (accessed January 28, 2015).

McNamara, Carter. "Group Dynamics: Basic Nature of Groups and How They Develop." *Free Management Library*. http://managementhelp.org/groups/ dynamics-theories.htm (accessed January 5, 2015).

Myatt, Mike. "Five Keys of Dealing with Workplace Conflict." *Forbes*. http:// www.forbes.com/sites/mikemyatt/2012/02/22/5-keys-to-dealing-with-workplace-conflict/ (accessed February 4, 2015).

Myers Briggs Foundation. http://www.myersbriggs.org/my-mbti-personality-type/mbti-basics/ (accessed December 13, 2014).

"Self-Management." *Trinity College Dublin.* https://student-learning.tcd.ie/undergraduate/topics/self-management/ (accessed December 15, 2014).

"The Simple Truth about the Gender Pay Gap." *American Association of University Women.* http://www.aauw.org/research/the-simple-truth-about-the-gender-pay-gap/ (accessed February 3, 2015).

Smith, Jacquelyn. "10 Ways to Get Your Colleagues to Work with You Better." *Forbes.* http://www.forbes.com/sites/jacquelynsmith/2012/10/03/10-ways-to-get-your-colleagues-to-work-with-you-better/ (accessed January 7, 2015).

Symons, Andrew B., Andrew Swanson, Denise McGuigan, Susan Orrange, and Elie A. Akl. "A Tool for Self-Assessment of Communication Skills and Professionalism in Residents." *BMC Medical Education.* http://www.biomedcentral.com/1472-6920/9/1/#abs (accessed February 4, 2015).

"Team Building." *Accel-Team.* http://www.accel-team.com/team_building/index.html (accessed January 5, 2015).

"Team Culture." *Cultural Orientations Approach.* http://www.culturalorientations.com/Articles/Team-Culture/70/ (accessed November 23, 2014).

"Teamwork Skills: Being an Effective Group Member." *University of Waterloo.* https://uwaterloo.ca/centre-for-teaching-excellence/teaching-resources/teaching-tips/tips-students/being-part-team/teamwork-skills-being-effective-group-member (accessed February 4, 2015).

"Teamworking Skills." *University of Kent.* http://www.kent.ac.uk/careers/sk/teamwork.htm (accessed February 4, 2015).

"What Are the Benefits of Having Teams in a Business Environment." *Call of the Wild.* http://www.callofthewild.co.uk/library/useful-articles/what-are-the-benefits-of-havingteams-in-a-business-environment/ (accessed January 26, 2015).

"Workplaces That Work: Work Teams and Groups." *Community Foundations of Canada.* http://hrcouncil.ca/hr-toolkit/workplaces-team-work.cfm (accessed January 7, 2015).

Negotiation Skills

What Is Formal Negotiation?

Formal negotiation is a discussion process that allows two or more parties to resolve matters of mutual concern or disagreement. This process is necessary when the parties cannot resolve a problem independently. For the process to work, all who are involved must agree to negotiate and then schedule a time to meet to talk about the issue in a formal setting.

In a negotiation, the parties discuss their interests in order to determine an outcome that is acceptable to everyone. A successful negotiation is one that allows all participants to feel that their needs have been met and that all differences have been amicably resolved. Negotiation is different from mediation in that there is no impartial, or neutral, party to assist in the process of reaching an agreement. It is also different from arbitration, in which two parties argue their case and a third party decides on the outcome.

What Kinds of Situations Require Formal Negotiation?

Formal negotiations can occur in business, the law, nonprofit work, government, and international relations. They often result in long-term

Legal negotiations are usually formal and legally binding. They should be the last choice of negotiation not the first.
© BIKERIDERLONDON/
SHUTTERSTOCK.COM.

and legally binding agreements, so they typically have established time limits and may have relatively high stakes. Some examples of formal negotiations include employee bargaining agreements, peace treaties, hostage negotiations, and terms of sale or purchase.

Formal negotiations are usually prearranged and include an agenda, or list of things that must be addressed. These meetings require high-level communications skills, so businesses and governments often choose to employ a trained negotiator to represent their interests. In academia and private industry, much time and money is spent on studying and perfecting effective practices and identifying the best negotiating strategy for each situation. The study of negotiation is called negotiation theory.

How Is Formal Negotiation Different from Informal Negotiation?

While the skills and strategies used in formal negotiation are the same as those used in informal negotiation, the situations that require these processes differ greatly. Informal negotiations occur frequently in our personal lives with family and friends, as well as in the workplace. They generally have lower risks than formal negotiations and tend to be spontaneous. For example, parents often negotiate with each other about issues such as child care and free time.

Roger Fisher: Negotiation Theorist

Roger Fisher (1922–2012) is remembered for his contributions to negotiation theory. Fisher earned a degree from Harvard Law School in 1948 and practiced law in Washington, D.C., before returning to Harvard as a law professor in 1960. As an attorney he had worked on several international negotiations, and as a professor he became increasingly interested in what makes a good negotiator and a successful negotiation. In 1979 he cofounded the Harvard Negotiation Project with William L. Ury to promote the study and practice of negotiation and conflict resolution.

Fisher is perhaps best known for the 1981 book *Getting to Yes: Negotiating Agreement without Giving In*, which he coauthored with Ury. Influenced by Fisher and Ury's work at the Harvard Negotiation Project, the book outlines a strategy for negotiation that can be applied in both personal and professional life. Among its key features are a call to separate people

and emotions from the problem that needs solving, figuring out the real interests at stake and focusing on those rather than on strict positions, looking for opportunities for mutual gain, and always using objective criteria. The book was a huge international success and has been translated into 36 languages. Although approaches to negotiation have evolved in the decades following its initial publication, *Getting to Yes* continues to enjoy a wide circulation, and it is considered a foundational text on negotiation theory.

During the 1980s and 1990s Fisher was active in working to bring peace to the Middle East and El Salvador and supported the fight against apartheid in South Africa. He is also said to have helped initiate a meeting between President Ronald Reagan and Soviet leader Mikhail Gorbachev. He remained active in diplomatic consulting throughout his life. He died on August 25, 2012.

Formal negotiations deal with more serious issues and have farther-reaching effects that are sometimes legally binding. The meetings are scheduled and planned in advance, which gives those involved in the discussion time to learn about the others' interests and goals in order to prepare a strategy.

What Is the Role of Formal Negotiation in Business?

Formal negotiation is a major part of doing business. It occurs at high levels, such as in *mergers* of companies, and also at lower levels, such as in individual employee contracts. Many transactions in different areas of business require formal negotiation, from sales to human resources, so the ability to negotiate is a highly valued professional skill.

Merger: *The combination of operations and management of two firms to establish a new legal entity.*

Good negotiation practices can build positive relationships between companies, which may leave openings for further collaboration or transactions. Successful formal negotiations can also forge long-term solutions to disagreements. Less structured or hurried agreements can break down more easily, leaving room for renewed conflict or bad feelings.

What Steps Are Involved in Formal Negotiation?

Accomplished negotiators follow several steps to reach the agreements they want. They prepare by learning ahead of time about all parties involved, as well as about the issues of concern. Through their advance research, they work to determine what the minimum and maximum acceptable outcomes will be for themselves as well as for the other participants. Preparation is vital to a successful outcome, so it is important for those involved in a negotiation process to gather as much information as possible.

Once the process begins, all parties present their arguments. Dialogue follows, as they discuss possibilities and solutions and decide whether they are willing to agree to or compromise on any of the issues. Once the parties reach an agreement, the discussion ends with the creation of a binding contract that documents the outcome.

What Are the Types of Negotiable Issues?

There are three types of negotiable issues: compatible, distributive, and integrative. If an issue is compatible, all parties want the same outcome. This type of issue is the easiest to resolve in a negotiation. A savvy negotiator will be able to identify compatible issues in order to build positive feelings of agreement between the parties.

Distributive issues involve a fixed sum that the parties must divide like a pie. Distributive negotiating is often described as win-lose, since the parties are competing for a limited quantity of a resource. This type of negotiation can be confrontational and can lead the participants to stand firm to protect their interests and avoid compromise. Distributive negotiations are best suited to situations in which the parties' relationships will be short term, and they often involve the use of aggressive, adversarial tactics.

Integrative issues allow the interested parties to view their dispute as having multiple possible solutions. Integrative negotiating helps the participants make compromises and look for mutually beneficial options. In a way, finding and capitalizing on integrative issues is like enlarging the pie of resources. It is often referred to as win-win negotiation.

In recent decades, negotiators have been increasingly looking for ways to take integrative approaches to distributive issues, shifting their thinking from win-lose to win-win. Integrative methods require negotiators to listen to the other parties' needs and find creative ways to help everyone reach a satisfactory outcome. Parties involved in integrative negotiations cooperate with one another to find the maximum possible benefit for all interests.

How Do Negotiating Parties Set Goals?

Before a negotiation, the participants should analyze and set their own goals for the desired outcome. Each negotiator should determine the least amount of value he or she can accept, which is known as the Least Supportable Outcome (LSO). Conversely, each negotiator should know the most value he or she can reasonably expect, or the Maximum Supportable Outcome (MSO). Finally and most importantly, each participant should have a Best Alternative to the Negotiated Agreement (BATNA).

The BATNA is a backup plan if those involved are unable to reach an agreement. This plan should include the actions to take or settlements to accept if negotiations fail. Expert negotiators use BATNAs as leverage in the negotiating process, but they do not usually disclose the details of their BATNA to the other parties. However, it can be useful for them to learn as much as possible about the other party's BATNA.

What Are Some Strategies and Tactics Used in Negotiations?

Successful negotiators are familiar with many different strategies that can range from aggressive to passive. It is often up to the negotiator to determine whether or not to view the other party as an adversary or as a partner in the process, and the strategies he or she chooses will reflect that view.

One kind of aggressive tactic is known as brinkmanship, or pushing the other party to the brink of their comfort level to force an agreement. Some adversarial negotiators attempt to force the other party to back down because of fear that they will not get a deal they can live with. Softer tactics can include making frequent concessions to maintain positive relationships or asking lots of questions to keep the discussion going.

What Happens during the Negotiation Process?

After preparing strategies and approaches, the bulk of the negotiation process occurs when the parties sit down together for a formal discussion. Negotiations generally begin with representatives of each party presenting a case for what they want and, if the discussion is not adversarial, stating what they are willing to bend on. Then the parties discuss possible solutions and outcomes. This part of the process can take minutes, days, or months, depending on the nature of the issues and what is at stake.

The discussions include exploration of possible concessions, LSOs, MSOs, and BATNAs and the search for common ground. All parties must settle on agreements about various smaller points before they can secure the overall agreement. Once all parties agree to the terms of all issues, the agreement is documented in a formal written contract. In most cases, this document must be officially signed and approved by those in authority before the terms can be implemented.

Even for the most prepared, experienced negotiators, it is not always possible to reach an acceptable agreement, and negotiations can sometimes fail. Having a BATNA in reserve can reduce the pressure on the participants in a negotiation if the discussions are not going well. It also can allow negotiators to walk away from the proceedings, which can sometimes be a powerful persuasive tactic. If the parties need to remain in negotiations after a deadlock, they may need to employ a mediator or an arbitrator to solve the conflict.

How Can I Build My Negotiation Skills?

Good negotiation skills are valuable in many different settings and can help build strong relationships. To be successful in negotiation, you should be confident and have an assertive communication style, and you should be considerate of others. Effective negotiators maintain a strong position while focusing the conversation on finding the best agreement for everyone involved. You should base your statements on facts instead of emotion and avoid criticism and aggressive confrontation. These efforts can help you maintain goodwill among the interested parties.

Good listening skills will allow you to be flexible and ready to hear others' perspectives, which may provide opportunities for building common ground. Creativity is vital to integrative negotiation in order to find unexpected solutions. You will also need to be able to communicate well. Negotiators must be able to explain their ideas, terms, and concessions clearly in order to ensure understanding.

The best way to hone formal negotiation skills is to practice and experiment. There are numerous books, articles, and online resources that teach formal negotiation skills. Many colleges, universities, and private companies also offer courses that can help. Studying the techniques and strategies of negotiation is important, but gaining experience is vital. *Role-playing* with others who are learning negotiation skills is the safest way to practice, since the stakes will be low or nonexistent. However, you can also learn by participating in negotiations with experienced professionals or teams.

Role-play: *To act out a situation before it actually takes place to prepare for a variety of potential reactions.*

Informal Negotiations

What Is Informal Negotiation?

Negotiation is a process of dialogue that allows two or more parties to resolve matters of mutual concern or disagreement. It is common in both professional and everyday life. While formal negotiations involve a set agenda and allow both parties to prepare in advance, informal negotiations generally occur without an agenda or prior planning. This type of negotiation does not include legal counsel, even though some informal negotiations can result in legally binding agreements.

Informal negotiations generally occur as a conversation between two or more individuals. During the negotiations, which can take minutes or hours, participants discuss issues related to the dispute and ideally reach a resolution that benefits everyone. Informal proceedings can create a friendly, relaxed atmosphere that can positively influence an outcome. Furthermore, the conversational nature of the discussion can leave the involved parties unaware that they are even negotiating.

In What Situations Do Informal Negotiations Occur?

 Negotiations occur frequently in business, government, and foreign affairs as well as in our family and personal lives. In fact, you probably find it difficult to get through a day without negotiating. Informal negotiations are more typical in personal settings but can also be used by professional negotiators in high-stakes situations. Formal negotiations, because they are planned and structured, are less common in personal or family life.

Informal negotiations can occur in many places and at different times. For example, you may engage in informal negotiation during a chat over coffee, during a chance meeting in an office break room, or even during a formal meeting. Common examples of informal negotiation topics include parents deciding on work and child-care schedules, workers persuading a boss to support an initiative, and employees working out the details of a policy with others in their department.

Informal negotiations can also take place as a part of more extensive formal negotiations. For example, if world leaders are negotiating a complex international issue, members of the involved parties may hold informal negotiations during breaks or over dinner to form alliances on issues or to settle smaller matters. These informal negotiations allow for conversations that are less restrained by formal, legal terms.

Informal negotiations also happen in everyday situations.
© RIDO/SHUTTERSTOCK.COM.

How Is Informal Negotiation Different from Formal Negotiation?

Informal negotiations differ from formal negotiations in that they are not planned, structured, or even anticipated. When you are involved in formal negotiations, the expectation is that you will prepare, often extensively, in order to learn about the other parties' goals, relationships, and approaches. This knowledge can help you predict how the other party might react to your goals, how hard they will fight to meet their own, and how you should approach the negotiation as a result.

When you are engaged in informal negotiations, especially in personal settings, you most likely already know the other parties' goals and interests well enough to negotiate without research. In situations in which you are negotiating informally with strangers, it is often over low-stakes issues, such as the price of a food item, that do not require intimate knowledge to ensure a satisfactory outcome.

Reaching a solution that everyone can agree on while maintaining positive relationships through respectful communication is the ideal result of any kind of negotiation. Even so, formal negotiators have more freedom to bargain hard and use harsher language without worrying about damaging relationships. As informal negotiations often are between friends, family members, or colleagues, it is usually not advantageous to sacrifice relationships for the sake of a desired outcome.

The Art of Conversation

During an informal negotiation, it is important to remain relaxed and put the other person at ease. One way to do this is by thinking of the negotiation as a simple conversation. This can reduce tension and make both parties feel more comfortable. Here are some techniques to help you improve your conversation and, ultimately, negotiation skills.

- Keep an inventory of your skills and personal strengths. During any conversation, remind yourself of those strengths in order to keep yourself relaxed and focused.

- During a conversation, it's important to listen to the other person. Feel free to ask follow-up questions so they know you're really listening.

- Remain positive and keep your responses brief and constructive. Focus on the topic and avoid boring the other person with too much information or too many of your own opinions.

- Ask people you trust to assess your conversation skills and offer tips on how you can improve. Once they've provided feedback, you can practice with them to avoid common mistakes such as talking too much about yourself or looking uninterested in what the other person is saying.

However, informal negotiation still uses many of the strategies and approaches found in formal situations.

What Are the Steps of Informal Negotiations?

In informal negotiations, the first step is to know what you hope to achieve. While extensive preparation is not part of informal negotiations, the most effective negotiators are prepared for the conversation before it happens. If you are starting the negotiation, you will typically have thought about your position ahead of time. At the least, you should know your limits, including your ideal outcome and the least that you will settle for. You should also know what you will be willing to give in to, if anything.

Once you are aware of your goals and limits, the next step is to open the conversation. In many cultures, people begin negotiations by making small talk to build or maintain positive relationships and connections. Depending on your culture and the culture of the other party, as well as the relationship you share, the extent of this small talk can vary greatly; in some cases, it may be nonexistent.

When it is time for the negotiations to begin, whether that is right away or after small talk, you and the other party will take turns presenting your arguments for what you want. Using a variety of strategies, you and the other party will then discuss the dispute until an acceptable solution is reached. Keep in mind that it is not always possible to reach an acceptable agreement or solution. In these cases you will need to decide on an appropriate next step.

If you do reach an agreement, it is important that everyone involved understands the terms and will follow up by completing the actions to which they agreed. In some cases it might be necessary to document the agreement and even have it made more formal through a legal process. In other cases, a handshake or verbal agreement might be sufficient. Either way, you and the other party should end by clarifying how the agreement will be put into action.

What Types of Issues Are Often Addressed during Negotiations?

Some negotiation styles work better with certain types of issues than with others. As a result, it is vital to understand the three major types of negotiable issues: compatible, distributive, and integrative.

If the negotiated issue is compatible, then you and the other party both want the same outcome. These issues are the easiest to resolve, provided that all parties recognize that they exist. For example, if you want to borrow your roommate's car to go to a concert on the same night your roommate wants peace and quiet in order to study for a big test, you have compatible issues.

Distributive issues are those that appear as a fixed or finite sum that parties must divide like a pie. Even a limited resource, however, can be divided in various ways, some which are more equal than others. Distributive negotiating is often described as win-lose: parties compete for a limited quantity of a resource, and, when one party gains more, the other has to lose some. For example, if you buy a stereo from your roommate and negotiate on the price, you get a good deal, but your roommate receives less money as a result.

Integrative issues are those that allow parties to view disputes as having multiple possible solutions. These solutions may include mutually beneficial options that allow everyone to achieve their desired outcome, such as is possible for compatible issues. For instance, if you share a car with your parents, and you each have urgent errands to run, you may find that carpooling to the various locations is easy to arrange. However, it is important to note that integrative issues are different from compatible issues, because in integrative issues you and the other party at first want very different outcomes.

What Are Some Common Negotiation Styles?

There are a variety of strategies you can use to argue for your goals and reach your desired outcome. As mentioned, certain types of issues are more likely to invite the use of particular negotiation styles. For example, distributive negotiation, because it deals with a finite resource, can be confrontational and can lead parties to take a hard line to protect their interests and avoid compromise. Maintaining a distributive view of an issue is best suited to parties whose relationship will be short term. Distributive negotiations are often characterized by an aggressive, adversarial, inflexible style of discussion.

In contrast, an integrative negotiating style helps parties look for mutually beneficial options that allow everyone to gain value. In essence, finding and capitalizing on integrated issues is like enlarging the pie of resources. It is often referred to as win-win negotiation because everyone leaves happy.

Although each type of issue naturally invites a particular style of negotiation, sometimes it is beneficial to use a different approach. For example, if you choose to approach a seemingly distributive issue as integrative, you are likely to find an acceptable outcome that results in a positive relationship with the other party. This is because integrative negotiating asks negotiators to listen to the other party's needs and creatively find ways to provide everyone with value. Encouraging a more aggressive or inflexible party to question the nature of the issue can help guide them toward a more integrative approach. For example, if both you and your parents want to use the car at the same time, asking them if carpooling is an option could shift their thinking to a more integrated style.

Furthermore, there are many formal negotiations strategies that can be used in informal situations. Having a realistic outcome in mind, walking away when negotiations go sour, and keeping the big picture in mind are all helpful strategies. The best results, however, happen between parties who are respectful, listen closely to each other's interests, and are in control of their emotions and communication. In addition, an assertive communication style, which is at the same time confident and considerate of other parties, is advantageous when negotiating. Being assertive means holding firm to your position while focusing the conversation on finding solutions for everyone involved. Assertive communicators use facts instead of emotion to build their arguments and avoid criticizing the other party or engaging in aggressive confrontation.

What Skills Are Necessary for Success in Informal Negotiating?

In order to be an effective negotiator, you need to possess certain skills. In general, you should be positive, empathetic, and reasonable. You should also strive to be an excellent verbal and nonverbal communicator and engage in *active listening*. Good listening skills allow negotiators to hear opportunities for finding common ground. In addition, you should be in control of your communication habits and strategies and use them to both gain advantage and maintain goodwill.

Being a good negotiator also means having a good idea of what is at stake for everyone involved and being ready to hear others' perspectives. In turn, you need to be able to clearly explain your ideas, terms, and concerns in a way that ensures that everyone understands. Once everyone involved is clear on the desired outcomes, it is important to be flexible and creative. Creativity is vital to integrative negotiation because it can help you identify unexpected solutions.

When negotiating, it is important to be able to discuss the issue at hand without getting overly emotional. Positive resolutions happen most often when the negotiations are based on facts and logic. Learning to predict when certain topics or actions will trigger strong emotions can help you prevent them from disrupting the negotiation. If emotions become heated anyway, the simple act of pausing the negotiation for a while can reset and fix the situation. In addition, it is important to know that *nonverbal communication* can cause strong emotions in others. For example, a simple eye roll can cause an intense negative reaction in the other party. Conversely, a welcoming smile and uncrossed, relaxed arms can calm a tense situation.

Active listening:
The act of mindfully hearing and attempting to comprehend the meaning of words spoken by another in a conversation or speech. It can involve nodding one's head, making sounds that indicate attentiveness, and paraphrasing what the other person said.

Nonverbal communication:
Communication without words. It includes facial expressions, eyes, touching, and tone of voice, as well as less obvious messages such as dress, posture, and distance between people.

How Can I Learn to Be a Good Negotiator?

The best way to improve negotiation skills is to learn as much as possible about the art and then to practice and experiment. There are many books, articles, and web resources that teach various forms of negotiation, including Patrick Collins's book *Negotiate to Win* and Harvard University's Program on Negotiation publications. Most business and law schools offer courses on negotiation, including Columbia University, Notre Dame, and the University of Baltimore. Private, for-profit companies that offer negotiations training include Karrass, Edge Negotiation, and ENS International.

Role-play: *To act out a situation before it actually takes place to prepare for a variety of potential reactions.*

However, while studying the techniques and strategies of negotiation are important, practicing is the only way to improve. *Role-playing* with others who are also interested in improving their skills is the safest way to practice, since the stakes are low to nonexistent. You can also improve your skills by becoming more aware of the information negotiations you participate in every day. By increasing your awareness of yourself, the other party, and the most effective practices, you can increase your success as a negotiator.

How Are Persuading, Influencing, and Negotiating Skills Related?

What Are Persuading, Influencing, and Negotiating Skills?

Persuading, influencing, and negotiating are closely related interpersonal skills that people use in both their professional and private lives to achieve desired outcomes. To successfully persuade, influence, and negotiate, it is necessary to communicate calmly and respectfully while keeping emotions in check.

The term *persuading* describes the act of creating a well-reasoned argument to convince a person or group of people to accept a particular position. In practice, persuading requires directly and intentionally convincing others to change, or in some way alter, their opinions or actions. To effectively persuade, an individual must be prepared to back up points with clear and convincing examples and evidence. For instance, if you want to persuade people to shop only with local merchants, you might explain that locally owned stores sell products not available elsewhere, that the products are better made and less expensive than in chain stores, and that shopping in locally owned businesses helps the local economy.

Although the words *influence* and *persuade* are often used interchangeably, they have distinct meanings. Persuasion tends to be obvious and outright, whereas influence is often an indirect mode of communication. For example, if you bring a healthy, tasty lunch to work every day, you may be influencing others to eat healthier. Even if you never say anything about eating healthy and it is not your intention to change the eating habits of other people, your behavior may prove to be influential.

If you are unable to change someone's mind using both your persuading and influencing skills, negotiation may be a good option. Negotiation occurs when two or more people who don't agree try to work

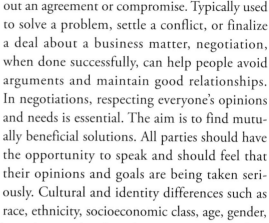

Contract negotiations involve settling the terms and conditions of the legal document that governs the business relationship between the parties. © PRESSMASTER/ SHUTTERSTOCK.COM.

Nonverbal communication: *Communication without words. It includes facial expressions, eyes, touching, and tone of voice, as well as less obvious messages such as dress, posture, and distance between people.*

out an agreement or compromise. Typically used to solve a problem, settle a conflict, or finalize a deal about a business matter, negotiation, when done successfully, can help people avoid arguments and maintain good relationships. In negotiations, respecting everyone's opinions and needs is essential. The aim is to find mutually beneficial solutions. All parties should have the opportunity to speak and should feel that their opinions and goals are being taken seriously. Cultural and identity differences such as race, ethnicity, socioeconomic class, age, gender, religion, and sexual orientation need to be taken into account when entering into negotiations.

Why Are Interpersonal Skills Important in Getting Your Point Across?

You use interpersonal skills to communicate and interact with other people every day, so you need to be able to express your views clearly and directly. Although some people believe interpersonal skills are innate, such abilities can often be learned or improved. Influencing, persuading, and negotiating are types of interpersonal skills.

Strong verbal communication is key to successful influencing, persuading, and negotiating. A good sense of humor helps, as does being an active listener. When you practice being an active listener by reflecting people's ideas back to them, you can build trust and lead to better solutions in the long term. *Nonverbal communication* plays an important role as well. The ability to read facial expressions and body language can help you determine whether people agree or disagree with you. Be sure to account for cultural differences in both verbal and nonverbal communication.

What Are Some Examples of Effective Persuading Skills?

To be successful at persuading, you need to have a clear and definite reason for trying to convince someone of something. You also need evidence to support your opinion. For example, a conservation biologist

How Can You Be a Successful Negotiator?

To be a successful negotiator, it is crucial to show respect for all parties and their opinions. You need to be impartial, showing respect for people who come from different cultural, religious, economic, social, or other backgrounds. You must also be comfortable working with people who have varying positions of power or responsibility in an organization. The more respect you demonstrate, the more trust is built and the easier it will be to find solutions, even when there are conflicts.

During a negotiation, gather as much information and as many ideas as possible from all sides. Encourage teamwork and collaboration. Don't stop the negotiation process when one possible solution is conceived; instead, try to look for a few possible outcomes. Some solutions may favor one party or the other, so it's important to look for one that works for everyone. Clarifying the problem and demonstrating openness to all ideas will help everyone create multiple solutions.

You may find that tensions and emotions rise during a negotiation. As the negotiator, it's important to remain calm and emotionally neutral. Although feelings such as anger, sadness, frustration, excitement, or happiness can help people come to a better understanding of the obvious and underlying issues, negotiators should be neutral so they can fairly diffuse emotions that might interfere with the process while also using such feelings to help everyone come to a better understanding of the situation. You should be empathetic toward emotional responses to build trust but also calm emotions when needed.

who opposes the damming of a river will know all the reasons such an action is harmful to the river. He or she might call on previous scientific research, use graphs and tables, and quote experts to show that the argument is grounded in evidence. Having examples to call on when persuading others not only will strengthen your argument but also will lend you credibility. People will be more likely to trust you based on your careful preparation and knowledge of the subject matter.

Effective persuaders work to convince people who may be open to persuasion, not people who are permanently rooted in their beliefs. Activists who are working to eliminate the death penalty, for example, may focus their efforts on convincing people who have not made up their mind about capital punishment and will avoid targeting people who are clearly in support of it.

People are most easily persuaded when they feel their own needs and opinions are being taken into account. As such, an effective persuader must genuinely listen to the person or group of people he or she is trying to convince. For example a furniture salesperson trying to sell a sofa will be more successful if she knows something about her customer. Does he have a family? Does he work a lot? Is his job stressful? Does it require manual labor? Knowing that her customer is a construction worker could help the salesperson tailor her pitch to that specific audience.

What Are Some Examples of Effective Influencing Skills?

Unlike persuasion, influencing others is often done in a more subtle, less apparent manner. Even though influencing is a more oblique approach, it can be just as effective as persuasion. Indeed, persuading and influencing often go hand in hand. For example, a manager who wants her employees to arrive at work on time may persuade her audience by telling them why it is important that they are not late. She may influence her audience by arriving to work on time herself.

Acting as you want others to act is an effective influencing tactic. A conservation biologist who wants to prevent a river from being dammed will attend anti-dam rallies and events, donate to conservation organizations that are fighting the dam, and contact local politicians and media outlets. This behavior may encourage other citizens who share such beliefs (or who have been persuaded to share such beliefs) to follow suit. These citizens may care about the health of the natural areas near them but did not know what to do to help out. By observing and then mirroring the actions of the conservation biologist, they are able to get involved and, in turn, influence others.

Involvement is another effective way to influence people. For example, a manager who wants her employees to arrive on time might involve them by asking for input on why people are arriving late to work and developing an action plan to encourage punctuality. This approach shows employees that their presence and ideas are valued, which may end up influencing them to be on time.

Win-win solution:
A solution providing a good result for everyone involved.

What Are Some Examples of Effective Negotiating Skills?

When entering into a negotiation, assume everyone is trying his or her best, that no one is out to get you, and that everyone is working toward a ***win-win solution***. Maintain respect for everyone involved in the process, and avoid threats, ultimatums, or being rigid. Try to understand all viewpoints, and listen carefully to what others are saying. Be open and flexible about where you might be willing to negotiate and about what values and opinions are most important to you.

Before you look for solutions, take the time to understand the problem. Once you analyze the problem, you may find that it is not as bad as you first suspected or that it is different than you originally thought. What began as an issue of overcrowding in the lunchroom is actually about teacher and student schedules. Once the problem is understood, you can work on solutions. Do not settle for just any solution. If both parties don't feel good about the negotiation, it won't work. It may take more time, but finding a win-win solution avoids problems in the future.

Consider the goals and needs of all parties. Before negotiations begin think about what you might be willing to compromise and what is nonnegotiable. Consider your past relationships with the other party and how that might impact negotiations.

What Do I Do If Persuading and Influencing Aren't Working?

If your persuading and influencing skills are not changing someone's viewpoint or actions, it is time to turn to negotiation. In negotiation, it is unlikely that both parties will get exactly what they want. They are far more likely to reach a compromise. Working toward a win-win situation is an important goal of negotiation. A win-win means all sides feel they have been listened to, have made positive gains, and are comfortable with any compromises made. Relationships are left in good standing or improved. Each side leaves the negotiation feeling satisfied that their needs have been met; each side wins.

Once negotiations begin, everyone should clarify their goals and expectations. It's useful to establish rules for how discussion will take place and how to move through conflicts or rough spots. Decide if you need a note taker and someone to keep track of time. Hopefully, you will move toward a win-win situation and come to an agreement. Often, it is necessary to develop a plan for implementing the agreement.

Make sure everyone is thanked for his or her efforts and work. Celebrate successes. Acknowledge any new and positive relationships formed during negotiations. Talk about ways new and stronger relationships can be built for further collaborations or to avoid future conflicts.

What Do I Do If Negotiating Isn't Working?

Most negotiations hit dead ends, so don't be discouraged when this happens. Sometimes a solution can be as simple as deciding to stop a particular session of the negotiation early. Giving people some time away from the negotiation can be useful, particularly if they are stuck in a loop of repeating the same issues again and again or are very emotional. Schedule a new meeting time, perhaps in a different location. A change of environment is sometimes just the thing for a fresh start.

Other logistical considerations can change a negotiation for the better. Rearrange the configuration of the seating. Make sure there are regular breaks, and perhaps have food and drinks available so people don't tire or become too hungry. Breaking a large group into smaller groups can help conflicts and stimulate creativity. Trust-building exercises can help build relationships that make it easier to negotiate.

Reviewing goals can help a negotiation move forward. You may need to change goals or decide you can only come to an agreement about some, but not all, of the issues. If you agree only some issues can be resolved, try to stay positive. Focus on how far you have come from where you first started. If a major roadblock can't be overcome, consider hiring a professional mediator who is specifically trained and experienced as a third-party intermediary to resolve disagreements.

The Art of Compromise

What Is Compromise?

Compromise is the process by which two or more parties settle a disagreement by making mutual concessions. This means that in order to reach an agreement, each party gives up something they wanted without completely giving up their original desires. Compromise can help parties involved in a negotiation avoid confrontations, animosity, and hostility.

Compromise is often considered a negotiation between different points of view, but it is more accurately described as a process by which parties split the difference between options or opinions and find middle ground. A good compromise benefits all parties. When reaching a compromise, all involved parties "win" on some issues and "lose" on others, but the ultimate outcome of forward motion should be the most important goal. Making sure both sides win and lose the right things is key, so the focus should be on the success of the end result.

What Conditions Are Necessary for Compromise?

For negotiation to be successful, you and the other party must be ready to come to a compromise. This means that everyone involved is willing to discuss options for resolving the conflict and is prepared to fairly consider each of the options available. It is also important that you take the process of preparing for and carrying out the negotiations seriously. Without a proper strategy in place, people may be hesitant to participate, thus making compromise difficult.

In addition, you must be ready and willing to find common ground. When the focus of a discussion is on continuing a conflict rather than on reaching a settlement, compromise is doomed. If even one party enters the negotiation unwilling to give in, a compromise is unlikely to be successful. It is also important that all parties are present

Shaking hands is one of the modern-day customs involved in sealing mutual agreement to a deal or negotiation.
© PHOTOGRAPHEE.EU/ SHUTTERSTOCK.COM.

at the negotiation. If a critical party or person is absent, the chances of reaching a common agreement are much lower.

When participating in a negotiation, you must be aware that there are multiple options for settling the conflict and that all parties can potentially benefit from reaching a compromise. Otherwise you are likely to see the negotiations as a win-lose situation, which may result in your unwillingness to take part in the conversation or to take the possibility of compromise seriously.

Finally, you should be certain that the proposed compromise is achievable. Many settlements may seem reasonable on paper but are actually impossible to put into practice. Make sure you have a realistic plan in place to execute the agreement once a compromise has been reached; otherwise the negotiations will seem pointless and impractical.

Why Is Compromise Important When Working with Others?

Compromise can help to settle disputes quickly, which is important when a time-sensitive project is being discussed. It can also keep a simmering argument from spinning out of control. Because there is no clear-cut winner, compromise allows you to feel you maintained your integrity without accepting defeat or disgrace.

Many times compromise is used not only to resolve disagreements but also to promote tolerance, which is an important factor when trying to accomplish a common goal. Quite often, all parties involved in negotiations have equally strong points of view. The key is that each side feels that all parties are sacrificing something and gaining something in order to achieve a greater goal. Organizations use compromise to ensure all involved achieve at least a partial victory. This helps to prevent lingering resentment and promotes a healthy environment for teamwork.

How Does the Process of Compromise Work?

When choosing to compromise, it's best to pick your battles. Not every dispute is important enough to be addressed. On the other hand, if you feel a subject is important, it is better to express your opinion than to keep quiet and end up feeling resentful.

Waiting until you are calm to seek a compromise is also helpful, as emotions can distort the source of the disagreement. Stating facts while trying to reach a compromise will give your opinions and emotions more credibility. Instead of criticizing the other party, be sure to speak only for yourself ("I'm concerned because …"), as this is an honest representation of how you view the situation.

Approach negotiations in a calm and balanced way. Never cross-examine the other parties. Asking a lot of yes-or-no questions can put others on the defensive and can make them feel as if you do not take their position seriously. Remember that compromise is a conversation, not an interrogation.

Finally, aim to clear the air rather than to win an argument. The most important factor in compromise is understanding the other person's viewpoint and why that person's opinion is different than your own. This way, common ground can be found in a space where everyone involved feels heard and validated.

When Is Compromise Appropriate?

You can use compromise to resolve disagreements and disputes, particularly when the relationship or situation will benefit from all parties giving in on some of their demands. Also, when the goals of the parties are equally important, compromise can help combine the best of all ideas, creating an even stronger end solution.

Compromise is also useful when significant time and energy are being spent on outcomes that are of moderate importance or when quick resolutions require only temporary fixes. When parties can agree to disagree, compromise is an excellent tool to air differences and keep moving forward.

What Are the Benefits of Compromise?

There are a number of advantages to compromise, the first of which is that everyone involved feels at least partially satisfied. Not everyone in a compromise gets exactly what he or she wants, but each individual gets the sense that the end result satisfies each party equally.

Compromise also offers relatively quick results. This is most important when deadlines are the top priority and conflict is standing in the way of completing tasks or making progress. Reaching a compromise quickly keeps everyone moving forward and erases petty conflicts, forcing all parties to focus on the bigger picture.

When you compromise, you also let others know that you are willing to give and listen rather than simply pushing your own agenda. Demonstrating your willingness to compromise may make future cooperation more likely. By being willing to work with others, you show that, when upcoming activities call for teamwork, there will be a smooth and fluid resolution to conflict.

Compromise also showcases a factor that is often overlooked in personal and business relationships: everyone benefits. By seeking compromise, you show precisely what you stand to lose and gain from the situation and highlight what others stand to lose and gain. With this type of transparency, there is never a question about who has benefited more and who has benefited less.

Are There Situations during Which I Shouldn't Compromise?

Compromise is a vital part of healthy personal or work relationships. However, constantly feeling like you have to compromise with an associate, a business, or another party may have negative consequences. Trying to use compromise to save a personal or professional relationship that is beyond saving can be a mistake. In a partnership that is only being held together by desperation, compromise can be unhealthy and can prolong the process of realizing that the relationship isn't working for either party.

In personal relationships, compromise can sometimes be used to manipulate others into thinking that you are giving in a little, all the while still having all of your needs met. Using compromise as a tool to come out ahead in a competitive-style relationship is very unhealthy.

Small compromises are unavoidable and completely natural, but if you find yourself compromising to the point that your own needs aren't being met at all, then you have likely taken compromise too far. Protecting needs that are vital only to constantly surrender them to compromise does more harm than good for all involved.

What Are the Downsides of Compromising?

Compromise is a useful tool, but you should take care not to rush into it too quickly. Problems can arise when parties with differing needs jump straight into negotiating a compromise and skip the process of finding out what each person needs. In such cases the involved parties may focus too much on what they gave up to make things work, which can lead to resentment and detachment.

A larger problem with compromise is that if you make a concession without a strong and obvious reason, the other party might assume that you will continue to make sacrifices without reasoning down the line. As such, you might be expected to make most of the concessions the next time a disagreement arises.

You may encounter another possible negative if you are in a management position and are negotiating on behalf of other people. Your employees might get upset if you reach a compromise with which they disagree. For example, if your compromise temporarily decreases bottom-line sales for your sales team, this could anger those working beneath you, as they aren't looking at the big-picture plan you have formulated for the future.

Other dangers of compromise include finding all people involved in a lose-lose situation, such that no one is satisfied with the outcome. In some cases compromises need close monitoring to ensure all agreements are met. If a compromise turns foul after a period of time, trust can be shattered in the long run, affecting future endeavors.

What Steps Can I Take If Compromise Isn't Working?

Ego is a dangerous element when trying to smooth out a bumpy compromise. It often prevents you from seeing other people's points of view and, worse, seeing the value of their ideas and opinions. Many strong-willed people immediately reject others' points of view during the process of compromise, denying their validity without fair consideration.

Ego: *One's sense of self-esteem or self-importance.*

In such a situation try to lead others in the group with open-ended questions and statements such as "Tell me about——." "Why do you feel like that?" "How can we make an improvement?" "Please explain further to help me see this better and more clearly."

Stimulating the conversation in this way helps others share their viewpoints and even creates space for them to make suggestions. If this isn't working, try to visit the opposing parties in their workspaces so you can see what shapes their points of view. If all else fails, you may need to get superiors involved to see if they would be open to a compromise.

Ultimately, it is crucial to show and ask for respect in a situation where compromise is rocky. Treating a person with an opposing opinion with respect allows you to disagree, even heatedly at times, and still drive toward a constructive conversation and create an end result that appeases all involved. A respectful attitude will also encourage those with whom you seek compromise to treat you with respect in return.

For More Information

BOOKS

Chaturvedi, P. D., and Mukesh Chaturvedi. *Business Communications: Concepts, Cases, and Applications*. India: Pearson Education, 2011.

Collins, Patrick. *Negotiate to Win: Talking Your Way to What You Want*. New York: Sterling Publishing, 2009.

Diamond, Stuart. *Getting More: How You Can Negotiate to Succeed in Work and Life*. New York:Crown Business, 2012.

The Essentials of Negotiation. Boston: Harvard Business School Publishing, 2005.

Fisher, Roger, William L. Ury, and Bruce Patton. *Getting to Yes: Negotiating Agreement without Giving In*. New York: Penguin Books, 1991.

Patterson, Kerry. *Crucial Conversations: Tools for Talking When Stakes Are High*. New York: McGraw-Hill, 2012.

PERIODICALS

Sanibel, Michael. "The Art of Negotiating: A Practical Guide to Getting What You Want, When You Want It, at the Price You Want." *Entrepreneur*, August 24, 2009. This article can also be found online at http://www.entrepreneur.com/article/203168.

Sherwin, David. "Twelve Essential Negotiating Strategies for Consultants." *Fast Company*, February 4, 2013. This article can also be found online at http://www.fastcodesign.com/1671787/12-essential-negotiating-strategies-for-consultants.

WEBSITES

Baldoni, John, "Compromising When Compromise Is Hard." *Harvard Business Review*. October 12, 2012. http://blogs.hbr.org/2012/10/compromising-when-compromise-i/ (accessed January 8, 2015).

Coburn, Calum. "Negotiation Conflict Styles." *Harvard University*. http://hms.harvard.edu/sites/default/files/assets/Sites/Ombuds/files/Negotiation ConflictStyles.pdf (accessed January 8, 2015).

Fiske, Christine, and Janet A. Clark. "Negotiation Skills." *University of Missouri Extension*. http://extension.missouri.edu/p/gh6830 (accessed December 1, 2014).

Joseph, Chris. "Strengths of Compromise as a Conflict Resolution." *Houston Chronicle*. http://smallbusiness.chron.com/strengths-compromise-conflict-resolution-10502.html (accessed January 8, 2015).

Messinger, Eric. "How to Disagree Agreeably." *Real Simple.* http://www
.realsimple.com/work-life/how-to-disagree-agreeably (accessed January 8,
2015).

"Negotiating Successfully." *Queensland Government Business and Industry Portal.* https://www.business.qld.gov.au/business/running/managing-business-
relationships/negotiating-successfully (accessed October 4, 2014).

Nunberg, Geoff. "What the Word 'Compromise' Really Means." *National Public Radio.* July 19, 2011. http://www.npr.org/2011/07/19/138468870/what-
the-word-compromise-really-means (accessed January 8, 2015).

Shpungin, Elaine, "The Danger of Compromise." *Psychology Today.* February
26, 2012. http://www.psychologytoday.com/blog/peacemeal/201202/the-
danger-compromise (accessed January 8, 2015).

White, Mark. "Maybe It's Just Me, But ..." *Psychology Today.* http://www
.psychologytoday.com/blog/maybe-its-just-me/201106/how-much-should-
you-compromise-your-relationship (accessed January 8, 2015).

Leadership Skills

What Does Effective Leadership Mean?

Leadership is a concept that is widely studied and discussed. Perhaps this is because it is valued in all walks of life. In the business world, *entrepreneurs* and CEOs aspire to be models of leadership. Politicians seeking votes for office present themselves as leaders. All sorts of organizations, whether local or global, from the Parent-Teacher Association (PTA) to the American Medical Association (AMA), thrive when they are properly led. A Marine battalion and a ragtag outfit of guerrilla fighters both depend on skillful leadership in order to succeed in combat.

Defining effective leadership isn't difficult. Broadly and simply, it's a process of bringing a group together to help that group accomplish its goals. The debate lies in identifying the particular actions, attitudes, and qualities that outstanding leaders have in common. No magic formula has been used, but there are some general common traits among leaders, including confidence, vision, passion, and a desire to learn.

Entrepreneur: *A person who takes the risk of organizing and operating a new business venture.*

How Is Vision Essential to Leadership?

Every organization has a purpose and objectives. An effective leader has a clear, compelling vision for the group's success, and that vision, or mission, becomes the organizing principle behind everything the leader does. Effective leaders are forward-looking and directed, and because they know where they're going, in all likelihood they'll get there. It helps to have confidence, both in yourself and in your vision. People look up to leaders who convey positive thinking, patience, persistence, and passion.

Profits: *The money left over from a business's sales after all costs of production have been paid.*

A positive vision is always about something larger than yourself. It's about making the world a better place rather than merely making a *profit*, winning a prize, or reaching some random measure of success. Richard Branson, who plotted an unorthodox course to wealth and success as the founder of the Virgin companies, writes in *The Virgin Way: Everything I Know about Leadership* that leadership vision is, in essence, about dreaming: "People who have the courage to spend their time working on things they love are usually the ones enjoying life the most. They are also the ones who dared to take a risk and chase their dreams."

How Does Vision Relate to Action?

A vision by itself is, of course, not enough. You also need a plan to take it forward. One hallmark of an effective leader is strategic thinking, which is a creative approach to the question of how to get from here to there. With a realistic understanding of your organization and its industry or market, you can assess opportunities and dangers, perceive various possible courses of action, and, relying on a balance of logic and intuition, take appropriate risks.

According to the U.S. Bureau of Labor and Statistics, in 2012 women comprised 38.6% of the chief executives in the United States. © ALWAYS JOY/ SHUTTERSTOCK.COM.

A strategic leader's choices have the power to shape the future of the organization. Effective leadership depends on sensitivity and awareness of the circumstances of the moment, but its essence is proactive, not reactive. In brief, leaders are people who are able to make things happen, take decisive actions, and get results. In business and in life, you will often face complex and difficult situations, with competing interests or conflicting values that create confusion. Effective leaders make decisions quickly when necessary but with neither undue haste nor costly delay, taking advantage of all the resources and information available at the moment.

Furthermore, you should have the determination to carry out your decisions and see them through, even if it takes time to bring about their intended effects. You should realize that meaningful changes rarely happen overnight, and you need to be prepared to stick to your decisions and accept the consequences. On the other hand, it is important to keep an open mind and even change your mind or make adjustments as situations unfold and new information becomes available.

Project management is part of a capable leader's skill set. Large projects need to be broken down into smaller tasks. You should be able to determine which tasks you should accomplish yourself and which ones to delegate to others. It is necessary to coordinate the efforts of a group or team, keeping the big picture in mind and not getting bogged down in details. In the world of politics, leadership often lies in building alliances and agreement to achieve the most that can be achieved within the capabilities and limitations of the group. Legislators refer to this as "the art of the possible."

Management versus Leadership

Management Doing things right	Leadership Doing the right thing
Administration	Innovation
Maintenance	Development
Systems/Structures	People
Short Range	Long Range
How?	What/Why?
Compliance	Commitment
Control	Empowerment/Trust
Reactive	Proactive

SOURCE: ECEOnline. *Leadership and Management.* http://eceonline.core-ed.org/groupcms/view/13898/leadership-and-management.

ILLUSTRATION BY LUMINA DATAMATICS LTD. © 2015 CENGAGE LEARNING.

How Is Communication Related to Leadership?

Strategic thinking plus a proactive approach to decision making form a powerful combination for leadership. Together, they produce what business consultant and former White House official James Rosebush, in a 2014 article on the website *Business Insider*, calls "ideation," the dynamic process of shaping ideas into effective real-world solutions. But one more element is needed, Rosebush notes, to turn ideas into gold. He calls it "radiation," which is "the ability to apply, spread, sell, market, and literally 'radiate' the idea or invention and innovation, to the user, the community, the marketplace, and the buyer."

Rosenbush was writing about persuasive communication. In U.S. senator Dianne Feinstein's words, "Ninety percent of leadership is the

Public relations: *The practice of building and maintaining an organization or individual's relationship with the public.*

Active listening: *The act of mindfully hearing and attempting to comprehend the meaning of words spoken by another in a conversation or speech. It can involve nodding one's head, making sounds that indicate attentiveness, and paraphrasing what the other person said.*

ability to communicate something people want." Effective or charismatic leaders use conversation, public speaking, and writing to articulate their vision in a compelling way, to inspire confidence, and to influence the views and actions of other people. These are also the core techniques of sales, marketing, and ***public relations***. Within an organization, effective communication can rally the members of a team around a common vision, resolve disputes and disagreements, and increase motivation. Popular leaders express their ideas, suggestions, and instructions in clear language and are generous with their encouragement and praise for their colleagues, especially in public settings.

Perhaps the most important communication skill for leaders is the one that's easiest to overlook: listening. Few people are aware of it, but skillful, ***active listening*** is a powerful way of exhibiting leadership. In any dialogue, the listener is the one doing the most learning and, in subtle ways, actually controls the interaction.

Make sure to focus on the other person's words rather than your own thoughts. Ask open-ended questions or invite others to share more deeply by remaining silent. Notice tone of voice and body language and become aware of what's not being said. Using these skills will build trust and may lead to creative proposals and solutions neither party would otherwise have conceived.

What about Interpersonal Factors and Ethics?

Listening does more than provide useful feedback and a source of new ideas, however. It generates empathy and builds relationship bonds that can pay enormous dividends in worker satisfaction. Researchers at Columbia Business School found that executives who combine workplace power with empathy, or "perspective-taking," are most likely to find the best solutions to difficult situations. Recognition of the significance of such factors is beginning to spread slowly through the business world. A qualitative study of the global workforce, published in 2014 by the consulting group Towers Watson, reported that only 40 percent of employees are highly engaged in their work. The main driver of sustainable workplace engagement, the survey concluded, is effective leadership. In particular, managers should treat employees with respect and understand their needs at least as well as workers are trained to perceive the needs of customers. Less than half of the workers surveyed, across more than 30 countries, said they had such a relationship with their employers.

Effective leaders inspire a sense of loyalty from their colleagues and subordinates, in no small part because they demonstrate that same loyalty themselves. It is fundamental that you earn respect by acting with integrity and ethical values suitable to your industry and position. Lead by example, revealing a humble recognition that the group or organization matters more than your own personal success. You should be fair, honest, and impartial in your dealings, which will help ensure the trust of both your coworkers and the wider public.

Organizations that establish a caring internal culture often find that it brings huge payoffs in productivity. In his book *Leaders Eat Last: Why Some Teams Pull Together and Others Don't*, Simon Sinek calls such a culture a "circle of safety." Sinek's key example of this team-oriented leadership model is a military unit on the battlefield, in which every soldier takes responsibility for watching everyone else's back. The circle of safety works, he writes, because "the leaders provide cover from above and the people on the ground look out for each other. This is the reason they are willing to push hard and take the kinds of risks they do. And the way any organization can achieve this is with empathy."

How Do Effective Leaders Respond to the Group's Needs?

From this standpoint, a major attribute of effective leadership is being able to foster a sense of security and loyalty in the group environment. The organization's members or employees will then feel safe to contribute their most enthusiastic and creative work. What's more, they will be empowered to take initiative, take risks, and speak openly and truthfully about their views and concerns, even if they question or disagree with certain decisions or policies of the leadership. This level of engagement is likely to result in higher job satisfaction and group performance.

In addition to these attributes, the business world widely acknowledges that leaders must be skilled at supervising, managing, and directing talent. With responsibility for the group's work output, managers must organize the workforce efficiently. You should assign and delegate tasks, set standards and ensure accountability, seeing to it that the efforts of many are directed toward fulfilling the group's mission. It is also important to engage current talent while nurturing future talent, providing mentorship and opportunities for workers to develop their skills and realize their own leadership potential. In the words of leadership scholar Rex Campbell, "No person is a leader all of the time. Everyone is a leader at some time. Anyone may be a leader at any time."

Effective leaders also understand that different groups and working conditions call for different styles of leadership. Management scholars Paul Hersey and Ken Blanchard elaborated on this notion in developing their theory of "situational leadership." In their model, groups that are low in motivation or competence require intensive, authoritative, hands-on leadership. The more confident and capable the group is of achieving its goals, the more leaders can refrain from personally taking charge of every aspect of the work, shifting to a coaching or delegating style. It follows from this theory that no single approach to leadership will succeed in all cases. Rather, effective leadership is adaptable and sensitive to the needs of the group at any particular time.

What Other Leadership Qualities Can You Develop?

One trait found in all the best leaders, across all areas, is a relentless zeal to learn and improve themselves. Leaders are learners. Their drive to succeed spurs them to invest in themselves and never stop growing. Make a habit of honestly assessing your personal strengths and weaknesses. Consider your weaknesses as areas where you can benefit by focusing on building proficiency. Effective leaders also make a point of recruiting colleagues with complementary skills, or as they put it in the business world, "Hire your weaknesses." Similarly, your mistakes can be among your most powerful learning opportunities, provided you have the security to face them and learn from them.

The psychologist Daniel Goleman, author of the landmark book *Emotional Intelligence* (1995), argues that the qualities that comprise emotional intelligence are more central to effective leadership than technical competence or analytical intellect. These qualities include self-awareness, self-regulation (the ability to control your impulses and emotional reactions), motivation, empathy, and good social skills. At one time people with such characteristics were considered too soft to be outstanding leaders, but, according to Goleman's research, the value of emotional intelligence increases at the highest levels of a company or organization. People whose abilities in these areas are strong will naturally be able to coordinate teams, build positive working relationships, and help organizations adapt to changing conditions. Best of all, you can develop the skill set of emotional intelligence with intention and practice.

Developing Leadership Skills

Why Are Leadership Skills Important in Business?

The overall success of any company depends on the leadership skills of its employees at all levels. When all employees are involved in leadership skill development, businesses have a better chance at success. The most successful businesses and agencies recognize the importance of each employee's potential, and they support the development of leadership skills in everyone, from aspiring leaders to new supervisors to senior managers.

Perhaps one of the most important reasons leadership skills are important in business is that leaders inspire and motivate others to get the job done. As a leader, you can inspire others by learning to communicate a vision, keeping your goal in mind, and seeing the big picture. Taking initiative and accepting responsibility are also inspirational skills.

Resources: *The ingredients of production, including land and natural resources, the size and characteristics of the labor force, and the amount and variety of equipment available for production.*

Once you have inspired others, you should try to motivate them to get involved and to empower them to accomplish tasks. One way you might do this is by focusing on the strengths rather than the weaknesses of those you lead. The ability to recognize and value others' innovative thinking is a motivational leadership skill, as are the abilities to effectively coach and mentor those around you.

A leader must also be able to facilitate the completion of a task or project. In other words, you need to create the conditions necessary to get the job done. This may require a variety of skills, including the ability to make an overall plan and daily detailed plans, to apply procedures and work rules to specific situations, and to distribute *resources*.

What Are the Different Styles of Leadership That I Might Use?

Your workplace may require particular styles of leadership. Various styles emphasize different skills, so the preferred style at your company may be based on the values of the business or the kind of work that needs to be done. Common styles of leadership are authoritarian, procedural, participative, and laissez-faire.

Authoritarian leadership is a directing and controlling style of leadership. It is sometimes called transactional leadership because it is associated with delegating specific work for specific pay. It is best used only on short-term or crisis projects because it may alienate workers over the long term. An authoritarian leader needs to be able to take charge, communicate effectively, and delegate tasks.

Effective leaders usually develop the mentoring and supportive skills needed to help their team members thrive. © DUNCAN ANDISON/SHUTTERSTOCK. COM.

Transformational and procedural leadership styles often go hand in hand, and they are frequently used by project managers, especially when they are working on projects that involve a high degree of risk or large sums of money. Transformational leaders focus on the big picture to inspire a vision, and they are involved in communicating ideas and encouraging teamwork. Procedural leaders need the abilities to plan, delegate responsibilities, stay focused, and motivate team members to follow routines, rules, and policies.

Participative leadership is also called democratic or consulting leadership. This style of leadership is useful when teamwork is essential and when quality of outcome is more important than speed. Participative leaders are skilled at listening, being flexible, and building consensus. Conflict resolution skills are important to participative leadership.

Laissez-faire, or delegative, leadership facilitates decision making, monitors achievements, and communicates with the team, but this style ultimately takes a "hands-off" approach to leadership. Laissez-faire leadership requires the ability to convene meetings but not control the outcomes. This style of leadership is most effective when all members of a team have areas of expertise, because they will be expected to work independently and with little oversight.

What Leadership Skills Will I Need to Succeed in a Changing Business Environment?

The business world is an area of constant growth and change. Frequently, businesses will merge, change ownership or direction, or implement new technology. Leaders for the future will need to be skilled in adaptability and versatility, and they will need to be able to implement change in a positive way.

Adaptability includes being able to adjust goals when situations or conditions change. It also requires continuous learning. When someone introduces a new idea or way of doing something, try saying "yes" before you say "no." This is a great way to learn new skills, and it shows that you are able to adapt to new conditions and methods of execution.

Globalization has been a major source of change in business environments. As a result, one of the most required skills in twenty-first-century businesses is multicultural awareness. It is important that you recognize that your workplace and the businesses it is connected to are part of a global community.

Leaders in particular need to be aware of the cultural contexts, issues, and behaviors of coworkers, business partners, and customers. Leaders with multicultural skills are also self-aware and have empathy for others. They know that communication is key to multicultural awareness. Experts suggest that face-to-face communication is important in addition to e-mail or other forms of remote communication.

Globalization: *A process involving the merging of economies, governmental policies, political movements, and cultures around the world.*

What Are Some Other Skills That Will Help Me as a Leader?

One of the most important leadership skills is the ability to communicate effectively, whether during a presentation to a group or in a one-on-one conversations. To give good presentations you need to learn to consider your audience, summarize important information, and learn how to deliver information in several ways without being repetitive. Skills needed for effective communication during one-on-one conversations include being able to make your point and knowing when you are understood. As a leader, these conversations will also often require you to possess coaching and mentoring skills.

Active listening: *The act of mindfully hearing and attempting to comprehend the meaning of words spoken by another in a conversation or speech. It can involve nodding one's head, making sounds that indicate attentiveness, and paraphrasing what the other person said.*

It is also important to note that there is more to effective communication than just expressing your own views and disseminating your own information and ideas. As a leader, you should possess good listening skills and know when and how to ask the right questions. *Active listening* goes beyond just hearing the words of others and is a skill that can be learned and practiced.

Another important skill for a leader is self-motivation, which includes setting personal goals and having the self-assurance that you can meet those goals. You also need to be able to keep going despite setbacks and unexpected challenges. Self-motivation does not necessarily come naturally, but it can be developed by creating visions of success, practicing goal setting, and revising goals based on experience. Self-motivation can also be nurtured by focusing on your own strengths rather than your weaknesses, having supportive relationships at work, and aligning your work goals with a personal sense of purpose.

Businesses need leaders who know how to collaborate. In order to build the consensus and trust needed for effective collaboration, conflict and disagreement between team members must be faced and resolved before they turn into emotional fights. As a leader, you will need to be able to build the necessary structures to facilitate teamwork. When done properly, this will allow team members to learn, make decisions, communicate effectively, and appreciate each other's work.

How Can I Develop Leadership Skills on the Job?

Every job offers numerous opportunities to further develop leadership skills. Look for opportunities to inspire, motivate, and enable your coworkers to reach goals. This could be as simple as showing enthusiasm, listening to and supporting others, or offering up a new idea. In addition, you should make good use of a coach or mentor—someone more experienced in the work you are doing or would like to do. You can also offer to be a mentor to new employees or to other people you supervise.

The best way to learn how to be a leader is to take on leadership responsibilities, being conscious of the skills you have and the skills you need to strengthen. For example, you could offer to facilitate a team in which the members are experts in areas that you are not. Alternately, you could act as a liaison between a department you are familiar with and a department you are unfamiliar with.

Are There Opportunities to Develop Leadership Skills Outside of the Work Setting?

There are many ways you can develop leadership skills outside of work. For instance, you could volunteer to take on responsibilities in civic or religious organizations, or you might volunteer to coach a youth sport team. Many experts advise that taking on leadership responsibilities is the best way to learn leadership skills.

Another option is to take classes, such as at a community college, in leadership development. These courses typically start with an assessment of your communication, time management, and interpersonal skills. The courses then prepare you to work in a team to design and accomplish a set of goals. You will learn about conflict resolution, how to motivate and inspire others, and how to coach future leaders.

Books, websites, and motivational speakers also provide ways to learn leadership skills. Some focus on youth leadership and have developed programs designed to promote group interaction, build self-confidence, and allow students to explore personal understanding. Others use books, curricula, and study guides for different ages, professions, and countries, which present various leadership theories. Some books include online assessment tools for determining your strengths and the skills you need to work on.

How Can I Demonstrate the Leadership Skills I Have Developed?

If you want to jump-start being a leader at work, use initiative to take advantage of opportunities. For instance, if there is a procedural problem that everyone is aware of, think about ways to solve it. Find out if your superior is open to suggestions. You may also try to anticipate challenges and problems at work and be the first to take action to solve them. Set priorities and goals for yourself that support the goals of the business and take responsibility to meet them.

When you are given leadership responsibilities at work, demonstrate your skills by motivating your team to reach its goals. Be sure to set up good methods for communication, develop plans for meeting goals, and build trust among team members. You should also be sure to give serious thought to task delegation and solicit feedback from coworkers and clients.

Different Leadership Styles

What Is a Leadership Style?

Just as there are different conceptions of what it means to be a leader, there are many different leadership styles. Leadership style is how a leader goes about accomplishing his or her goals. It comprises approaches to leadership tasks such as making and implementing plans, defining roles and tasks, and communicating with and motivating team members.

Leadership styles are developed over time. Your leadership style may evolve with experience, and it may change depending on the task and the team involved. There is no one single leadership style that is right for every leader or situation. You will likely find a style that is comfortable and that works well for your team. You may also decide to remain flexible, adapting your style as necessary.

What Are Some Different Leadership Styles?

In "Leadership That Gets Results," an article in the March 2000 issue of the *Harvard Business Review*, Daniel Goleman presented the results of a three-year study of a random sample of 3,871 executives. Based on the data collected, he proposed that there are six distinctive leadership styles: coaching, pacesetting, affiliative, authoritative, coercive, and democratic.

The statement that can best describe the coaching leadership style is, "Try this." The coaching leader helps team members develop personal strengths that will benefit them over time and have lasting effects. By building people up for the future, the coaching leader ensures future successes down the line.

Pacesetting leadership is used when a team is already skilled and motivated and the leader assumes the position of "Do as I do, now." This style is best suited for times when results need to be expedited quickly and efficiently.

DIFFERENCE BETWEEN
BOSS VS. LEADER

BOSS
- Drives employee
- Depends on authority
- Inspires fear
- Says, " I "
- Places blame for the breakdown
- Knows how it is done
- Uses people
- Take credit
- Commands
- Says, " Go "

LEADER
- Coaches them
- On goodwill
- Generates enthusiasm
- Says, " We "
- Fixes the breakdows
- Shows how it is done
- Develops people
- Gives credit
- Asks
- Says, " Let's go "

Leadership styles definitely differ in the workplace as shown in this picture noting some marked differences between a boss and an effective leader. © KEEPSMILING4U/ SHUTTERSTOCK.COM.

The affiliative leader creates emotional and personal bonds that promote the feeling of belonging to a team. The phrase that best sums up this style of leadership is "People come first." This style works well when a team is in a period of healing from a trauma and needs to rebuild trust within the group.

Authoritative leadership involves the leader keeping an eye on the end goal and allowing each individual team member to decide on the means to get there. This style can best be explained by the sentence "Come with me," and it should inspire and motivate the team to achieve its vision.

Coercive leadership happens when the leader takes the stance of "Do what I tell you." This style demands a team immediately comply with the leader's wishes. The coercive leadership style is most effective in times of crisis. Coercive leaders are quick to make decisions without input from team members.

The final leadership style, democratic, involves building harmony by allowing all to participate. The democratic leader is the type who asks his or her team members, "What do you think?" in order to create a common goal that considers everyone's opinions.

What Are the Positives and Negatives of the Coaching Leadership Style?

Coaching leadership provides a relaxed, friendly work environment, which helps team members recognize both their strengths and their

Daniel Goleman on Emotional Intelligence and Leadership Style

Prior to writing about leadership styles, Daniel Goleman made a name for himself as an expert on the concept of emotional intelligence, sometimes known as EQ or EI. Although Goleman was not the first to use the term, his 1995 book *Emotional Intelligence: Why It Can Matter More than IQ*, helped to popularize it. The book outlines Goleman's argument that emotions have a significant, but underacknowledged, impact on decision making and success. For Goleman, emotional intelligence comprises such skills as empathy, impulse control, self-awareness, and social awareness. In his next book, *Working with Emotional Intelligence* (1998), he considered the role of emotional intelligence in the workplace and most notably how emotional intelligence is a predictor of career success.

Goleman's work on leadership style draws heavily on his work on emotional intelligence.

In "Leadership That Gets Results," the 2000 article that introduced his idea of the six leadership styles, he suggested that these styles are tied to different aspects of emotional intelligence. The article paved the way for new ways of thinking about leadership. Goleman elaborated on his ideas in his 2004 book *Primal Leadership: Realizing the Power of Emotional Intelligence*. Cowritten by Richard Boyatzis and Annie McKee, the book makes a case for the place of emotions in a business environment.

Since the publication of *Emotional Intelligence*, Goleman's work has had a global impact. Its influence is broad, reaching from classrooms, where emotional development is fostered, to boardrooms, where it is often used in the process of interviewing for executive positions.

weaknesses. Coaching leaders want employees to understand how different aspects of a project all fit together. The coaching leader also encourages team members to express and share their opinions in a safe setting and offers positive feedback and support for their ideas. This serves to validate team members' values and shapes a better vision of the overall strategy, helping to improve team performance.

While there are advantages to the coaching leadership style, there are drawbacks as well. The employee must want to be coached; employees who are not interested in professional development might feel the coaching leader is *micromanaging* them, which can in turn wear down an employee's self-confidence. In addition, Goleman noted that the coaching style "flops if the leader lacks the expertise to help the employee along."

Micromanage: *To control every part, no matter how small, of an activity or enterprise.*

What Are the Positives and Negatives of the Pacesetting Leadership Style?

The pacesetting style is very effective in driving a project to its goal as quickly as possible. With the leader literally "setting the pace," the team has a clear-cut lead to follow. Team members never have to question what or where the next step is. By demanding excellence from the team, the pacesetter aims to build a stronger unit, eliminating workers who cannot produce quickly and efficiently. The pacesetting style works well when all the team members are highly skilled and self-motivated.

The problem with pacesetting leaders is that they often believe that they can do a better job than their subordinates and will consequently take on too much responsibility. The reaction from the team can quickly turn hostile, because they are not being trusted to do their jobs. By taking away subordinates' responsibilities, a pacesetting leader is also limiting what the team learns. Over time, pacesetting leaders tend to demotivate team members by making them feel like they are always being corrected or having their tasks taken over by the leader.

What Are the Positives and Negatives of the Affiliative Leadership Style?

An affiliative leader is highly aware of the need for teamwork and values harmony within the group. This style of leadership fosters high morale, communication, and flexibility among team members. By rewarding their team with positive feedback, affiliative leaders hold animosity at bay and manage headstrong team members who feel they must prove their worth. Affiliative leaders establish emotional bonds with their employees and create a work environment where employees have a sense of belonging. As a result, employees often develop a strong loyalty to the company.

One potential pitfall of affiliative leadership is that the emphasis on positive feedback to motivate subordinates can lead to the perception that poor performance will be tolerated. Affiliative leaders may hesitate to provide constructive criticism when their team is headed down the wrong path, consequently allowing them to fail. Weaker team members who are never corrected may not learn how to improve, which can cause deterioration in team performance.

What Are the Positives and Negatives of the Authoritative Leadership Style?

A conceptual thinker with the ability to establish a vision for an organization, the authoritative leader creates clear goals and implements strategies to move the organization into the future. The authoritative leader ensures that the team understands exactly what these goals are, then he or she steps back, allowing team members freedom to accomplish tasks in a timely manner. Because the authoritative leader is a proponent of innovation, he or she welcomes new ideas and strategies that will help the organization accomplish its overarching goals more effectively.

Focused on the future of the company, the authoritative leader may not be interested in improving the day-to-day running of an organization unless it specifically assists in achieving a goal. Also, such a leader may not welcome or take into consideration the input of team members who disagree with his or her goals or the implementation of them (even if these team members have more experience or expertise than the leader). In addition, team members who need precise direction and personal feedback on their work may find the authoritative leader's style too vague and hands-off.

What Are the Positives and Negatives of the Coercive Leadership Style?

Coercive leaders hold a great deal of control over their team and staff. While providing direction, they demand conformity from those beneath them in reaching goals. This leadership style can work well when an organization is in trouble. Coercive leaders are quick to make decisions and helm the project, directing team members toward their end goal by insisting they be given complete power to do so.

The work climate for those who must work under someone using the coercive leadership style can be unhealthy. The coercive leader is inflexible, usually providing workers with little or no reward and removes all responsibility from workers' actions, demanding they simply get the job done. Many employees may actually enjoy being told exactly what to do and how. However, others might see this leadership style as unbearable over the long term.

What Are the Positives and Negatives of the Democratic Leadership Style?

Democratic leaders are excellent at solving complex problems. They do so by collaborating with their team in innovative ways and encouraging all team members to participate in finding solutions to intricate problems. They also build strong teams by being supportive and honest. Creative people thrive under democratic leaders, because their talents are supported and appreciated, and they can feel nurtured and respected.

The democratic leadership style is only effective when employees have enough competence and skills to provide useful input. Another limitation of this style is that it may prevent decisions from being made and can in fact lead to conflict. Democratic leadership also takes time; if a fast turnaround is the goal, a democratic leader may refuse to cut corners and continue to seek out the thoughts of others, delaying necessary action. In an emergency, when quick actions must be taken, there normally is not enough time to find out how everyone involved feels.

How Can I Decide Which Leadership Style Is Best for Me?

Studying leadership styles is the first step in deciding what leadership style works best for you. As you consider each style, think about your own personality. If, for example, you are someone who naturally seeks consensus, you may find that the democratic style of leadership is a good match for you. When choosing a style that is well within your comfort zone, however, it is especially important to consider the pitfalls associated with that style of leadership. Consensus can make your team members feel valued, but as a leader you must make sure you are also providing them with a vision for success.

Although choosing a leadership style is in some ways a personal decision, it is important to take team members into consideration. Remember that not all members of your team will respond in the same way to each style of leadership. Be prepared to adapt your style, venturing out of your comfort zone as necessary to meet the needs of your team and its tasks. You may fear that a shift in your leadership style will signal to your team that you are indecisive, inexperienced, or grasping. On the contrary, a strong and decisive leader reacts to situations in a way that will benefit the team. Communicating the reasons for major shifts in your leadership style will let your team know that you are in tune with the situation and that you are open to trying new ideas for the benefit of the project.

What Should I Do If My Boss's Leadership Style Isn't a Good Fit for Me?

If you regularly work as part of a team, you will be most productive if you respond well to the leadership style of your team manager. At some point in your career, however, you will probably encounter a manager or team leader whose leadership style you find difficult to work under. How you respond to this challenge may determine the success of your team.

If you are struggling with your manager's leadership style, the first step is to get some perspective on the situation. Be objective and professional. Do not allow personal emotions to cloud your thinking. Avoid venting to other team members about your manager or attempting to undermine him or her in team meetings. Instead, think about what specific aspects of the manager's style are impeding your work. Do you need more frequent communication, or is the problem that your manager's desire to communicate frequently is limiting your ability to get your work done? Do you need more direction, or do you feel like you are being micromanaged? Once you have come up with notes about the situation, schedule a time to meet with your manager. Be open and honest about what you are experiencing. Be prepared for your manager to offer suggestions for how you might improve your performance as well.

For More Information

BOOKS

Branson, Richard. *The Virgin Way: Everything I Know about Leadership*. New York: Portfolio/Penguin, 2014.

Bridges, William. *Managing Transitions: Making the Most of Change*. London: Nicholas Brealey Publishing, 2012.

Hersey, Paul, and Kenneth H. Blanchard. *Management of Organizational Behavior: Utilizing Human Resources*. 3rd ed. Englewood Cliffs, NJ: Prentice Hall, 1977.

MacGregor, Mariam G. *Building Everyday Leadership in All Teens: Promoting Attitudes and Actions for Respect and Success: A Curriculum Guide for Teachers and Youth Workers*. Minneapolis: Free Spirit Publishing, 2006.

Sinek, Simon. *Leaders Eat Last: Why Some Teams Pull Together and Others Don't*. New York: Portfolio/Penguin, 2014.

PERIODICALS

Benincasa, Robyn. "Six Leadership Styles, and When You Should Use Them." *Fast Company*, May 29, 2012. This article can also be found online at http://www.fastcompany.com/1838481/6-leadership-styles-and-when-you-should-use-them.

Economy, Peter. "The Nine Traits That Define Great Leadership." *Inc.*, January 24, 2014. This article can also be found online at http://www.inc.com/peter-economy/the-9-traits-that-define-great-leadership.html.

Galinsky, Adam D., et al. "Acceleration with Steering: The Synergistic Benefits of Combining Power and Perspective-Taking." *Social Psychological and Personality Science* 5, no. 6 (2014): 627–35.

Goleman, Daniel. "Leadership That Gets Results." *Harvard Business Review*, March-April 2000, 78–90. This article can also be found online at https://hbr.org/2000/03/leadership-that-gets-results.

———. "What Makes a Leader?" *Harvard Business Review*, January 2004.

Tokar, Jennifer, and John Tindal. "Lessons from the Best: The #1 Place to Work in the Federal Government Shares Its Leadership Development Best Practices." *T+D*, April 8, 2014. This article can also be found online at http://www.astd.org/Publications/Magazines/TD/TD-Archive/2014/04/Lessons-from-the-Best?mktcops=c.govt%7ec.human-capital&mktcois=c.leadership-development%7ec.engagement&mkttag=c.original-official-blog-cat-astd-membership.

WEBSITES

Campbell, Rex. "Leadership: Getting It Done." *University of Missouri*. http://web.missouri.edu/~campbellr/Leadership/ (accessed January 1, 2015).

Fraser, Simon. "What Makes a Good Leader?" *GOV.UK*. May 12, 2014. https://www.gov.uk/government/speeches/what-makes-a-good-leader (accessed January 20, 2015).

"How to Find Out Your Style of Leadership." *University of Kent*. http://www.kent.ac.uk/careers/sk/leadership.htm (accessed November 14, 2014).

The Leadership Challenge: Achieve the Extraordinary. http://www.leadershipchallenge.com/about.aspx (accessed November 14, 2014).

"Leadership Skills: Become an Exceptional Leader." *MindTools: Essential Skills for an Excellent Career*. http://www.mindtools.com/pages/main/newMN_LDR.htm#start (accessed November 14, 2014).

Murray, Alan. "Leadership Styles." *Wall Street Journal*. http://guides.wsj.com/management/developing-a-leadership-style/how-to-develop-a-leadership-style/ (accessed January 20, 2015).

Rosebush, James, "The Most Effective Leaders Have These Two Traits." *Business Insider*. December 2, 2014. http://www.businessinsider.com/effective-leaders-have-these-traits-2014-12 (accessed January 1, 2015).

"The 2014 Global Workforce Study: Driving Engagement through a Consumer-Like Experience." *Towers Watson*. August 2014. http://www.towerswatson.com/en-US/Insights/IC-Types/Survey-Research-Results/2014/08/the-2014-global-workforce-study (accessed January 1, 2015).

Resources for More Information

The following is an alphabetical compilation of books, periodicals, and websites relevant to the topics found in this volume of the *Life and Career Skills Series*. Although the list is comprehensive, it is by no means exhaustive and is intended to serve as a starting point for gathering further information. Gale, Cengage Learning, is not responsible for the accuracy of the addresses or the content of the materials or websites.

Books

Bolton, Robert. *People Skills: How to Assert Yourself, Listen to Others, and Resolve Conflicts*. New York: Simon & Schuster, 1986.

Chan, Janis Fisher. *E-mail: A Write It Well Guide*. Oakland, CA: Write It Well, 2008.

Dale Carnegie Training. *The Five Essential People Skills: How to Assert Yourself, Listen to Others, and Resolve Conflicts*. New York: Simon & Schuster, 2009.

DuBrin, Andrew J. *Leadership: Research Findings, Practice, and Skills*. 8th ed. Boston, MA: Cengage Learning, 2016.

Ellis, Donald G. *From Language to Communication*. New York: Routledge, 2012.

Friedman, Stewart D. *Leading the Life You Want: Skills for Integrating Work and Life*. Boston, MA: Harvard Business Publishing, 2014.

Garner, Alan. *Conversationally Speaking: Tested New Ways to Increase Your Personal and Social Effectiveness*. Chicago: Contemporary Books, 1997.

Glickman, Jodi. *Great on the Job: What to Say, How to Say It: The Secrets of Getting Ahead*. New York: St. Martin's Griffin, 2011.

Goman, Carol Kinsey. *The Nonverbal Advantage: Secrets and Science of Body Language at Work*. San Francisco: Berrett-Koehler, 2008.

———. *The Silent Language of Leaders: How Body Language Can Help—or Hurt—How You Lead*. San Francisco: Jossey-Bass, 2011.

Jamieson, Harry G. *Visual Communication: More than Meets the Eye*. Chicago: University of Chicago Press, 2007.

Kallet, Michael. *Think Smarter: Critical Thinking to Improve Problem-Solving and Decision-Making Skills*. New York: Wiley, 2014.

Keller, Ed, and Brad Fay. *The Face-to-Face Book: Why Real Relationships Rule in a Digital Marketplace*. New York: Free Press, 2012.

Lerner, Marcia. *Writing Smart: Your Guide to Great Writing*. New York: Princeton Review, 2001.

Levi, Daniel Jay. *Group Dynamics for Teams*. Thousand Oaks, CA: Sage Publications, 2013.

Levine, Stewart. *Getting to Resolution: Turning Conflict into Collaboration*. San Francisco: Berrett-Koehler Publishers, 2009.

Mackin, Deborah. *The Team-Building Tool Kit: Tips and Tactics for Effective Workplace Teams*. New York: AMACOM, 2007.

McKay, Matthew, Martha Davis, and Patrick Fanning.*Messages: The Communication Skills Book*. Oakland, CA: New Harbinger Publications, 2009.

Navarro, Joe, and Marvin Karlins. *What Every BODY Is Saying: An Ex-FBI Agent's Guide to Speed-Reading People*. New York: Collins Living, 2008.

Nazario, Luis, Deborah Borchers, and William Lewis. *Bridges to Better Writing*. 2nd ed. Boston, MA: Wadsworth, 2013.

Nightingale, Virginia. *The Handbook of Media Audiences*. Malden, MA: Wiley-Blackwell, 2013.

O'Hair, Dan, and Mary Wiemann. *Real Communication: An Introduction*. Boston, MA: Bedford/St. Martin's, 2012.

Raines, Susan S. *Conflict Management for Managers: Resolving Workplace, Client and Policy Disputes*. San Francisco: Jossey-Bass, 2013.

Robbins, Stephen P., and Tim Judge. *Essentials of Organizational Behavior*. 13th ed. Upper Saddle Hill, NJ: Prentice Hall, 2015.

Webb, Christina. *Writing for Publication*. Hoboken, NJ: Wiley-Blackwell, 2009.

Periodicals

Burg, Natalie. "How Technology Has Changed Workplace Communication." *Forbes*, December 12, 2013. This article can also be found online at http://www.forbes.com/sites/unify/2013/12/10/how-technology-has-changed-workplace-communication/.

Davey, Liane. "Conflict Strategies for Nice People." *Harvard Business Review*, December 25, 2013. This article can also be found online at https://hbr.org/2013/12/conflict-strategies-for-nice-people/.

Halzack, Sarah. "A Lesson in the Art of Business Etiquette." *Washington Post*, February 15, 2013.

Johnson, Chandra. "Face Time vs. Screen Time: The Technological Impact on Communication." *Deseret News*, August 29, 2014. This article can also be found online at http://national.deseretnews.com/article/2235/Face-time-vs-screen-time-The-technological-impact-on-communication.html#Vz4TEhyEQ3UO6TGX.99.

Kasanoff, Bruce. "10 Ways to Build a Winning Team." *Business Insider*, November 13, 2014. This article can also be found online at http://www.businessinsider.com/ways-to-build-a-winning-team-2014-11.

Mickan, Sharon, and Sylvia Rodger. "The Organisational Context for Teamwork: Comparing Health Care and Business Literature." *Australian Health Review* 23 (2000): 179–92.

Moulesong, Bob. "Listening Skills Are an Important Part of Effective Communication." *Times of Northwest Indiana*, December 19, 2010. This article can also be found online at http://www.nwitimes.com/business

/jobs-and-employment/listening-skills-are-an-important-part-of-effective-communication/article_b4d0940a-f919-5d1a-be45-05da2c6752c2.html.

Parker-Pope, Tara. "When the Bully Sits in the Next Cubicle." *New York Times*, March 25, 2008, F5. This article can also be found online at http://www.nytimes.com/2008/03/25/health/25well.html.

Websites

"Building a Collaborative Team Environment." *Office of Personnel Management*. http://www.opm.gov/policy-data-oversight/performance-management/teams/building-a-collaborative-team-environment/ (accessed March 30, 2015).

Cardinal, Rosalind. "Managing Conflict at Work." *Huffington Post*. January 12, 2015. http://www.huffingtonpost.com/rosalind-cardinal/managing-conflict-at-work_b_6446928.html (accessed March 28, 2015).

"Conflict Resolution." *University of Wisconsin-Madison*. https://www.ohrd.wisc.edu/onlinetraining/resolution/resources.htm (accessed March 25, 2015).

"Creating a Great Team Culture." *Global Leadership Foundation*. https://globalleadershipfoundation.com/deepening-understanding/creating-a-great-team-culture/ (accessed March 30, 2015).

"Effective Communication: Improving Communication Skills in Business and Relationships." *Helpguide.org: Your Guide to Better Mental and Emotional Health*. http://www.helpguide.org/articles/relationships/effective-communication.htm (accessed March 25, 2015).

"How to Improve Listening and Conversation Skills." *Erupting Mind: Intelligent Advice for Intelligent People*. http://www.eruptingmind.com/how-to-improve-listening-skills-in-conversations/ (accessed March 24, 2015).

"List of Free Online Communications Courses and Classes." *Education Portal*. http://education-portal.com/articles/List_of_Free_Online_Communications_Courses_and_Classes.html (accessed March 24, 2015).

Rowe, E. "Team Leadership." *University of Vermont*. http://www.uvm.edu/extension/community/buildingcapacity/?Page=teamleadership.html (accessed March 31, 2015).

"The Seven Challenges Workbook: Communication Skills for Success at Home and Work." *The New Conversations Initiative*. http://www.newconversations.net/ (accessed March 25, 2015).

"The Seven Cs of Communication: A Checklist for Clear Communication." *Mind Tools: Essential Skills for an Excellent Career*. http://www.mindtools.com/pages/article/newCS_85.htm (accessed March 25, 2015).

Stewart, Jill. "The Most Enjoyable Way to Improve Your Writing Skills." *Ragan's PR Daily*. December 30, 2013. http://www.prdaily.com/Main/Articles/The_most_enjoyable_way_to_improve_your_writing_ski_14300.aspx (accessed March 15, 2015).

Suttle, Rick. "Importance of Writing Skills in Business." *Houston Chronicle*. http://smallbusiness.chron.com/importance-writing-skills-business-845.html (accessed December 15, 2014).

"Why Communication Skills Should Matter to You." *Working World.* http://www.workingworld.com/articles/why-communication-skills-should-matter-to-you (accessed March 25, 2015).

Wray, Amanda. "What to Think about When Writing for a Particular Audience." *Writing Commons.* http://writingcommons.org/open-text/writing-processes/think-rhetorically/711-what-to-think-about-when-writing-for-a-particular-audience (accessed March 25, 2015).

List of Key Organizations

The following is an annotated alphabetical compilation of organizations and advocacy groups relevant to the topics found in this volume of the *Life and Career Skills Series*. Although the list is comprehensive, it is by no means exhaustive and is intended to serve as a starting point for assembling further information. Gale, Cengage Learning, is not responsible for the accuracy of the addresses or the contents of the websites, nor does it endorse any of the organizations listed.

American Arbitration Association

A nonprofit organization that helps people solve problems through mediation and not litigation.

> *Phone: (800) 778-7879*
> *Website: https://www.adr.org/*

American Association of University Women (AAUW)

An organization with local chapters dedicated to advancing equity for women and girls through advocacy, education, philanthropy, and research. They provide information and classes on their website.

> *1111 Sixteenth St. NW*
> *Washington, DC 20036*
> *(800) 326-2289*
> *Email: connect@aauw.org*
> *Website: http://www.aauw.org/*

American Institute of Stress

An organization that provides education on stress management to professionals and the public.

> *6387B Camp Bowie Boulevard, #334*
> *Fort Worth, TX 76116*
> *Phone: (682) 239-6823*
> *Fax: (817) 394-0593*
> *Website: http://www.stress.org/*

American Management Association

An organization that provides professional development training for companies.

> *1601 Broadway, #8*
> *New York, NY 10019*
> *Phone: (877) 566-9441*
> *Fax: (518) 891-0368*
> *Website: http://www.amanet.org/*

American Psychological Association

A nonprofit organization that supports the practice of psychology and the use of psychological knowledge to help the well-being of Americans.

> *750 First Street NE*
> *Washington, DC 20002*
> *Phone: (800) 374-2721*
> *Email: customerservice@apa.org*
> *Website: http://www.apa.org/*

American Psychological Center for Organizational Excellence

A nonprofit organization that is a part of the American Psychological Association and supports the psychological health of Americans in the workplace.

750 First Street NE
Washington, DC 20002
Phone: (202) 336-5900
Website: http://www.apaexcellence.org/

Association for Conflict Resolution

A professional organization that provides continuing education and information to conflict resolution professionals and others.

1959 South Power Road, Suite 103-279
Mesa, AZ 85206
Phone: (202) 780-5999
Email: corbett@acrnet.org
Website: https://www.imis100us2.com/ACR
/ACR/Default.aspx

Association for Psychological Science

A nonprofit organization that promotes psychology based in scientific research.

1133 15th Street NW, Suite 1000
Washington, DC 20005
Phone: (202) 293-9300
Fax: (202) 293-9350
Website: http://www.psychologicalscience.org/

Association of Image Consultants International

A professional association with chapters worldwide that provides education and certification courses for image consultants and related professionals.

1000 Westgate Drive, Suite 252
St. Paul, MN 55114
Phone: (651) 290-7468
Fax: (651) 290-2266

Email: info@aici.org
Website: http://www.aici.org/

Center for Creative Leadership

An organization with offices in the United States, Belgium, and Singapore that provides education on professional leadership.

Phone: (800) 780-1031
Email: info@ccl.org
Website: http://www.ccl.org/leadership/index
.aspx

coursera

An education platform that partners with top universities and organizations worldwide, to offer courses online for anyone to take, for free. Course topics include discussion and arguing, and public speaking.

381 E. Evelyn Ave.
Mountain View, CA 94041
Website: https://www.coursera.org/

Dress for Success

With local chapters worldwide, this global not-for-profit organization promotes the economic independence of disadvantaged women by providing professional attire, a network of support, and the career development tools to help women thrive in work and in life.

32 East 31st Street
New York, NY 10016
Phone: (212) 532-1922
Website: https://www.dressforsuccess.org/

Editorial Freelancers Association

A professional organization that provides support to freelance writers, editors, and those in related fields.

71 West 23rd Street, 4th Floor
New York, NY 10010
Phone: (866) 929-5425

Fax: (866) 929-5439
Email: office@the-efa.org
Website: http://www.the-efa.org/

Ethics and Compliance Officers Association

A professional association that supports ethics and compliance officers through professional development and education.

411 Waverley Oaks Road, Suite 324
Waltham, MA 02452
Phone: (781) 647-9333
Fax: (781) 647-9399
Website: http://www.theecoa.org/

Ethics Resource Center (ERC)

A nonprofit, nonpartisan research organization, dedicated to independent research that advances high ethical standards and practices in public and private institutions.

2345 Crystal Drive, Suite 201
Arlington, VA 22202
Phone: (703) 647-2185
Fax: (703) 647-2180
Website: http://www.ethics.org/

Federal Bureau of Investigation (FBI)

A federal government organization that is a part of the U.S. Department of Justice and investigates crime.

935 Pennsylvania Avenue NW
Washington, DC 20535
Phone: (202) 324-3000
Website: http://www.fbi.gov/

Fierce

An organization that trains personnel to communicate more effectively in the workplace.

101 Yesler Way, Suite 200
Seattle, WA 98104

Phone: (206) 787-1100
Fax: (206) 787-1120
Email: info@fierceinc.com
Website: http://www.fierceinc.com/

International Association of Business Communicators (IABC)

A professional organization that supports professional communicators through education, professional development, and community.

601 Montgomery Street, Suite 1900
San Francisco, CA 94111
Phone: (800) 776-4222
Fax: (415) 544-4747
Email: member_relations@iabc.com
Website: http://www.iabc.com/

Institute for Challenging Disorganization

A professional organization that provides information and resources about chronic disorganization.

1693 South Hanley Road
St. Louis, MO 63144
Phone: (314) 416-2236
Email: icd@challengingdisorganization.org
Website: http://www
.challengingdisorganization.org/

Institute for the Study of Conflict Transformation

An academic organization that researches conflict resolution.

371 West Second Street, 3rd Floor
Dayton, OH 45402
Phone: (937) 333-2360
Fax: (937) 333-2366
Email: admin@transformativemediation.org
Website: http://www.transformativemediation
.org/

International Institute for Conflict Resolution and Prevention

An organization that helps companies resolve commercial conflicts through mediation and not litigation.

575 Lexington Avenue, 21st Floor
New York, NY 10022
Phone: (212) 949-6490
Fax: (212) 949-8859
Email: info@cpradr.org
Website: http://www.cpradr.org/Home.aspx

International Society of Protocol and Etiquette Professionals

An organization that offers certificate programs for protocol and etiquette professionals.

13116 Hutchinson Way, Suite 200
Silver Spring, MD 20906
Phone: (301) 946-5265
Fax: (240) 371-0080
Email: info@ispep.org
Website: http://ispep.org/

The Leaders Institute

An organization that provides team-building events and public speaking and leadership skills training to businesses.

6703 Coronation Court
Arlington, TX 76017
Phone: (800) 975-6151
Website: http://www.leadersinstitute.com/

National Association of Professional Organizers

A professional organization that supports professional organizers and offers information to people who want help with organization.

1120 Route 73, Suite 200
Mount Laurel, NJ 08054
Phone: (856) 380-6828
Fax: (856) 439-0525
Email: napo@napo.net
Website: http://www.napo.net/

National Ethics Association

An organization that helps businesses act in an ethical manner.

12707 High Bluff Drive, Department 200
San Diego, CA 92130
Phone: (800) 282-1831
Fax: (760) 462-3333
Website: http://www.ethics.net/

National Institute of Mental Health

A federal government organization that is a part of the National Institutes of Health and promotes research on mental health for the well-being of Americans. Their website provides information on a variety of topics include social phobias.

Science Writing, Press, and Dissemination Branch
6001 Executive Boulevard, Room 6200,
MSC 9663
Bethesda, MD 20892
Phone: (866) 615-6464
Fax: (301) 443-4279
Email: nimhinfo@nih.gov
Website: http://www.nimh.nih.gov/index.shtml

National Public Radio

A nonprofit organization that broadcasts news, information, and entertainment radio programs across the United States through syndicate stations.

1111 North Capitol Street NE
Washington, DC 20002
Website: http://www.npr.org/

National Seminars Training

An organization that provides professional training to companies.

6901 West 63rd Street
Shawnee Mission, KS 6620
Phone: (800) 258-7246
Fax: (913) 432-0824
Email: cstserv@natsem.com
Website: http://www
.nationalseminarstraining.com/

The New Conversations Initiative

An online organization that provides free self-help information about communicating with others and conflict resolution.

Website: http://www.newconversations.net/

New Horizons Computer Learning Centers

An organization that provides computer instruction to companies.

100 Four Falls Corporate Center, Suite 408
West Conshohocken, PA 19428
Phone: (888) 236-3625
Website: http://www.newhorizons.com/

The Nonverbal Group

An organization that researches nonverbal communication and provides information on nonverbal communication to the public.

548 West 28th Street, Suite 221
New York, NY 10001
Phone: (212) 380-7944
Email: contact@nonverbalgroup.com
Website: http://www.nonverbalgroup.com/

Pew Research Center

A nonprofit organization that researches, analyzes, and provides information on trends in American culture, technology, media, religion, and other topics.

1615 L Street NW, Suite 700
Washington, DC 20036
Phone: (202) 419-4300
Fax: (202) 419-4349
Website: http://www.pewresearch.org/

Project Management Institute

A professional organization that provides continuing education to project managers.

14 Campus Boulevard
Newtown Square, PA 19073
Phone: (855) 746-4849

Fax: (610) 482-9971
Email: customercare@pmi.org
Website: http://www.pmi.org/default.aspx

Say It Social

An organization that trains businesses to use social media and develop digital strategies effectively.

1844 Sir Tyler Drive
Wilmington, NC 28405
Phone: (910) 550-0982
Website: http://www.sayitsocial.com/

Skillpath

An organization that provides professional training for companies.

P.O. Box 2768
Mission, KS 66201
Phone: (800) 873-7545
Fax: (913) 362-4241
Email: customercare@skillpath.com
Website: http://www.skillpath.com/index.cfm

SkillsYouNeed

A UK-based online skills development resource providing professional materials on a variety on social skills.

Email: hello@skillsyouneed.com
Website: http://www.skillsyouneed.com/

Society for Human Resource Management

A professional organization that provides support to human resource professionals through continuing education and research.

1800 Duke Street
Alexandria, VA 22314
Phone: (800) 283-7476
Fax: (703) 535-6490
Email: shrm@shrm.org
Website: http://www.shrm.org/

Society for Personality and Social Psychology

A professional organization that provides professional support and education for social psychologists.

1660 L Street NW, #1000
Washington, DC 20036
Phone: (202) 524-6545
Email: spspinfo@spsp.org
Website: http://www.spsp.org/

Tech Change: The Institute for Technology and Social Change

An organization that provides online technological education and resources to organizations that work to effect social change.

2001 13th Street NW, 3rd Floor
Washington, DC 20009
Email: info@techchange.org
Website: https://www.techchange.org/

Toastmasters International

A nonprofit organization of clubs that teaches public speaking and leadership skills to members.

P.O. Box 9052
Mission Viejo, CA 92690
Phone: (949) 858-8255
Fax: (949) 858-1207
Website: http://www.toastmasters.org/

U.S. Copyright Office

A federal government organization that is a part of the Library of Congress and determines and manages copyrights for intellectual works including books and articles.

101 Independence Avenue SE
Washington, DC 20559
Phone: (877) 476-0778
Website: http://copyright.gov/

U.S. Department of Justice

A cabinet department of the federal government that enforces U.S. law. Their website gives toll-free numbers for reporting fraud and white-collar crime among others.

950 Pennsylvania Avenue NW
Washington, DC 20530
Phone: (202) 514-2000
Website: http://www.justice.gov/

U.S. Department of State

A cabinet department of the federal government that manages diplomatic relations between the United States and other countries. Their website gives information about the No FEAR and Whistleblower Protection Acts.

2201 C Street NW
Washington, DC 20520
Phone: (202) 647-4000
Website: http://www.state.gov/

U.S. Equal Employment Opportunity Commission

A federal government organization that enforces equal employment opportunity laws. Their website contains information about sexual harassment and other types of discrimination in the workplace.

131 M Street NE
Washington, DC 20507
Phone: (202) 663-4900
Email: info@eeoc.gov
Website: http://www.eeoc.gov/index.cfm

U.S. Small Business Administration (SBA)

A federal government organization that supports small businesses in the United States. There website contains a learning center of videos, online training, and chat sessions.

409 Third Street SW
Washington, DC 20416
Phone: (800) 827-5722
Email: answerdesk@sba.gov
Website: https://www.sba.gov/

Index

This index is sorted word-by-word. Italic page locators indicate images. A *t* following a page number indicates the citation is to information in a table or other illustration.

D

Darwin, Charles, 62
Decision making, 168–172
    apps, *118*
    importance, 168–169
    leadership aspects, 334–335
    overview, 119–120, 168
    participatory, 274
    problem solving and, 121, 169
    process, 168, 171
    strategies, *169,* 169–172
    for teams, 274, 277–278
Decision matrix analysis, 120, 121
Deep breathing, 161, 197
Defense Industry Initiative on Business Ethics and
    Conduct, 220
Delegating tasks
    overview, 117–119
    as problem-solving skill, 154
    team leaders, 270
Delegative (laissez-faire) leadership, 271, 341
Democratic leadership, 341, 346, 350
Department of Health and Human Services, 195
Department of Workforce Development, 135
Developmental editors, 98
Diagrams (graphics), 110
Digital communication. *See* Computer communication
Digital Trends, 37
Dilated pupils, 48–49
Ding, Shujun, 232
Disciplinary procedures, employee misconduct, 216,
    228–229, 234, 235
Discrimination
    conflict from, 177
    diversity awareness and, 281, 285
    legal considerations, 219–220, 221, 226
    pay gap, 282
Disorganization, chronic, 145
Distractions, time management aspects, 130–131
Distributive negotiable issues, 308, 309, 315, 316
Diversity
    emoticons use and, 109
    teamwork considerations, 266–267, 274,
      280–287, *281, 283t*
    valuing, 280–281, 285

Diversity training, 286
Divisional organizational structures, 119
Divorce proceedings, active listening, 57
Documents, organizing, 145–146
Dodd-Frank Wall Street Reform and Consumer
    Protection Act (2010), 220
Donovan, Joe, 37
Doodle online scheduler, 144
Dress. *See* Clothing
Dress codes, 250
Dropbox, 146

E

Edge Negotiation, 318
Editors, 97–98
Editors in chief, 98
Education and training
    communication skills, 9–10, 25
    diversity, 286
    leadership skills, 338, 343–344
    negotiation, 311, 318
    organizational skills, 134–137
    professional ethics and conduct, 213,
      220, 231
    sexual harassment, 219, 225–226
    teamwork skills, 279, 286
Education Portal website, 9
Ego, 329
EI (emotional intelligence), 270–271, 289,
    338–339, 347
Ekman, Paul, 62
Elections, nonverbal communication role, 49
Electronic communication. *See* Computer
    communication
E-mail
    automatic reminders, 146
    emoticons use, 109
    history, 5
    professional *vs.* personal, 91–92
    subject headings, 89
    telephone communication *vs.,* 27
    workplace problem solving use, 166, 167
Emily Post website, 89
Emoticons, 109

J

Japan
  business etiquette, *256, 257*
  quality circles, 265
Jargon
  as communication obstacle, 6–7
  for texting, 29, 92
Jewelry, professional appearance, 253
Job interviews
  body language, 65
  etiquette concerns, 205
  first impressions, 204, 237, *238,* 242, 249
  nonverbal communication, 50
  via web conferencing, 28
Johari window, 291–292
Jokes and humor, 19, 183, 219, 226
Journals, 81–82, 94
Justice. *See* Law enforcement

K

Karrass Ltd., 318
Keeper (password manager), 147
Keeping an open mind, 157–159
Kennedy, John F., 49
Know your audience rule, 18–19

L

Laissez-faire leadership, 271, 341
Language
  communication obstacles, 6–7
  overview, 13–14
  reading audience concerns, 84–86
  spoken at home, *283t*
  team communication and, 296
  texting, 92–93
Law enforcement
  help with conflict, 187, 192
  nonverbal communication role, 50–51, 70
  reporting misconduct, 209, 233, 234
  sentencing guidelines, 220
Lawsuits
  mediation *vs.,* 188, 189, 191, 192
  proxies in, 187

Leaders Eat Last: Why Some Teams Pull Together and Others Don't (Sinek), 337
Leadership, 333–352. *See also* Team leaders
  conflict and obstacles role, 298, 301
  developing skills, 340–344, *341*
  management *vs.,* 335t
  qualities and skills, 270–271, 333–339, 334, *334*
  styles, 118–119, 183–184, 271, 338, 345–351, *346*
Leadership That Gets Results (article), 345, 347
Leakage, emotional, 75, 76
Learning opportunities, problems as, 156–157, 159–160, 338
Least Supportable Outcome (LSO), 309, 310
Left-handed and right-handed eating, cultural differences, 258
Legal concerns
  copyright, 98–99
  ethics policies and codes of conduct, 222
  lawsuits, 187, 188, 189, 191, 192
  workers' rights, 219–220
Lehman Brothers, 225
Letter writing, 87–90, *88*
Levi Strauss, 276
Liability, 227
Libraries, for research, 129
Liking (Facebook), 102
Line graphs, *108,* 110
LinkedIn, 204, 242
Links, short versions, 105
Listening audiences, 7–8, 18–19, 82
Listening skills. *See also* Active listening
  conflict resolution role, 185
  importance to communication, 4–5, 8–9, 24, 25
  for leaders, 336, 342
  negotiation role, 311
  for note-taking, 131–132
Lists
  for project management, 128–129
  to-do lists, 128–129, 130, 147
Literary agents, 96
Long-term *vs.* short-term solutions, 121–122
Long-term *vs.* short-term stressors, 194–196
Loyalty, leadership aspects, 337, 348

T